A Sunset Travel Book

HAWAII

BY THE SUNSET EDITORIAL STAFF

Research and text by Nancy Bannick,
Hawaii Editor of Sunset Magazine

Lane Books • Menlo Park, California

Above: Kalalau Valley, Kauai; photograph by Robert Wenkam.

PHOTOGRAPHERS: Nancy Bannick, pages 9, 15, 21, 25, 32, 34, 38, 42, 44, 45, 47, 54, 55, 57, 58, 61, 66, 71, 77, 82, 83, 86, 88, 93, 98, 100 top, 102, 103, 106, 107, 111, 118, 121, 124. **Glenn M. Christiansen,** pages 11, 69, 70, 81 top, 84. **Richard Dawson,** pages 7, 12, 18, 20, 22, 29. **Dole Photo,** page 122 right. **Norman Gordon,** pages 91, 99. **Hawaii Visitors Bureau,** pages 68, 81 bottom. **Island Holidays,** page 94. **Lahaina Restoration Foundation,** page 100 bottom. **Martin Litton,** pages 6, 40, 41, 112, 120. **Clarence Maki,** pages 14, 23. **National Park Service,** page 105 bottom. **Ray Piper,** page 45. **Salbosa/Wenkam,** page 31. **Darrow M. Watt,** page 48. **Robert Wenkam,** pages 13, 17, 24, 33, 36, 39, 43, 49, 51, 63, 64, 67, 73, 74, 75, 76, 79, 80, 85, 87, 92, 96, 97, 104, 105 top, 108, 109, 114, 115, 116, 117, 119, 122 left, 125. **George Woo,** pages 30, 35, 44. **James Y. Young,** page 40.

Cover photograph of Kailua, Hawaii, and title page photograph of Honokahua Beach, Maui, by Glenn M. Christiansen.

Third Printing June 1970

CONTENTS

An introduction to
THE ISLANDS

There are so many Hawaiis. The romantic scenes of the travel folders are very much present—blue-green lagoons and flaming sunsets, smooth sand beaches offset by frothy surf, jungled valleys, green-clad peaks, vivid flowers, puffs of clouds afloat in azure skies, glamorous hotels, and happy, brown-skinned people who play ukuleles, dance the hula, skim the crests of waves, or shinny up a palm for a coconut.

But Hawaii has other faces and moods. You will see awesome volcanoes that sometimes spew fire upon already blackened, scarred moon-like deserts; shiver in forests and ranges on the shoulders of snow-capped mountains; hear tales of mythical characters more respected than real people; drive through fields of sugar cane, undulating rows of pineapple, and plantation towns that look like sets on a stage; explore a big city as cosmopolitan and up-to-date as any of its size on the Mainland; cool off in drifting showers, run from sudden squalls, seek indoor diversion during several-day storms that make the land sodden.

Hawaii is the only American state in which two-thirds of the people had their beginnings in the Orient or Polynesia. It is probably also the only state where rice outsells potatoes, holidays commemorate royalty, and college graduates affect pidgin English. Car racks carry surfboards, visitors dress native style and natives take to Ivy League, secretaries wear orchids to work, teen-agers relish noodles with soda pop, and tourists leave fashionable resorts to sightsee in foreign compacts.

The Geography

Everywhere you go in Hawaii you will be on a volcano. The eight main islands — only seven of them populated — are peaks that rise out of the sea at the southeastern end of a great volcanic mountain range stretching across almost 2,000 miles of the Pacific. Volcanism appears to have started in the northwest, moved along a fissure in the ocean floor some 15,000 feet below sea level, and is still very much at work on Hawaii, youngest in the chain of 136 islands, islets, and atolls totaling 6,452 square miles.

More than 90 per cent of the native plants and birds that evolved in these isolated islands live only here; and scientists and conservationists are working to have selected wilderness set aside for their protection and rejuvenation.

The islands lie about 2,400 miles southwest of California. Kauai is the northernmost island in the main group, fourth in size, and the oldest and greenest. Tiny, parched Niihau, 15 miles southwest, is privately owned and off-limits to visitors. Its 292 inhabitants are mostly pure Hawaiians, work a cattle and sheep ranch, and by choice speak Hawaiian and live in a primitive manner without such 20th century trappings as automobile roads, electricity, plumbing, television, and movies. (They do have a telephone line to Kauai, kerosene, transistor radios, and newspapers which arrive by boat.)

Oahu, third-largest island and one of the Pacific's most important, is the first landing place for most visitors. It has Honolulu, the state capital and only real city, and such landmarks as Waikiki Beach, Diamond Head, and Pearl Harbor. The four islands in a cluster to the southeast include second-in-size Maui and three of the smaller islands—Molokai, Lanai, and Kahoolawe. Molokai has pineapple fields and ranch land—some now giving way to resort spreads. Most of Lanai belongs to the Dole Company (pineapple), but visitors are welcome. Both of these islands are popular with outdoorsmen. Kahoolawe is the island without people, and for good reason—since World War II it has been a military bombing and gunfire range. Maui, Hawaii (southernmost of the main islands and almost twice as big as the other seven put together), and Kauai are a mix of vast plantations and ranches, farm towns, and new and growing resort communities. Maui and Hawaii each have a national park (and one is proposed for Kauai). Hawaii has the state's highest mountain, its two active volcanoes, and its second overseas airport (at Hilo).

The History

Flying across the Pacific to Hawaii, you strain your eyes to see the first island. If you're approaching by ship, you watch a haze on the horizon take on distinct form. Either way, you'll wonder how explorers centuries ago ever found these bits of land. Actually, they discovered them by chance but through nonetheless impressive feats.

Polynesians from the Marquesas as early as 750 A.D. and from Tahiti about 500 years later crossed the uncharted ocean in large sailing canoes and landed in Hawaii with their families, plants, animals, and personal belongings. For hundreds of years they knew only a Stone Age life, making *tapa* cloth, grass houses, outrigger canoes and carvings, and subsisting on fish, *poi,* and other fruit of the land. When British navigator Captain James Cook discovered the islands in 1778 (he named them The Sandwich Islands for the Earl of Sandwich) during the third and last of his famous South Pacific voyages, he

The People

Most of Hawaii's some 800,000 people are American citizens even though they call each other *haoles,* Japanese, Chinese, Hawaiians (most now are just part), Filipinos, Samoans, Portuguese, Korean, Puerto Rican. Increasing numbers are of mixed parentage, their ethnic composition the object of many a guessing game.

You hear a lot about the Aloha spirit, the carry-over of the friendly, generous, unpretentious, carefree behavior of the first Polynesians. You get the feeling that everyone knows everyone else, or at least about him. You're struck by the leveling effect—people are pretty much the same in *mu'umu'us* and Aloha shirts; it's manner and attitude that count.

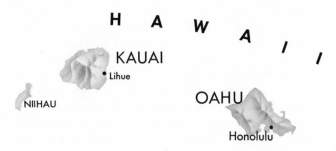

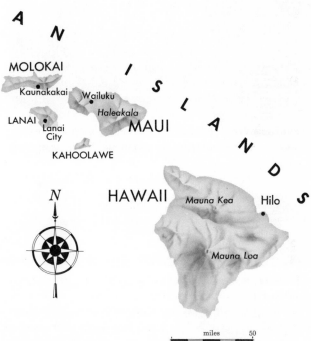

found each a separate kingdom organized in a feudal manner with chiefs, priests, and commoners. By 1810 the king of Hawaii island, Kamehameha, had brought all of the islands under his domain (by conquests and a ceding). He and his descendants reigned until 1872. They were succeeded by rulers from another ancient family of chiefs which included Queen Liliuokalani, who was ruler in 1893 when the monarchy was overturned. A provisional government was set up, and the following year, the Republic of Hawaii. The Islands were annexed by the United States in 1898 and made a territory in 1900. On March 12, 1959, Congress passed the bill that made Hawaii the 50th state and ended a campaign for statehood which Islanders had waged for half a century.

The waves of *haoles* (foreigners — the term used today for Caucasians) who came during the 19th century rearranged Hawaiian society. Traders came from Captain Cook's time on, and in the middle years, whalers came seeking provisions and entertainment. Companies of missionaries arrived starting in 1820. These stern, dedicated New Englanders braved the hazardous journey to the mid-Pacific to convert natives to Christianity and Western values, to introduce agriculture, commerce, democratic government. In the last half of the century Chinese came, then Japanese, and more recently Filipinos to work the sugar cane and pineapple plantations started by the early New Englanders and their descendants, many still prominent in the Islands today.

The Economy

The biggest contributor to the Hawaiian economy is the federal government, with military expenditures alone of more than $600,000,000. Other big income producers are tourism, construction, diversified manufacturing, sugar, and pineapple, in that order. The tourist industry is one of the fastest growing—some $1\frac{1}{2}$ million visitors a year now and expectations of $2\frac{1}{2}$ million by 1975 and 4 million by 1980. New and promising are scientific research and development, particularly in the fields of oceanography, geophysics, and astronomy. Various quests into the mysteries of the sea have started, including some from manned underwater laboratories. Mountaintop stations

The view from the air. *You look into the almost circular crater of Diamond Head, most famous Island landmark.*

track spacecraft, missiles, and satellites, and house telescopes for studying the sun, moon, stars, and planets.

The Climate

The Islands are in the tropics, but fresh trade winds from the east and northeast prevail most of the year and keep the air pleasantly balmy. In lowland areas, such as Waikiki, temperatures range from an average low of 65° to an average high of 80° in winter, and from 73° to 88° in summer. Atop the highest mountains, the temperature occasionally drops into the 20's, and in many upland sections the range is from the low 50's to low 70's.

Sometimes the trades break down and a spell of Kona weather sets in, with southerly breezes (Kona means leeward) and high humidity. In summer and early fall, a Kona wind is synonymous with sticky weather; in winter it brings a few storms (gales and torrential rain) but also some of the Islands' clearest days. Winter trades can get blustery and drop frequent showers even on dry areas such as Waikiki (with 20-25 inches of rain a year). In spring and summer, showers are few and come mostly at night, drifting down from mountain peaks which still receive frequent drenchings. The surprise of Island weather is that a year's rain may amount to more than 100 inches of rain in one place and less than 20 in another just a few miles away.

The State Trappings

Hawaii is the Aloha State. Its flag has eight red, white, and blue stripes (for the eight islands) and a field that resembles Great Britain's Union Jack. Its motto, *"Ua mau ke ea o ka 'aina i ka pono,"* which means "The life of the land is perpetuated in righteousness," has come down from King Kamehameha III who expressed it in 1843 at the time the British, after a short-lived, forced cession of the islands to them, restored sovereignty to the Hawaiians. The state anthem, "Hawaii Ponoi," is played at all ceremonious occasions; it was composed by King Kalakaua and Henri Berger, royal bandmaster. Queen Liliuokalani's "Aloha Oe," however, is the best known song.

Hawaii's official bird is the *nene,* a native goose; its flower, the native hibiscus; its tree, the *kukui (Aleurites moluccana),* whose pale green foliage makes groves of it stand out in mountain landscapes. Early Hawaiians used *kukui* nut kernels as candles, the nuts for meat accompaniments, soot from burned shells for black dye. They wore *leis* of satiny nuts, husked, filed, and polished with *kukui* nut oil—and you'll find similar craftwork in shops today.

How to Get to the Islands

The trip from the Mainland to Hawaii can be fast, by jet plane, or leisurely, by ocean liner or freighter. Or you can combine the two modes of travel, going one way by air, the other by sea. The Islands lie about 2,400 statute miles southwest of California. By air, the trip takes about 5 hours from West Coast cities, 9 hours from Chicago, 11 hours from New York. Luxury liners reach the Islands in 4½ days.

(Note: You cannot travel on a foreign carrier, air or sea, directly between two U.S. terminals, but you can stop over in Hawaii on a flight continuing beyond the Islands, and you can go to Hawaii by ship or plane from a foreign Mainland city like Vancouver, B.C.)

Air service. Most of these U.S. airlines serve both Honolulu and Hilo: American, Braniff International, Continental, Northwest Orient, Pan American, Trans World, United, and Western. American, Northwest, Pan Am, and TWA travel from Honolulu on across the Pacific and the last two, around the world.

These foreign airlines stop in Honolulu. Their Mainland terminal is a West Coast city (except Canadian Pacific which has some direct Toronto-Honolulu flights): Air New Zealand, British Overseas Airways Corporation, Canadian Pacific Airlines, Japan Air Lines, Philippine Air Lines, Qantas Airways, UTA French Airline, and

Varan-Air-Siam. Continental/Air Micronesia (a domestic line) has a service from Honolulu through the Trust Territory islands and Guam to Okinawa.

Consult travel experts on schedules, fares, and the itineraries possible on the various airlines. Three classes of service are available on most Mainland-to-Hawaii flights. On international flights, there are two (except for one-class Air Micronesia). Under the Common Fare plan offered to holders of Mainland-to-Hawaii round-trip tickets on the American carriers or CP Air, it is possible to route yourself from your landing place (Honolulu or Hilo) to each of the other islands for only $5 more for each stop (see Travel Between the Islands, page 8). If you hold a transpacific ticket, you may find the mileage allowance to your farthest point entitles you to a free flight from Honolulu to a Neighbor Island—the $5 payable only for an intermediate stop.

The American and Canadian airlines have various reduced-fare plans for Hawaii trips—for individual excursions and group travel. If you wish, you can combine them with an all-expense tour—either one in which you travel independently and at your own convenience but have air transportation, hotel rooms, and Island touring prepaid, or an escorted tour in which you travel in a group and on a schedule. The biggest low-cost-tour parties travel in planes chartered from supplemental or scheduled carriers.

Steamship service. For part of the year (usually March through October), Matson Lines operates the *Lurline* on "floating hotel" cruises from California to Honolulu and ports on three other islands (see Travel Between the Islands, page 8). You buy a 10, 15 or 20-day package—on the 10-day package, you fly both ways and sail to the Neighbor Islands when you arrive. On the 15-day package, you fly one way between California and Hawaii. (It can be either direction). Matson's *Monterey* and *Mariposa* call at Honolulu on the return voyage of 6-week South Pacific cruises—substituting for the *Lurline* —make occasional Hawaii-only excursions; both ships leave from California.

American President Lines offers passenger service to Honolulu on cruises from California to the Far East aboard the *Presidents Wilson* and *Cleveland*. Both Wilson and Cleveland depart from San Francisco and Los Angeles to Honolulu. P & O Lines' *Canberra, Oriana, Iberia, Arcadia, Orsova, Oronsay,* and *Himalaya* call at Honolulu on the circle-Pacific and around-the-world cruises originating in England. They connect Vancouver, San Francisco, and Los Angeles with Honolulu on voyages westbound to the Orient, Australia, South Africa, and Northern Europe, or eastbound to Europe through the Panama Canal. Mitsui O.S.K. Lines' passenger ships *Brazil Maru, Argentina Maru,* and *Sakura Maru* link

On "boat day" *you can sail from Waikiki on sleek catamaran to meet the incoming liner and escort it to its pier.*

Honolulu and California cities on cruises between Japanese and South American ports. Norwegian-America Line, Swedish-America Line, and Holland-America Line ships stop in Honolulu homeward bound from South Pacific and round-the-world cruises.

Matson and States Line have freighters, with limited passenger accommodations and variable schedules, that ply between West Coast cities and Hawaii. United States Lines sails from New York through the Panama Canal to Honolulu and the Far East. Foreign and other American passenger-freighters reach Honolulu at less frequent intervals. Among these are Hanseatic-Vaasa Line and Johnson Line from North Europe; Columbus Line from New Zealand and Australia; and Micronesia Interocean Line (MILI) from the West Coast through Hawaii to U.S. Trust Territory district centers.

To Ship Your Car . . . or Bring a Pet

If you plan to stay in Hawaii for several months or longer, you may wish to send your car over by ship. The one-way cost is about $255 for a standard size car, $145 for a small foreign car. To ship a car from Honolulu to another island costs from $32 to $61 one way depending on the size of the car and its destination. For a round trip, the range is $51-$94 for a 90-day voucher, $41-$71 if the trip is completed within 15 days. Reserve barge space at least a week ahead with Young Brothers, Pier 24, Honolulu.

Within 10 days of when your car arrives in Honolulu, you must get a temporary permit (it is free) at the Motor Vehicle Registration office, 1455 South Beretania Street; it is good until your Mainland license plates expire. You also need Oahu's annual car safety check permit; this costs $3.25 and is available at a number of service stations. Your Mainland driver's license is good for 90 days; by then you must have a Hawaii license ($4 for 4 years for persons 25 to 64 years old, $2 for 2 years for others).

Common pets such as dogs and cats are quarantined for 120 days upon arrival (for details, write State Department of Agriculture, Box 5425, Honolulu 96814).

Travel between the Islands

Inter-island jets fly frequently between all major island airports, and prop-jets serve smaller ones at least once a day. With a Mainland-to-Hawaii round-trip ticket on a U.S. airline or Canadian Pacific, you can arrange through airline offices or travel agencies on the Mainland or in Hawaii to take advantage of the Common Fare plan, which permits you to island-hop from your Honolulu or Hilo port of entry to any or all of the other islands for only $5 per stopover. In general, you won't have to pay any full-fare legs (required in certain instances of backtracking) if you land at one overseas terminal and leave from the other. You must travel between islands on Aloha Airlines or Hawaiian Airlines. If you're heading for some single Neighbor Island destination and stop in Honolulu or Hilo only to change planes, you can fly to one airport beyond either of these overseas terminals for just the Mainland-Honolulu or Mainland-Hilo fare.

For those not eligible for Common Fare travel, both Aloha and Hawaiian also offer a Family Plan and other discount fares for off-hour flying and for youths, oldsters, and servicemen. And if you are flying at regular or discount fare from Honolulu to an island southeast of Oahu, you can stop off at other islands en route for $5 each.

Twin-engine air taxis fly from Honolulu Airport to all other fields and airstrips, specializing in commuter service and charters to resort airstrips and fields Aloha and Hawaiian serve infrequently. The three that operate with published schedules are Air Hawaii (featuring lower-than-normal fares), Royal Hawaiian Air Service, and Sky Tours Hawaii. These inter-island taxis are for charter only: Air Molokai, Central Pacific Helicopters, Executive Aviation, Hawaiian Air Tour Service, Island Flight Center, Pacific Flight Service, Resort Airways, Polynesian Airways, Trans-Pacific Air Charter, Universal Enterprises, and Wai Manu Airways. See the separate chapters for information on each island's own air tour and charter services. You'll find a list of firms that rent small aircraft in the Oahu Telephone Directory Yellow Pages.

Package tours available range from a 1-day trip from Honolulu to one other island to a 10-day excursion covering four Neighbor Islands. You can elect to stay in either standard, superior, or deluxe hotel rooms (with or without meals included), and can travel in an exclusive car, 5 or 7-passenger limousine, 11-passenger "stretch-out," or air-conditioned bus. If you're going to travel on your own, be sure to reserve flights, a rental car, and hotel accommodations.

On a 1-day combination air and ground tour offered by Air Hawaii, Hawaiian Air Tour Service, Hawaiian Pacific Airline, and Sky Tours Hawaii, you fly over all eight islands and put down on three or more to eat and sightsee (itineraries vary).

Matson liners sail about the Islands a half dozen or more times a year on cruises from California (see Steamship Service, page 7). You can buy a 10-day, inter-island package, using the ship as your hotel in Honolulu; Nawiliwili, Kauai; Lahaina, Maui; and Hilo and Kailua on the Big Island. Or you can take a 1-day cruise around Oahu, or from Hilo to Kailua (Kona Coast).

For inter-island small boat cruising, see Outdoor Fun, page 12.

Getting Around on Each Island

Tours, rental cars, taxis, buses, aircraft. On all islands, you can buy a sightseeing tour, hire a taxi, and rent a car—upon landing at the airport, or at your hotel. In busy seasons, make advance car rental and tour arrangements.

Rental cars available on most islands range from foreign compacts for as little as $5 or $6 a day plus 5 or 6 cents a mile to 4-wheel-drives and dune buggies at $15 plus 12 to 15 cents a mile. All kinds of packages are offered (flat rates with no mileage charge, weekly specials covering cars on several islands, etc.). So investigate —one package may be more advantageous than another for the driving you expect to do.

On the major tourist islands, you can get from point to point or sightsee by helicopter or light plane. You can take buses in Honolulu and Hilo, and can cover parts of Oahu, Hawaii, Maui, and Kauai by bus or point-to-point taxi.

Roads, signs, place names. Route numbers on Hawaii's major state roads are on markers shaped like taro leaves. The first digit identifies the island: Hawaii, 1 and 2; Maui County (islands of Maui, Molokai, and Lanai), 3 and 4; Kauai, 5; Oahu, 6, 7, 8, and 9. Many of these roads are not really worthy of the description "highway," and Islanders, who have not had a numbered system for long, still call them by name or nickname.

On all islands, dirt roads criss-cross plantation lands. It is unwise to attempt these without getting permission and directions. It's easy to get stuck or lost on them, and you might meet a mammoth hauling truck.

You may be confused by names of places you see on maps or hear Islanders refer to that are not towns or even settlements. Generally they are the *ahupua'a* names — those of the historic district or land division that usually extended from the mountain slopes to the sea.

Most points of interest on all islands are identified by Hawaii Visitors Bureau red and yellow warrior markers. The sign figure faces the attraction and does not point to it (which would be thought impolite). Note the total absence of billboards and the restrained use of advertising signs. Control is by ordinances brought about by years of dedicated work by the Outdoor Circles — bands of volunteers who are also energetic in saving trees, planting more, and preserving and enhancing the Islands' beauty.

What to Wear

Lightweight clothing is the rule throughout the year. And leave room in your luggage for the Hawaiian apparel you'll want to buy and wear. Around resorts and for touring women wear shorty *mu'us,* shifts, shorts, or long pants; men wear sport shirts with shorts or slacks. Informal clothes are suitable for many restaurants, but some require men to wear a coat and tie. A sweater is enough wrap (unless you're spending time in the cool regions), although in winter some women show off furs. A raincoat, and for women, a scarf or net to protect hair from the breezes, are useful.

Honolulu *kama'ainas* dress more formally than in years past, partly because many places are air-conditioned, partly to defy the visitors—and some residents—who have invaded all parts of the city in resort garb. Many men wear coats over the white shirts and ties that once were the common business uniform, and many women still won't wear a *mu'umu'u* on the street.

What to Shop For

Waikiki has some of the Islands' finest stores as well as a repetition of Hawaiian clothes, handcrafts, and trinkets that is confusing. Other resort places have a smaller but similar clutch of shops eager to outfit you and send you off with appropriate gifts to take home. Prices vary little within quality brackets (you find several levels in every field of merchandise), but shop other places for different selections. Visit Honolulu's other shopping bases—Ala Moana Center, Kahala Mall, Fort Street Mall, the Oriental shopping district (Chinatown)—and specialty shops on all the islands. Here are some buying suggestions:

Clothes and fabrics. Hawaii's many garment manufacturers turn out sportswear (bikinis, surf trunks, pants outfits, Aloha shirts, Hawaiian-print sport coats), shorty-*mu'us,* and long *mu'umu'us* that range from Mother Hubbards to elegant gowns perhaps styled from the *kimono* or *cheongsam.* Many make children's clothes, and shifts and cocktail frocks. The choice of Hawaiian-wear is greater in the Islands than on the Mainland, but prices are similar.

You can buy fabrics by the yard. Look for Hawaiian cotton prints; Japanese printed *yukata* cotton; Japanese and Chinese silks and brocades; Thai silks; Indian *madras,* bedspreads, silks, and *saris.* Some shops make clothes to order from imported fabrics.

Handcrafts. Shop at gift and specialty houses, department stores, and small factories or plants for: Bowls and trays of monkeypod, *koa,* and some rare native woods

Hawaiian-designed *fabrics are a popular tourist buy. This shop is in Waikiki's open-air International Market Place.*

(factories have "seconds"). *Lauhala* handbags, hats, and mats for table or floor. Pottery bowls, ash trays, and planters; porcelain vases and figurines. Jewelry of seeds and shells, black and pink coral, obsidian, olivines, wood, ceramics, and hand-wrought silver. Hatbands of feathers, shells, and everlasting strawflowers. Ukuleles and Hawaiian hula accessories. Wall hangings loom-woven from many tropical plants. Curios of lava. Hawaiian dolls of all sizes, shapes, and materials.

Foods and plants. Many Hawaiian foods — papayas, pineapple, jams, jellies, syrups, macadamia nuts, coconut chips, Kona coffee — come gift-boxed, separately or in combinations. At street stands and in flower shops, you will find *leis* (plumeria, *pikake*, orchid, carnation, tuberose, crown flowers, ginger, jade), bold cut flowers such as anthurium and bird-of-paradise, dried arrangements of coconut sheaths, woodroses, papyrus, or *koa* pods. Hawaii's perfumes have the fragrances of its blossoms.

Oriental and South Pacific imports. The Island selection is greater and prices are a bit lower than in West Coast shops for Japanese, Chinese, Philippine, Korean, Indian, and South Seas products. Almost every store has imports and some shops are devoted to one nation's output. Consulates and ethnic Chambers of Commerce (page 16) can tell you where to buy the wares of the countries they represent. Besides fabrics, look for ivory, jade, and pearl jewelry; basketry and other woven articles; china, pottery, lacquer, bronze and brass ware; rattan and wicker furniture; masks; bamboo fishing poles, nets, floats, and reef-walking *tabi;* costly *objets d'art.*

The New Words You Will Hear

As you might expect, the English spoken in the Islands has been augmented with words and expressions from languages native to Hawaii's various ethnic groups. You will hear people pronounce vowel sounds in English words as they would in Hawaiian, Japanese, or one of the Romance languages. You'll also hear pidgin English, shortcut communicating that may be unintelligible but is always entertaining. Most Islanders, however, can and usually do speak good English; they just enliven their talk with Hawaiian words and turn the pidgin on and off. It's the local way of belonging, of not appearing snobbish. Phrases such as "da kine," "whassamattah," "hello, dere," "hey, bruddah" have become local dialect.

Names of most places and streets are Hawaiian; so some knowledge of the pronunciation rules of this language will be useful. The alphabet contains only 12 letters — the 5 vowels plus 7 consonants (h, k, l, m, n, p, w). Words seem to overflow with vowels, but pronunciation is not difficult if you remember to pronounce every letter separately. The vowel sounds are: a as in "arm," e as in "they" or "end," i as in "machine," o as in "old," u as in "rude." Consonants have the same sounds as in English except for the w. Some Hawaiians always pronounce it as a v unless it is preceded by an o or u; others do so only when it is the next-to-last letter in a word.

In diphthongs (ei, eu, oi, ou, ai, ae ao, au), stress the first member *(lei).*

If you see a glottal stop mark, or hamza, it indicates, in the Polynesian language, that the letter k has been omitted and there is a distinct break in sound between the letters it separates.

'ae	yes
ahupua'a	land division
aikane	friend (slang)
'aina	land, earth
akamai	wise, smart
ala	road, path
ali'i	royalty, a chief
aloha	greetings, welcome, farewell, love
aloha nui loa	much love
'a'ole	no
auwe	alas! ouch
Ewa	An Oahu town, used in Honolulu to indicate westerly direction
ha'ina	end of song
hale	house
hana	work
hana hou	encore
haole	Caucasian
hapa	half, part
hapai	to carry, be pregnant
Hauoli la Hanau	Happy Birthday
Hauoli Makahiki Hou	Happy New Year
haupia, kulolo	coconut puddings
heiau	temple, place of worship
hele mai	come here
hikie'e	large couch
holoku	fitted ankle-length dress with train
holomu'u	fitted ankle-length dress
ho'olaule'a	celebration
ho'omalimali	to flatter
huhu	angry
hui	club, association
hukilau	to fish with a seine
hula	Hawaiian dance
iki	small, little
imu	underground oven
ipo	sweetheart, lover
kahili	feather standard
kahuna	priest, expert
kai	sea
kala	money
kalua	baked underground
kama'aina	native born
kanaka	person, man
kanalua	doubtful, hesitate
kane	male, husband
kapakahi	crooked, lopsided
kapu	forbidden, keep out
kaukau	food (slang)
keiki	child
kokua	help
Kona	lee side, a leeward wind
kuleana	right, property, responsibility
lanai	porch, veranda
laulau	bundled food, packages of leaves containing fish and meat
lei	garland, wreath
lomi (or *lomilomi*)	rub, press, massage
lua	toilet
lu'au	feast, taro leaf
mahalo	thanks
maika'i	good, fine
makai	toward the sea
make	dead
malihini	stranger, newcomer
malo	a loin cloth
manu	bird
manuahi	free, gratis
mauka	inland
mauna	mountain
mele	song
Mele Kalikimaka	Merry Christmas
Menehune	dwarf, legendary race of dwarfs
moana	ocean
moemoe	sleep (slang)
momona	fat
mu'umu'u	long or short loose-fitting dress
nani	beautiful
ne'i	this place
nui	big, large, great
'okolehao	ti-root liquor

'okole maluna .... bottoms up	poi .... food prepared from
'ono .... delicious, tasty	taro root
'opu .... belly, stomach	popoki .... cat
Pake .... Chinese (slang)	pua .... flower, blossom
pali .... cliff, precipice	pua'a .... pig, pork
paniolo .... cowboy	puka .... hole, door
pau .... finished, done,	pune'e .... couch
the end	pupu ..... shell, hors d'oeuvre
pa'u .... wrap-around skirt	pupule .... crazy, insane
pehea 'oe .... how are you?	tutu .... grandmother
pikake .... jasmine	wahine .... a female, wife
pilau .... putrid	wai .... fresh water
pilikia .... trouble	wikiwiki .... fast, hurry
pohaku .... rock, stone	

Here are the English equivalents for Hawaiian names of fish, a list useful to gourmets as well as fishermen:

'ahi .... yellowfin	ono .... wahoo
aholehole .... perch-like fish	'o'opu .... goby
aku .... skipjack, bonito	'opae ...... fresh-water shrimp
akule .... big-eyed scad	'opakapaka ...... blue snapper
'ama'ama .... mullet	'opelu .... mackerel
a'u ...... marlin and swordfish	'opihi .... limpet
awa .... milkfish	papa'i .... crab
hihi-wai .. a kind of shellfish	papio ...... small form of jack
humuhumu-nukunuku-apua'a	puhi .... eel
trigger fish	uhu .... parrot fish
kaku .... barracuda	uku .... deep sea snapper
kawakawa .... bonito	'ula'ula .... red snapper
kumu .... goat fish	ulua .... crevalle or jack
mahimahi .... dolphin fish	'u'u .... squirrel fish
moi .... threadfin	wana .... sea urchin
'oama .... young weke	weke .... goat fish
'o'io .... bonefish	weke-'ula .... red goat fish

What to Eat . . . Night Life

Tourist hotels and restaurants on all of the islands serve mostly continental food or broiler specialties (just like home), but their menus are also long on fruits (pineapple, papaya, tasty local bananas, occasionally mangoes and litchis in season) and a few other local specialties: teriyaki steak, local fish (mahimahi always and sometimes ulua and 'opakapaka), coconut and pineapple waffles and pancakes, coconut and macadamia nut cream pies and ice creams, guava and liliko'i (passion fruit) sherbets and chiffon pies, curries, Kona coffee, and often Hawaiian laulaus and poi.

But on every island, you can make dining a cosmopolitan adventure. In Honolulu, in or not far from Waikiki, you will find Hawaiian, Cantonese, Mandarin, Japanese, Filipino, Tahitian, Mexican, French, German, Italian, and Kosher fare. In every community are plain little cafes that serve Chinese, Japanese, and Hawaiian favorites of the local people.

Try the various kinds of Chinese noodles and dim sum (stuffed pastries); the most popular is pork-filled and

Intriguing assortment of "crack seed"—dried, preserved whole fruits—may tempt you as it does these youngsters.

has a Hawaiian name, manapua. Sample the different kinds of Japanese sushi (stuffed rice), and sashimi (raw fish). Choose main dishes that are a departure from the standard fare in Mainland Oriental restaurants. Many hole-in-the-wall places feature saimin, a filling noodle soup that borrows from both Chinese and Japanese cuisines but is unique to the Islands.

For the accompanying ceremony, as well as to round out your acquaintance with Japanese food, dine at a tea house, where you slip into a kimono, sit on the floor, and eat sukiyaki or other specialties cooked at your low table; and most visitors want to join in at least one Hawaiian lu'au, either one of the Waikiki tourist parties or an organization benefit (see pages 20-21).

If you have a kitchen to putter in, shop supermarkets and Oriental sidewalk groceries for a fascinating array of strange vegetables, dried fish, cured meats, and tinned and packaged foods of all types including confections. At some bakeries you will find Portuguese sweet bread and malasadas (doughnuts), and at all markets, Portuguese sausage.

By all means sample "crack seed," the Chinese dried and preserved whole fruits that youngsters relish; you will find an assortment in small packages at most cash register counters, and big glass jars of them in markets and specialty stores that sell the snack by the pound. Everywhere you see children licking fruit-flavored "shave ice" (snow cones).

Any of the glamorous dining spots and cocktail lounges is apt to have a piano player, Hawaiian or jazz combo, or a show. The notable big Hawaiian-Tahitian-Samoan revues in Waikiki and Neighbor Island resorts may be a bit synthetic, but they are good entertainment. Some big hotels have dancing under the stars. In Honolulu you will find the assortment of nightclubs that are common to any big city; and here and in "big towns" on other islands, night spots with local color—impromptu music, audience participation, Japanese acts, and patter by local personalities. Worthwhile indeed are programs of music and dance by other ethnic groups—Filipino, Japanese, Korean, Chinese, Maori, Indian.

Outdoor Fun . . . and Some Precautions

The Islands are a year-round summer playground where you can lie in the sun on golden sands, or — if you are energetic — swim in calm bays or under tingling waterfalls; ride churning breakers on your belly, a board, or in an outrigger canoe; sail; skin-dive into underwater castles; troll the ocean waters or hook a fish off reefs or shores or from streams and ponds; play golf or tennis; ride horseback; hunt birds and wild game in grasslands and forests; camp out and live off the land; climb challenging volcanic peaks; and ride on a *ti* leaf down a wet mountainside.

Would-be hikers and campers, attracted by scenic trails which reach country untouched by roads, should be aware of certain dangers to one acquainted only with Mainland wilderness conditions. You needn't worry about poison oak or ivy, snakes, or insects. But in jungled valleys and upland forests (with 150 to 300 inches of rain a year), trails are muddy and get overgrown quickly. In dry areas, trail surfaces may crumble and slide. If you get lost thrashing through dense vegetation, follow ridges (not streams—many end on high cliffs) to get to open country or the sea. Wear long pants, take water, and don't hike alone. Get advice from state foresters or the Hawaiian Trail and Mountain or Sierra clubs (see page 25); or join the clubs' regular trips.

You can buy Wide World Outdoor Sports Maps for Oahu, Hawaii, Maui, and Kauai showing beaches, parks, camp sites, surfing and scuba diving areas, hunting and fishing grounds, back country roads and trails.

These firms rent campers on two or more main islands (Oahu, Hawaii, Maui, Kauai): Holo Holo Campers (Box 11, Hilo); Barefoot Campers, Ltd. (354 Olu St., Hilo, or 3745 Cahuenga Blvd. West, North Hollywood, Calif.); Camper Rentals Hawaii, Inc. (170 North Kainalu Dr., Kailua, Oahu); Campers International (6227 Sunset Blvd., Los Angeles, or 2424 Kalakaua Ave., Suite 10, Honolulu); Ecological Habitat, Inc. (826 Kaheka St., Suite 302, Honolulu). See pages 22 and 67 for firms only on Oahu or Hawaii.

Before taking the big plunge into unfamiliar waters, swimmers and surfers should make sure there are no hazardous currents, concealed rocks, or breakers too strong for them to handle. Not all dangerous or sometimes dangerous beaches are so posted.

Small boat cruising between islands is limited—as most channels are rough. But McWayne Marine Supply (1125 Ala Moana, Honolulu) can arrange a sail or power boat charter; Lahaina has charter sailing ships and a glass bottom boat that cruises the smooth sea to Lanai; and Pacific Game Fishing Unlimited (1777 Ala Moana, Honolulu) handles weekend fishing trips to Neighbor Islands aboard an Oahu tour boat and arranges charters on any island. Or check at the big fishing centers (Honolulu's Kewalo Basin and Kailua on Hawaii) for boats to hire for inter-island voyaging.

Skindiving Hawaii, based at Honolulu's Ala Wai Boat Harbor and with representatives on other islands, rents surface and scuba diving equipment, offers guided trips and instruction, can arrange other water sports.

Hawaii Hunting Information Center, Box 9242, Honolulu, can help you arrange a guided safari on any island.

The Hawaii Bicycling League (2620 East Manoa Rd., Honolulu), an affiliate of the League of American Wheelmen and American Youth Hostels, schedules regular Oahu outings for family groups and racers and occasional trips to other islands.

See the Recreation section for each island.

Lu'au specialty—*pit-roasted whole pig—is lifted from underground oven by brawny lavalava-clad Hawaiians.*

Festivals and Annual Events

Most of the events listed here are held in Honolulu, but some of the other islands have lesser versions of them and, in addition, some special events of their own (see chapters on each island). Check Hawaii Visitors Bureau on events with dates and places that vary.

Chinese Narcissus Festival. January-February; Honolulu. Five weeks of festivities coinciding with the beginning of the new year according to the lunar calendar. Highlights: New Year's Eve with feasting and firecrackers; Chinatown open-house; coronation of festival queen; lion, dragon dances; flower, fashion shows.

Opening of State Legislature. Third Wednesday in January; Honolulu, at State Capitol. The legislature begins its annual session with a colorful ceremony, Hawaiian music and dancing, and presentation of *leis*.

Haleiwa Sea Spree. February; one or more weekends; Haleiwa-Waialua area. Celebrates days of Queen Liliuokalani. Surfing contest, canoe races, carnival, *saimin* and *poi*-eating contests, torchlight pageant, international show, shell and art exhibits.

Carnivals. Two Honolulu private schools have exceptionally good carnivals: February; Punahou School (usually Friday and Saturday of second weekend). Mid-April; Iolani School. Good buys in paintings, handcrafts, plants, native fruits, vegetables, preserves. Old-fashioned carnival with rides, games, food booths.

Cherry Blossom Festival. February-March-April; Honolulu. Japanese community presents a series of events which include a Pan Pacific products show, queen pageant, coronation ball, cultural show (Japanese flower arranging, folk dancing, painting, tea ceremony), and imported East-West revue.

Kite-flying Contest. March; one of Honolulu's larger parks. Young and old compete with kites (mostly handcrafted) of all sizes, shapes, and colors.

Kuhio Day. March 26. A state holiday with major celebrations in Honolulu and on Kauai honoring Prince Kuhio, delegate to Congress 1902-22. Oahu events: *lu'aus*, ceremonies at Throne Room of Iolani Palace and Royal Mausoleum, Hawaiian services at Kawaiahao Church.

Kamehameha Schools Song Contest. A Friday evening in March; Honolulu International Center Arena. Annual contest between the Sophomore, Junior, and Senior classes of this school for children of Hawaiian ancestry—one of the finest programs of Hawaiian choral singing. Free tickets must be picked up in advance.

All Hawaii Spring Flower Show. March; Honolulu International Center. Emphasis on orchid displays. Spon-

For a delightful experience, *watch children perform in colorful Lei Day programs at the elementary schools.*

sored by Pacific Orchid Society of Hawaii. Admission charge.

Easter Art Festival. Precedes Easter; Ala Moana Center. One week. Exhibitions and demonstrations in various media presented by the Windward Artists Guild.

Easter Sunrise Service at Punchbowl National Memorial Cemetery of the Pacific. An hour-long, nondenominational service starting at 6 A.M. in Punchbowl Crater overlooking the city and a sweep of ocean.

Buddha Day. On the closest Sunday to April 8; Honolulu Concert Hall. The birth of Gautama Buddha is commemorated with a sweet tea ceremony, choir singing, and ritualistic Japanese dancing.

Pan Pacific Festival. April; University of Hawaii. Ethnic beauty pageant, dances, games, native foods.

Lei Day. May 1; all islands. Islanders don *leis* to greet spring. During the day at Waikiki Shell you can see contests and exhibits of *leis* made from shells, seeds, and feathers, as well as flowers. Visitors are welcome at delightful programs held at all schools. In the evening, a *hula* pageant at Waikiki Shell is highlighted by coronation of the *lei* queen. All events are free.

Children's Day. May 5; all islands. Celebrated by the

There's excitement aplenty *when world's top surfers vie for honors in international championships at Makaha.*

Japanese community. Gaily colored paper carp (symbol of courage) flying outside many homes indicate families who have sons of pre-school age. Homes and stores set up tiered doll displays for girls.

Fancy Carp Festival. May; Ala Moana Center. Exhibit of hundreds of beautiful carp and tropical fish. Carp and goldfish clubs also have some smaller shows.

Hawaiian Song Festival. Third Sunday in May; Honolulu. Adult and children's groups sing old and new Hawaiian songs. Original compositions are judged and prizes awarded the winners.

Hibiscus Show. May; Honolulu. Several hundred varieties in exhibits, arrangements. Free.

Memorial Day. The 21,000 markers at National Memorial Cemetery of the Pacific in Punchbowl Crater are heaped with flower *leis* strung by school children on all islands. A memorial service is held in the morning.

Fiesta Filipina. May-June; Honolulu. A month-long program of Philippine folk dances, music, sports, fashion and handcraft shows.

Kamehameha Day. June 11. A state holiday, with parades and pageantry on most islands. Honors King Kamehameha I, who founded the all-islands kingdom. Honolulu highlights are draping of his statue in Civic Center with 40-foot *leis*, parade with colorful *pa'u* riders (women riding bareback, in long, divided skirts).

Festival of the Arts of This Century. Mid-June through July. University of Hawaii. Experimental music, dance, theater, films, and art of Asian and Western origin. Free tickets must be picked up in advance.

50th State Fair. Late June and early July; Honolulu. Ten days. Arts, crafts, commercial displays, produce and livestock exhibits, ethnic dances, food booths, rides.

Samoan Flag Raising Day. Saturday closest to July 7; Ala Moana Park. Day-long program includes Samoan song competition, dances, ceremonies, sporting contests.

Japanese Bon Dances. Every weekend during July and August at Buddhist temple grounds. All islands. To honor the dead, masses of dancers in colorful *kimonos* circle a decorated tower on which musicians sit, drumming and chanting. A few temples hold spectacular nighttime lantern ceremonies to close a Bon celebration.

Tanabata Festival. July; one day. Japanese celebration, 3,000 years old, features parade, group dances.

Outrigger Canoe Racing. Main Oahu races of the season, from June to August, are the Walter MacFarland Canoe Races on July 4 at Waikiki Beach, and the Oahu Championships, in some protected bay on a Saturday in August.

Junior Surfing Championships. Second weekend in July; Honolulu. Nine to sixteen-year-old surfers compete for awards at Kuhio Beach.

Transpacific Yacht Race. July of odd-numbered years. Boats leave San Pedro, California, on July 4, cross Diamond Head finish line from 9 to 25 days later. Celebrations follow in Honolulu. Multihulls race same course July of even-numbered years.

Other Yacht Races. The season is February to October, with inter-island races in summer from Honolulu to Molokai; to Hanalei Bay, Kauai, in odd-numbered years; and from Lahaina, Maui, to Waikiki.

Windward Oahu Fair. July or August. Three days. Hawaii's biggest agricultural show, with orchids, anthurium, *bonsai*, home show, arts and crafts, livestock, poultry.

Chinese Feast of the Homeless Souls. Late July or early August; Honolulu. Three days. Kwan Yin Temple welcomes the souls of the departed during their annual sojourn on earth with ritual music, offerings of food, bonfires of paper money and clothing. The public is welcome.

Festival of Old Hawaii. A Sunday in August in private Honolulu garden. Hawaiian entertainment; demonstrations of native crafts; exhibits of artifacts, fashions. Sponsored by Outdoor Circle. Admission charge.

Hula Festival. August; Honolulu. Young and old, amateur and professional dancers perform the entire range of *hulas* from ancient to modern comic. Several Sunday afternoons at Kapiolani Park. Free.

Hawaii State Surfing Championships. August-September. Intrastate competition for men and women of all ages held on the south shore in or near Honolulu.

Waialua Country Fair. Late summer; Haleiwa Beach Park, Oahu. One weekend. Hawaiian-style country fair in sugar-mill community; auctions of art works and orchids, sales of paintings and handcrafts, fishing in a tank for tilapia, and a supper of *huli-huli* chicken.

Queen Liliuokalani Quilt Show. September; Ilikai. Display of authentic Hawaiian quilts, for awards; quilting demonstrations. Admission charged. Some libraries have annual Quilt Day (notably Waianae, in June) with exhibit, traditional patterns for tracing; all free.

Chinese Moon Festival. September; Honolulu. A festival in Chinatown with lion dances, sales of Chinese moon cakes, selection of a Moon Goddess.

Annual Artists of Hawaii Exhibition. All October; Honolulu Academy of Arts. Excellent juried show open to all artists, all media.

Honolulu Orchid Society Show. October; Honolulu International Center. Three days. Several thousand flowering plants on display and seedlings and plants on sale in the biggest orchid show of the year. Demonstrations of *lei* and corsage making and Oriental arranging.

Aloha Week. Third week in October on Oahu. (Neighbor Islands celebrate before or after.) Everyone wears a *mu'umu'u* or Aloha shirt during Hawaii's major celebration. The week begins with the presentation of the Royal Court at Iolani Palace and ends with the Flower Parade, Aloha Ball, and Monarchy Ball. During the week you can see dance programs, the finish of the Molokai-Oahu Outrigger Canoe Race, the Waikiki Water Carnival, and special displays and presentations at Ulu Mau Village and the Bishop Museum.

Hawaiian Malacological Society Shell Fair. November; Honolulu. One week. Exhibits of world-wide as well as Hawaiian marine shells, a shell sale, and film on shell-collecting. Admission charge for adults.

All Islands Makahiki Festival. Late November.

Filipino children *do a "surtido," several folk dances arranged as one, in the annual month-long Fiesta Filipina.*

Korean girls, *in bright skirts and rainbow-sleeved blouses, dance the "happy dance" at state fair.*

Variety of events to celebrate the harvest time of Old Hawaii. Honors Hawaiian God Lono.

Bodhi Day. Closest Sunday to December 8; Honolulu Concert Hall. A Buddhist celebration commemorating the enlightenment of Gautama Buddha beneath the Bodhi, or Bo, tree *(Ficus religiosa),* where he meditated. Religious services followed by entertainment. The public is welcome.

Festival of Trees. Early December; Honolulu International Center Exhibition Hall. Several days. An exhibit and sale of "everlasting" Christmas trees and ornaments, many handcrafted by members of Queen's Medical Center Auxiliary and the community.

Kamehameha Schools Christmas Song Festival. Mid-December. Two nights, Honolulu Concert Hall. A program of Hawaiian, traditional and popular Christmas music by the Glee Clubs and Ensembles of the Kamehameha Schools.

Duke Kahanamoku International Surfing Classic. One week before Christmas vacation; North Shore, Oahu. Televised invitational Big Wave contest for 24 top surfers in the world.

Makaha International Surfing Championships. First week of Christmas vacation. The world's top men and women surfers compete for honors in the big winter waves at Makaha Beach.

Christmas Eve. Kawaiahao Church in Honolulu welcomes visitors to its beautiful candlelight services with choral singing in both English and Hawaiian.

Horse Shows and Rodeos. Among the horse shows or rodeos held almost every month on Oahu, three of the best are the Horse Trials (spring and fall) and shows of the Hawaii Preparatory Academy (in May) and the Hawaii Horse Show Association (in early September). There are rodeos on Memorial Day, Fourth of July, and Labor Day, and shows by the Quarter-horse Association, Pony Club, and 4-H Horse group. For information call the New Town and Country Stables, Waimanalo.

East-West Center Shows. Students celebrate their different national holidays throughout the year. Main offering is the East-West Center Students Association International Show featuring national songs, costumed dances, skits, plays of various Pacific and Asian countries.

Art Shows. Honolulu. Shows are put on each year by the Hawaii Painters and Sculptors League, Association of Honolulu Artists, Honolulu Printmakers, and Hawaii Craftsmen, and there are frequent one-man exhibits in the galleries. For art news, check the *Aloha* magazine supplement of the *Sunday Star-Bulletin & Advertiser*.

Flora Pacifica. One week (varying dates); Honolulu. Exposition of plants in the domestic and artistic life of Pacific peoples. Call Friends of Foster Garden for date and location. Admission charge.

Hawaiian Open Invitational Golf Tournament. One week (dates vary) at Waialae or Makaha club. Top professionals compete for $50,000 in prize money.

Sources of Information

The Hawaii Visitors Bureau has offices on major islands and in several Mainland cities where you can take questions on almost anything — hotels, restaurants, recreation, tours, transportation, clubs, annual and special events. If staff members do not have the answer, they'll direct you to the right source. The all-island center is in Waikiki Business Plaza, 2270 Kalakaua Avenue, Honolulu. Information offices are at 2285 Kalakaua Avenue; in Hilo and Kailua, Hawaii; Wailuku, Maui; and Lihue, Kauai (see Getting Around section for each island). Other offices are: Tishman Building, 3440 Wilshire Boulevard, Los Angeles; Welcome Wagon Building, 209 Post Street, San Francisco; Wrigley Building, 400 North Michigan Avenue, Chicago; KLM Building, 609 Fifth Avenue, New York; 142 New Kokusai Building, 4, 3-chome, Marunouchi, Chiyodu-ku, Tokyo, Japan.

Hawaii State Visitor Information Centers are located at these airports: Honolulu (overseas and interisland terminals); Hilo and Kona, Hawaii; Kahului, Maui; Lihue, Kauai; and at Honolulu passenger ship piers.

The Chamber of Commerce of Hawaii, Dillingham Building, Honolulu, can give you the names and addresses of Chamber offices in cities and towns throughout the Islands and of the Chambers of various ethnic groups; these are primarily in Honolulu.

The State Department of Planning and Economic Development, 1010 Richards Street, Honolulu, has the latest information for businessmen.

The Consulates for Hawaii's main ethnic groups can also give you shopping and cultural information. They are all in Honolulu.

The State Department of Land and Natural Resources, 465 South King Street, Honolulu, has three divisions: **State Parks** handles reservations for cabins it maintains; **Fish and Game** sells hunting and fishing licenses (none needed for non-commercial salt-water fishing), sets hunting and fishing seasons and other regulations, can direct you to hunting guides; **Forestry** has trail maps. The Department has branches in Hilo, Hawaii; Wailuku, Maui; Lihue, Kauai; Lanai City, Lanai; Kaunakakai, Molokai.

Honolulu Department of Parks and Recreation, 1455 South Beretania Street, can supply information on the city's parks and playgrounds and Oahu's beach parks.

Hawaiian Trail and Mountain Club, Box 2238, Honolulu, and **Hawaii Chapter, Sierra Club,** 1372 Kapiolani Boulevard, Honolulu, can tell you about trails, help you plan hikes.

The Pacific Scientific Information Center, Bishop Museum, Box 6037, Honolulu, has information on the Islands, their people, animals, and plants.

Foster Botanic Garden, 180 North Vineyard Boulevard, Honolulu, can give you information on the Islands' plants and trees, garden clubs and shows.

Hawaii Audubon Society, P.O. Box 5032, Honolulu, can tell you where to find the Islands' interesting birds.

The State Foundation on Culture and The Arts, 250 South King Street, Honolulu, publishes a monthly calendar of Cultural Events, has information on plays, art shows, concerts.

Publications. These list current goings-on: Hawaii Visitors Bureau's weekly *Calendar of Events* (posted in hotels); *Honolulu Advertiser's Honolulu Calendar; Honolulu Star-Bulletin's The Pulse of Paradise; Waikiki Beach Press* (complimentary at hotels, Waikiki street stands; distributed Monday and Friday on Oahu; the Friday edition includes *Neighbor Island News* supplement, which also goes to other major islands); *Hawaii Tourist News* (distributed on Wednesday on all major islands; complimentary at hotels, Waikiki street stands); *Honolulu Weekly Snooper* (give-away available at hotels, shops, restaurants); *This Week on Oahu* (give-away at travel counters, restaurants); *This Week on the Neighbor Islands* (available on Hawaii, Maui, Kauai); *Aloha* magazine supplement of the *Sunday Star-Bulletin & Advertiser;* free tourist supplements published by major Neighbor Island newspapers.

Waikiki from plane off Diamond Head. *Open spaces are Kapiolani Park and, in distance, Ala Wai Canal, Golf Course.*

OAHU . . . the Capital Island

Oahu, the main island, is only the third largest, but it has four-fifths of Hawaii's people, almost half of whom live in Honolulu.

The 607.7-square-mile capital island, 40 miles long and 26 miles wide, lies between Kauai and Molokai. The Koolau Range that runs from northwest to southeast and the Waianae Mountains along the west coast are the remains of two volcanic domes which formed the island. Lava flows and erosion from both volcanoes joined the two, creating the fertile Leilehua plain where much of Oahu's sugar and pineapple is grown today.

People were living on Oahu before 1,000 A.D. Waikiki, with its coconut groves, fishponds, and walled taro patches, was a favorite seaside resort of early monarchs. Oahu was added to the all-island kingdom in 1795 when King Kamehameha and his warriors from Hawaii island landed at Maunalua Bay and took the Oahu king's forces in a famous battle in which they supposedly pushed some of the Oahu men all the way up to Nuuanu Pali and forced them to leap from the precipice to their deaths.

With its fine harbors, the island gradually developed into the state's political, economic, military, educational, and cultural center. Honolulu Harbor, discovered just before 1800, became a key Pacific port of call for whalers and sandalwood and fur traders. The sailing vessels used a mere reef-protected slip at the mouth of Nuuanu Stream; since then men have dredged and widened it, carved two inlets, and added fill to make shelter and berths for the world's largest liners and freighters. Pearl Harbor (once pearl oysters were abundant) came into importance decades later when ships exchanged sails for engines and nations set about building strategic bases.

By 1850 the court had moved permanently to Honolulu, which has been the seat of the Islands' governments—monarchy, republic, territory, state—ever since. For 75 years the capitol was Iolani Palace, the only royal residence in the nation. Now the Governor and Legislature work in the monumental new State Capitol, also in Honolulu's Civic Center, and the picturesque old palace is being restored to its original grandeur.

Although today Oahu is the only island on which other economic activities overshadow agriculture, it also has more land planted to pineapple than any of the others; its sugar plantations produce about 20 per cent of the state's crop; its truck farms and orchards yield 25 to 30 per cent of all Hawaii's fruits and vegetables.

Most of the state's servicemen and their families (in recent years about 110,000 people) live on Oahu, where all the big military bases are. They have helped to swell the island's population—which has been growing by nearly 17,000 civilians annually—to almost 650,000.

Oahu hosts virtually all of the tourists—now approaching 1½ million—who come to the Islands each year. A lot of new buildings, roads, even new land, are needed to take care of all these people; it is no wonder the dredge, bulldozer, pile driver, and jackhammer chorus never stops. Construction is big business, but so is manufacturing—everything from petroleum and steel products to surfboards and Hawaiian-style clothing.

People and goods from the Mainland, the Orient, and the South Pacific flow in and out of Oahu's sea and air terminals at a dizzying rate. The Pacific and its far-flung islands and opposite shores are about as strongly reflected in the island's educational and cultural life as is the Mainland U.S.A.—in oceanographic research, in the University of Hawaii's tropical agriculture and linguistics programs, and in its campus companion, the East-West Center, which attracts Asian and Pacific island scholars; in the museums, music, dance, movie-houses; in Oriental-language newspapers, radio, and TV shows.

All ages enjoy the beach *at Waikiki. This is Halekulani cove, midway in series of beaches that front hotels.*

How to Get There

Almost all flights across the central Pacific stop at Honolulu International Airport, and it is the destination of all Mainland-to-Hawaii flights except some that go direct to Hilo. Most inter-island flights are routed through the Oahu terminal, and Hawaii-bound ships call at Honolulu Harbor. For names of carriers which go in and out of Honolulu on domestic, international, or inter-island runs, see opening chapter.

Where to Stay

Waikiki, Honolulu's resort district, is a thicket of hotels and apartment-hotels with about 16,500 rooms. More than 20 hotels are right on the beach, the others a few blocks away at most. You can choose between high-rise towers (mostly air-conditioned) and wooden cottage clusters, a bedroom, a room with kitchenette, or a housekeeping apartment (weekly, monthly rates common).

Waikiki's congestion has resulted in tourist development in other parts of the island—almost 3,000 rooms now. The biggest new and growing resort is in Makaha Valley on the Waianae Coast, and another will be spread on Oahu's northern tip. You will find hotels Downtown, at the airport, in residential parts of the city such as Kahala, on Windward Oahu and the North Shore, and at Wahiawa and Waipahu. For more on the larger places, see Waikiki (pages 28-31), Makaha (page 50), and Kahuku (page 44). Travel agents and the Hawaii Visitors Bureau have names, descriptions, and rates of all hotels.

Getting Around on the Island

There is scheduled ground transportation between air or ship terminals and hotels. If you want a fast taxi, charter a Central Pacific helicopter to Waikiki or outlying spots—the Kahala Hilton, Makaha Inn. Kenai Helicopter Service can take you from Waikiki's Ilikai to Makaha.

In Honolulu you can get about on buses. Honolulu Rapid Transit Company has a free city map for sightseers (at travel desks, or send a stamped, self-addressed envelope) showing its routes which extend from Pearl Harbor to Koko Head. The HRT also runs buses to Sea Life Park.

Wahiawa Transport System runs buses from downtown Honolulu to Schofield-Wahiawa. City Bus Service provides transportation from Wahiawa to Kahuku; from Honolulu to Makaha and points en route; and from Honolulu to Waimanalo, Kailua, and Kaneohe. There is shuttle service several times a day from the Ilikai to Makaha Inn. Point-to-point taxis go from downtown to most Oahu towns for fares far lower than metered taxi rates. For a list of these, call Taxi Control at the Police Department.

Kaena Point

Mokuleia
Beach Park

missile tracking station
(99)
Dillingham Field

YOKOHAMA BAY
Keawaula Beach
Mokuleia
(82) KAIAKA
Alii Beach
WAIALUA
BAY
Haleiwa Beach Park

Makua
Beach
Waialua
Haleiwa
Kawailoa

Sunset Beach
Paumalu Beach
Ehukai Beach Park
Pupukea Beach Park
KAWELA BAY
Pupukea
(3)
Puu-o-Mahuka Heiau
Waimea Bay Beach Park
1
Kahuku

aau Beach Park
Kaneana Cave
Weed Junction
Thompson Corner
WAIANAE MOUNTAINS
Polynesian
Cultural
Center
Mormon Temple
Laie-Maloo Beach
Laie
Laie Point

Beach Park
Makua Valley
(82)
(99)
Puu Kainapuaa
Hauula Beach Park
Aukai Beach Park

Makaha
Makaha Valley
△ Kaala
Schofield
Barracks
Whitmore Village
Hauula

na Lahilahi Beach Park
(90)
Waianae Valley
Kolekole Pass
Lake Wilson
(80)
(804)
Wahiawa
Botanic Garden
KOOLAU RANGE
Sacred
Falls
Punaluu
Punaluu Beach Park

ai Bay Beach Park
Waianae
Lualualei Naval
Ammunition Depot
Wahiawa
Kahana Bay Beach Park
Swanzy Beach Park

lualei Beach Park
Maili
Lualualei
Valley
Wheeler Air Force Base
(99)
Kahana Valley
Kaaawa Beach Park
Kalae-Oio Beach Park

li Beach Park
Mililani
Kualoa Point
Mokolii

hawa Beach Park
Nanakuli Valley
(H-2)
(83)

nakuli Beach Park
Nanakuli
Palehua
Kipapa
Gulch
Waiahole
Ditch
Waiahole Valley
Waiahole Beach Park

he Point Beach Park
(75)
(H-1)
(73)
Keaiwa Heiau
State Park
Waiahole

lighthouse
Ewa
Waipahu
Pearl City
Kahaluu
Laenani Beach Park

rbers Point Beach Park
Campbell Industrial Park
Barbers Point Naval Air Station
(90)
(76)
Arizona Memorial
PEARL
HARBOR
Aiea
(71)
Camp Smith
Kahaluu Valley
Ahuimanu Valley
KANEOHE BAY
Ulu Mau Village
Heeia-kea Pier
Coconut
Island
Kaneohe Marine Corps
Air Station
Moku Manu

Nimitz Beach (military)
Oneula Beach
Park
Ewa Beach Park
Hickam Air Force Base
Honolulu International Airport
Keehi Navy Beach
(67)
(72)
Salt Lake
(H-3)
Kaneohe
Haiku Valley
Kawainui Swamp
(63)
Kaneohe
Beach Park
(63)
Mokapu
Peninsula

(90)
(63)
Nuuanu
Valley
Nuuanu Pali
Tantalus
(61)
1
(61)
Kailua
KAILUA BAY
Kalama Beach
Kailua Beach Park
Mokulua Islands

(90)
Manoa
Valley
Maunawili Valley
Puu Konahuanui
Olomana Peak
Lanikai
Bellows Field Beach Park

Honolulu
(See map on
pages 26-27)
(92)
(H-1)
Aina Haina Valley
(72)
Waimanalo
Waimanalo Beach Park
Manana
Kaupo Cove

Wailupe
Kuliouou Beach Park
MAUNALUA BAY
Koko Head
(72)
Kuapa
Pond
Sea Life
Park
Koko
Crater △
Kaiona Beach Park
Makapuu Beach Park
Makapuu
Lighthouse
Koko Head Sandy Beach Pa
Blow Hole
Halona Cove
Hanauma Bay Beach Park
Hawaii-Kai

N

0   miles   5

1   Golf Course
✕   Airport
       Paved road
═══ Unpaved road
       Jeep road
------ Trail
✕   Restricted access
━━ Proposed or
       under construction

OAHU   19

Honolulu tour agencies sell sightseeing trips of the city (half day); the greater Oahu circuit (all day)—it excludes the Waianae Coast; and the Koko Head-Waimanalo loop (3 to 5 hours). Air Safari will take you around the island in a Cessna (two tours daily), or you can charter a Central Pacific or Kenai helicopter for an overall view.

Rental-car agencies offer all kinds of vehicles—even motorcycles—at a variety of rates (see page 8). For location of the Hawaii Visitors Bureau and State Information counters, see page 16.

To see Oahu from a car, make three separate trips: (1) a circle tour of the greatest part of the island (about 80 miles), crossing the Koolaus on Pali Highway (route 61) or Likelike Highway (route 63), going around the north end, and returning to Honolulu via Wahiawa and Pearl Harbor (page 40); (2) the Koko Head-Waimanalo loop (35 miles) around the island's east end (page 47); (3) the Leeward Oahu-Waianae Coast trip (about 40 miles) as far as Makua (page 49). Side trip possibilities are everywhere, but note especially those in the Waianae section (pages 49 and 50).

Regular Events

In addition to the festivals and annual events listed in the opening chapter of this book, these events and activities take place regularly on Oahu, many of them in Waikiki.

Honolulu Symphony. October through April season includes concerts and 2 operas at Honolulu Concert Hall. In summer, there are Starlight Concerts at Waikiki Shell.

Royal Hawaiian Band Concerts (free). Bandstand in Kapiolani Park (Sun. 2 p.m. except during August); bandstand on Iolani Palace grounds (Fri. 12:15 P.M.).

Concerts by the Sea (Sun. 7:30 P.M.; free). Banyan Court at Moana Hotel. Weekly outdoor recitals by local or visiting musicians. (To combine concert with dinner, make reservations.)

Theater. These groups are either first-class amateur, experimental, or professional: **Honolulu Community Theatre** does contemporary plays and musicals throughout the year at Fort Ruger Theatre; **Lyceum Series** (University of Hawaii) schedules 8 events—theater, dance, visual arts, music—for all islands (October through May); for **Oumansky Magic Ring Theatre** plays you sit at tables on the Terrace Lanai at Hilton Hawaiian Village; **Theatre for Youth** performances (intermittent) appeal to grown-ups, too; **University Theatre** productions run throughout the year except August at Kennedy Theatre, East-West Center; **Windward Theatre Guild** stages 4 plays at Kailua Elementary School; both the **Mallory Players** at Tenney Theatre, St. Andrews Cathedral, and the Hawaii Performing Arts Company presents new theatrical works several times a year.

Bishop Museum Planetarium has regularly scheduled skyshows (page 35).

Movies. Waikiki has 3 attractive first-run theaters: the Waikiki, the Kuhio, and the Royal. You'll find a Cinerama Theatre, several centers for foreign and American art films, and a handful of Japanese theaters (sub-titles in English)—including the Toho notable for quality films and the Toyo for its architecture.

Arts, crafts, flower arranging. You can watch craftsmen at work at the **International Market Place** (page 30); **Ceramics Hawaii**, 629-C Cooke St. (page 37); **Kawa'u Kilns**, 650 Ala Moana (page 37); **The Foundry**, 899 Waimanu St. (page 37); **Olde Harbour Forge**, 1349 Kamaile St. (page 38); and **Crossroads Ceramic Center**, 1212 University Ave. (page 40). At the **University of Hawaii**, daytime classes are held at ceramics and sculpture labs, textile design, printmaking and weaving studios. Visitors welcome. Many arts and crafts centers and art galleries are described in area sections of this chapter. For more information call the State Foundation on Culture and the Arts. Flower arrangement demonstrations are given at various hotels.

Art Mart (Sat. 10-4; free) at Honolulu Zoo fence. Colorful outdoor display and sale of paintings by Island artists.

A Day in Japan (summer only; Sun. 2 P.M.) at the Japanese Chamber of Commerce, 2454 So. Beretania St. Tea ceremony, flower arranging, *bonsai* exhibit, bridal dress demonstration, music and dancing.

Senior Citizens activities. There are several clubs open to anyone over 50. Visitors should note Honolulu Senior Citizens Club which meets Wednesdays at 9 A.M. at Ala Wai Clubhouse, gathers other times for dinners, outings. Central Union Church has Senior Citizen activities Tuesdays at 8 A.M.

"Hawaii Calls" broadcast (Sat. 2 P.M.; free) rotates to Moana, Reef, Ilikai, Hilton Hawaiian Village hotels.

Kodak Hula Show (several times a week, 10 A.M.; free) in Kapiolani Park. Long-standing program of Hawaiian music and dancing staged especially for photographers.

Lu'aus. Many hotels regularly, churches and clubs periodically (and for lower price) hold Hawaiian feasts with pig

Traditional *Hawaiian floral greeting is given to most new arrivals. Lei sellers are at pier on boat days.*

roasted in the *imu* (underground oven), raw fish, *poi, laulaus* (taro tops or spinach, chicken, and fish steamed in *ti* leaves), coconut pudding, fresh fruits. Guests wear gaily colored *mu'umu'us* or Aloha shirts, watch Hawaiian entertainment. A *hukilau* (fishing with a big net) followed by a *lu'au* is staged weekly at the Kahala Hilton and once a month at Laie Beach by the Hawaiian-Samoan community there.

Tours and Cruises

In addition to regular around-the-island and around-the-city tours, here are a number of special interest and industrial tours.

Folkways Hawaiiana (several times a week). A 9-hour round-the-island guided tour geared to historical and cultural interest; 24 stops, including *heiaus,* Polynesian Cultural Center, and a *poi* factory.

Chinatown tours. Two regular walking tours of Chinatown start at 9:30 A.M., visit temples, jade, herb, and fabric shops, end with Chinese luncheon (optional). **Cathay Chinatown Tour** leaves (Mon., Wed., Fri.) from China Emporium, 1029 Maunakea St. (make reservations there); **Chinatown Shopping and Temple Tour,** every Tuesday, starts at Chinese Chamber of Commerce, 42 N. King St. The Chamber takes reservations, will arrange the trip for groups on other days, or set up a food tour that visits markets, cafes, and a noodle factory. The YWCA sponsors a **Walking Tour of Chinatown,** and a **Temple Tour;** call Richards St. headquarters for schedules, reservations.

Guide-yourself tours. To walk through Honolulu Civic Center's many historical spots, pick up a *Monarchy Promenade* descriptive map-folder at the Hawaii Visitors Bureau or travel desks. A low-cost paperback, *Old Honolulu: A Guide to Oahu's Historic Buildings,* is available at bookstands.

University of Hawaii campus tour (Mon.-Fri. 1:30; free). One-hour tour of campus buildings and art works starts from Bachman Hall, finishes just before East-West Center tour begins.

East-West Center tour (Mon.-Fri. 2:30; free). International guides take you on a 45-minute tour of the East-West Center starting at Jefferson Hall lounge and including the Kennedy Theatre and Japanese garden. To plan for a large group, call East-West Center Community Relations Office.

Perfume factories. Hula-Lei, 1225 Hopaka Street, and **Liana,** 2051 Kalakaua Avenue, welcome visitors but conduct no tours (Mon.-Fri., 9-4).

Woodworking factories. You can see native hardwoods cut, carved, and finished into bowls, figurines, and furniture, and buy seconds, at **Hardwoods Hawaii,** 850 Waimanu St. (7 days, 8-4, call for transportation), and at **Blair, Ltd.,** 404 Ward Ave. (Mon.-Sat.).

Sugar mill tour. Free tours through **Ewa Sugar Company** mill at Ewa are given weekdays at 10 A.M. and 2 P.M. during most of year. Call company to check.

Pineapple cannery tour. Check with **Dole Company** for tour days and hours, February to September; adm. fee.

Garden tours. Garden Club of Honolulu arranges tours for visiting groups through some of Honolulu's loveliest homes and gardens. Other organizations schedule such tours from time to time.

Night club tour of several Polynesian shows leaves major Waikiki hotels at 7:30 nightly except Sundays.

Camera shoots. Several Polynesian shows are staged especially for photographers. The Rainbow Camera Club schedules a camera shoot once a month; visitors are welcome. Call *Star-Bulletin* camera columnist for days.

Pearl Harbor cruises. Daily 3-hour trips by yacht or catamaran leave from Kewalo Basin at 9:30 A.M. and 1:30 P.M. You hear the story of the 1941 attack, pass the Arizona Memo-

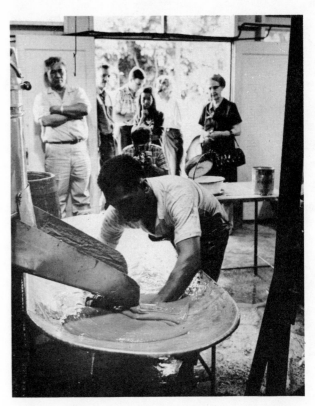

Folkways Hawaiiana tour *takes you to a poi factory where taro root is turned into favorite Hawaiian staple.*

rial, which bridges the sunken battleship, and the half-submerged *Utah,* tour current operations of the Navy base. (Some boats swing around Honolulu Harbor on return trip.) Complimentary trip on Navy barge departs from Halawa Landing at Pearl Harbor weekdays only; make reservations far in advance with the 14th Naval District PIO office. The Navy runs a free launch several times daily, except Mondays, to the Arizona Memorial from Halawa; you go inside, get impressive history lesson.

Ship arrivals and departures. Don't miss the colorful ceremony accompanying the arrival and departure of each passenger liner, starting a half hour ahead. *Lurline* alohas are the most festive. The Royal Hawaiian Band plays stirring music, hula dancers perform, and crowds hurl streamers back and forth. You can also sail on a catamaran to greet some liners off port.

Glass bottom boat trips. The Coral Garden Glass Bottom Boat, Heeia-kea pier (46-499 Kamehameha Hwy.) makes 4 trips daily except Tuesday over Kaneohe Bay's gardens. Glass Bottom Boats Hawaii, Kewalo Basin, has hourly cruises every day over the reef off Ala Moana (free transportation from Waikiki).

Other cruises. You can go for a ride on one of the catamarans moored along Waikiki Beach during the day and leaving hourly (depending on wind), or enjoy a leisurely sail and Hawaiian entertainment while dining aboard a catamaran or barkentine at the twilight hour—the "Sunset Dinner Sail." Pacific Game Fishing Unlimited, 1777 Ala Moana, books day-long excursions to Makaha, evening shoreline cruises, weekend fishing to other islands on the *Kona Princess.*

Special destination tours go to more distant spots: **Paradise Park** (page 39), **Sea Life Park** (page 48), **Ulu Mau Village** (page 42), **Polynesian Cultural Center** (page 43). The sea is the theme of the **Oceanic-Sea Life Park Tour** (daily except Mon.), a 3-hour excursion from Waikiki through Wilson Tunnel to Kaneohe, returning via Blow Hole and Hanauma Bay.

Catamarans *sail alongside liner as it heads into pier next to Aloha Tower for welcome by band, hula dancers.*

A Sea Life Park Express Bus picks up at major hotels daily except Mondays, starting at 11 and 1, with 2 afternoon return trips. The Honolulu Rapid Transit also runs buses directly to the park.

Recreation on Oahu

Camping and Picnicking

Oahu's shoreline is edged by more than 40 beach parks that attract swimmers, surfers, fishermen, or all of these. Many have pavilions, showers, rest rooms, fresh water, picnic tables, and grills. Honolulu's Department of Parks and Recreation, 1455 South Beretania Street, publishes a folder (available at the Hawaii Visitors Bureau Information Center) that gives the location and facilities of each park.

Camping. These are the beach parks at which camping is permitted, tents at all, campers at most: Hanauma Bay, Kaupo, Kaiona, Waimanalo, Bellows Field (weekends, holidays), Kailua, Kaaawa, Swanzy, Punaluu, Hauula, Pupukea, Haleiwa, Mokuleia, Keaau, Makaha, Pokai Bay, Lualualei, Maili (by 1970), Nanakuli, Kahe Point, Oneula (by 1971), and Ewa. At big Waianae Coast parks, campgrounds are widely separated and noted by Hawaiian plant names on bathhouses. The parks department requires permits (issued for an annual year) and limits camping periods.

To use Keaiwa Heiau State Park campground or reserve Waahila Ridge State Recreation Area for group camping, check with the State Parks Division, 465 South King Street. Local people also camp on Anuenue.

Hawaii Outings, 708 Keeaumoku Street, Honolulu, rents campers as do some firms noted on page 12.

Picnicking. You can picnic at any beach, mountain, or city park, or along mountain trails. At parks, campfires and cooking fires are permitted in designated areas. Bring charcoal as beaches are almost devoid of driftwood.

About the island, or right in the city, you will find lovely spots at the end of short trails. Some suggestions: Nuuanu Petroglyphs and Jackass Ginger pools along Nuuanu Stream; Manoa Falls; Sacred Falls (near Hauula); Puu Ualakaa State Park and Waahila Ridge Recreation Area (forest retreats with city panoramas). If you want to avoid walking, you can ride to Waimea Falls (adm. fee) near Waimea Bay; or try Wahiawa Botanic Garden, with paths to stroll; or close to downtown, Liliuokalani Gardens, with Waikahalulu Falls and swimming hole, or Thomas Square, with fountain and banyans. Don't overlook the big city parks, Ala Moana and Kapiolani. On all weekends you'll see crowds of local people at their fun, and in summer, the huge picnics of Oriental societies. Yet weekdays during the school year, or late in any day, you can stake out a large retreat. The Honolulu Zoo picnic grounds are often alive with colorfully-dressed children feeding the pigeons.

(Note descriptions on these and other parks in area sections of this chapter.)

Swimming, Surfing, Skin Diving, Shelling

As a general rule, swimming is safe in reef-protected areas at all times and in open ocean when the sea is calm. Beware of swimming where waves are very large, a beach is steep, or the coastline is rocky.

Here are beaches—most of them beach parks—where you will find fair-to-excellent and generally safe swimming: Ala Moana, Magic Island, all sections of Waikiki from Duke Kahanamoku Beach to Diamond Head, Kaalawai, Waialae, Hanauma Bay, Kaiona, Waimanalo, Bellows, Lanikai shore, Kailua, Kalama, Kualoa, Kaaawa, Kahana, Punaluu, Hauula, Kawela Bay, Pupukea, Haleiwa, Alii, Makua, Makaha, Mauna Lahilahi, Pokai Bay, Lualualei, Maili, Ulehawa, Nanakuli, Kahe, Nimitz, Oneula, Ewa.

Spots that look inviting but are hazardous are Halona Cove (rocks), Koko Head Sandy Beach (treacherous waves and currents), Makapuu (powerful waves, some undertow), and Waimea Bay (a dangerous riptide except when absolutely placid). When the sea is agitated, any of the north and west side beaches from Kahuku to Barbers Point—except for Kawela, and Pokai—can become dangerous.

For names of several easily-accessible natural fresh-water pools, see Picnicking.

Surfing. Waikiki, shallow and with a gradually-sloping floor inside the reef, has surf all year, and its various grounds, although crowded, are best for beginners and for "hot dogging" (experimenting, stunting). For safety—yours and the other surfers'—start out with lessons. The Kalama shore has small, windchop waves all year, for youngsters and their unskilled elders (a section is reserved for swimmers). Barbers Point and Hau Bush surf (Oneula Park) are also popular all year.

In summer, Waikiki has south swells and occasionally, waves of 15 feet or more. For other good summer surf, go off Ala Moana and Magic Island, Diamond Head, Black Point, and Koko Head. In winter, swells from the north and northeast are large enough to bring awesome 30-foot waves to the North Shore—to Sunset Beach, Banzai Pipeline (Ehukai Park), Waimea Bay, Haleiwa—and northwest swells create breakers that challenge experts at Yokohama Bay, Maili, and Mahaka (for surfing meets, see Annual Events, pages 13 to 16). Many surf grounds are also dangerous: beaches drop off, currents are tricky.

Makapuu is the king of body surfing spots, but don't attempt its powerful waves unless you know how. Be careful, too, at Koko Head Sandy Beach, a great place for *paipo* (belly) boards. You'll have gentler waves at Waikiki (especially off Kuhio Beach pier), Waimanalo, Bellows, and Kalama. You can body surf waves at Makaha, Barbers Point, Black Point, and Koko Head when they're too small for surfboarding.

You'll find licensed instructors and surfboards to rent at concessions all along Waikiki Beach. For more information, write Hawaii Surfing Association, Box 8125, Honolulu; it represents more than two dozen surf clubs.

Skin Diving. You can rent surface or scuba diving equipment, take lessons, charter a boat for a guided trip, or line up other water sports at Skindiving Hawaii, Ala Wai Boat Harbor, Hawaii's oldest and largest firm of underwater specialists, and from others listed in the Yellow Pages of the Oahu Telephone Directory.

In Hanauma Bay, a Marine Life Conservation District (no boats or removal of sea life, geological material), divers will see all the corals and colored, odd-shaped fish exhibited at Sea Life Park or the Aquarium. An underwater park (with onshore chart of various areas, their topography, marine life, and access point) is being created. Fin-a-Rama (Suite 1205, 2222 Kalakaua Avenue) offers day-long Hanauma snorkeling tours.

For shells, comb wave-swept sands in the least-searched areas—windward beaches north of Kaneohe Bay, and the North Shore. When there are Kona winds, choose beaches on south and west coasts. To skin dive for shells, go off Waimanalo, out to Rabbit Island; to Pupu-

kea Cove; Haleiwa Bay; the Waianae Coast (if you're an experienced diver). For information on Hawaiian shells, or to plan a shelling expedition, get in touch with the Hawaiian Malacological Society through Waikiki Aquarium—it meets there the first Wednesday of each month at 7:30 P.M.

Fishing

Kewalo Basin charter boats will take you trolling off the Waianae Coast for all the big fish (marlin, *mahimahi, aku, 'ahi,* barracuda, *ulua, kawakawa*), or through choppy waters off Koko Head or to the Penguin Banks near Molokai for *mahimahi* and *ono* and sometimes marlin and *aku*. On fast-moving trips across the channel you can surface-fish (using artificial lures) over and back, and anchor at the Banks for a few hours or overnight and bottom-fish ledges along the outer edge. Rates include tackle. Make arrangements with booking offices: Island Charters, 1089A Ala Moana, and Sport Fishing Hawaii, 1089 Ala Moana. Deep-sea fishing is also productive along the Windward Coast, notably in the open sea off Kaneohe Bay.

Spear fishing is good wherever the shore is rocky and the bottom is a mixture of sand and rock, and along reefs—particularly in caverns at the outer edges. Waianae's deep and inshore waters are excellent.

Best spots for spin fishing, surf casting, and poling from lava ledges are the rocky coast beyond Koko Head, Koko Head Sandy Beach, Waimanalo Beach, some parts of Kaneohe Bay, and selected spots along the entire north and Waianae coasts.

You can try your luck mullet-fishing the Ala Wai Canal or Boat Harbor; some of the chairs on stilts at water's edge are always vacant. In summer, *'oama* (tiny goat fish) and *moi-lii* (baby *moi*) run for short periods. You can join resident families who stand hip deep in Kuhio, Ala Moana, and windward shoals and hook

A "sliding board." *Falling off requires skill; surfer must thrust board aside, dive deep to avoid possible blow.*

Hikers in Maunawili Valley *follow trail toward Olomana Peak on Hawaiian Trail and Mountain Club trip.*

dozens of them with crude tackle. September and October are the months for clamming (if clams are plentiful) in Kaneohe Bay, from Kaneohe Marine Corps Air Station to Kaneohe Beach Park.

Lake Wilson (Wahiawa Public Fishing Area) is well-stocked with bass, bluegill, tilapia, giant channel catfish, and tucunare. Wahiawa Sporting Goods, almost on the banks, runs monthly fishing contests. Fishing from shore is practical, or the reservoir has a small boat ramp. Nuuanu Reservoir Number 4 has channel catfish and tucunare, is open for fishing on a limited basis—check State Fish and Game Division, 465 South King Street. You can buy your fresh-water license and pick up an area permit there or at tackle stores.

Boating

There are a number of ways to get out on the water. For charters, see Outdoor Fun, page 12, and note the cruises described on page 21. Through the Kewalo fishing agencies (see page 23), you may come upon boats to rent and skipper yourself, or try at the small boat harbors: Ala Wai, Keehi Lagoon, Pokai Bay, Haleiwa, Heeia-kea.

Areas protected enough for water skiing are Keehi Lagoon (best place), Kaneohe, Kahana, and Pokai bays, beyond the channel out from Duke Kahanamoku Beach, off Lanikai, Hawaii-Kai Marina. For boats, equipment, and instruction, get in touch with Hawaii Water Sports, Box 75, Building 2, Sand Island Road; Aeromarine, Inc., Building 210, Lagoon Drive; or Hilton Hawaiian Village.

Mainland yacht club members are welcome at the Hawaii (ocean-going craft) and Waikiki (class boats) yacht clubs at Ala Wai Boat Harbor, and at Kaneohe Yacht Club (class boats) on Kaneohe Bay. Visiting sailors sometimes are invited to crew in races, held all year but most frequently in summer.

Waikiki concessions sell outrigger canoe trips; each is a ride in on three waves. Hilton Hawaiian Village has U-Drive glass bottom tubs. For Ala Wai Canal U-Drive boats, see page 29.

Soaring

Sightseeing flights by sailplane are offered by the Hawaii Soaring Club, as well as instruction and sail plane rental. From the club's base of operations at Dillingham Field in Mokuleia (later at Bellows Field in Waimanalo), you soar along Oahu's coastal palisades. Trade winds blowing against them produce consistently good ridge soaring conditions—the best to be found anywhere, according to local enthusiasts. Phone the club to check weather and make reservations.

Bicycling

You can rent bicycles from Eki Cyclery, Ala Moana Center and 681 South King Street. Sometimes there are concessions in Waikiki. Makaha Inn and Country Club has bikes for guests. Visitors are welcome to join excursions of the Hawaii Bicycling League—some for speedsters, some leisurely family outings. Write 2620 East Manoa Road for schedule.

Horseback Riding

In several parts of the island you can rent horses and ride scenic trails. Most stables are open every day and have guides, but telephone ahead. From Koko Head Stables, you can explore Koko Crater Botanic Garden or go above Hawaii-Kai Golf Course to lookouts over Windward Oahu. At Waimanalo, in foothills of Oahu's most spectacularly-fluted mountains, are The New Town & Country Stables (horses rented only to riding students), Waimanalo Riding Academy, and Saddle City. To ride in Makaha Valley (3-hour guided trips from Hale O Lio Makaha Ranch a specialty), make reservations with Makaha Inn. Polo club members can join Wednesday afternoon scrimmages at Mokuleia Polo Club (check Waikikian hotel).

Hiking

Oahu's mountains abound in waterfalls, swimming holes, wild fruit, land shells growing on trees (supposedly a different variety on each ridge), forests, and viewpoints that are the exclusive domain of the hiker.

Both the Koolaus and Waianaes are criss-crossed by trails, some 66 described on sectional maps available from the State Forestry Division, 465 South King Street. Only the most traveled are maintained. Many are off-limits: they cross restricted watershed, private land, or military-lease land sometimes in use weekdays (particularly Koolau trails between Wahiawa and Kahuku). Check with Forestry, or better, join the hikes taken regularly by members of the Hawaiian Trail and Mountain Club (Box 2238, Honolulu) and the Hawaii Chapter of the Sierra Club (1372 Kapiolani Boulevard, Honolulu).

The Trail and Mountain Club schedules day-long hikes almost every Sunday, leaving Iolani Palace grounds at 8 A.M., and easy, short hikes two Saturday afternoons and one or two Sunday afternoons a month, leaving at 1 P.M. Non-members pay a small fee and everyone chips in on transportation. The Sierra Club has all-day hikes most Sundays; there's a transportation charge but no fee. Both groups secure necessary trespassing permission, publish schedules, and make periodic several-day hiking and camping trips to Neighbor Islands.

Here are a few trails easy and safe enough to do on your own (most are on club schedules): Judd Trail—and a spur loop past Jackass Ginger pool—and the petroglyphs—stream bank walk in Nuuanu Valley; the Tantalus complex—Manoa Cliffs, Manoa Falls, Makiki Valley; trails up or down the ridge from Waahila Recreation Area—from atop St. Louis Heights to Woodlawn, or the University of Hawaii; NaLaau Hawaii Arboretum trail on Diamond Head, or the course to the summit from inside the crater; Lanipo (from atop Maunalani Heights); old Pali road, below Pali Lookout; Lanikai Hills (by moonlight); Aiea Loop; Sacred Falls (Hauula); Laie; and Kealia and Palehua (with Campbell Estate permission) in the Waianaes. You can also walk the shore from Diamond Head to Black Point and Hanauma Bay to the Blow Hole. (See further descriptions on some of these in area sections of this chapter.)

Bird Walks

Visitors are welcome to join Hawaii Audubon Society walks to study native birds in the mountains or observe migratory and local shore birds. The group goes the second Sunday of each month at 8 A.M. from Hawaii State Library (Punchbowl Street side); there's a small transportation charge. The society (Box 5032, Honolulu) meets the third Monday of every month at 7:30 P.M. at Waikiki Aquarium.

Ti Leaf Sliding

There are slides on Tantalus and in back of Haiku Plantations, Kaneohe, where you can try this thrilling, but sometimes dangerous, sport—riding a *ti* leaf down a steep,

Sailboats, houseboats, fishing craft *crowd Ala Wai Boat Harbor. In distance: Ala Moana Building.*

wet, and often muddy bank which may end in a clump of trees or a drop-off. Also, you get quite a workout scrambling up the slope to start another run. Go in rainy months and just after a rain or during a light drizzle. The Hawaiian Trail and Mountain Club (this page) holds a *ti* leaf sliding party every New Year's Day on Tantalus, and can give you directions to various slides.

Golf

Oahu has two dozen golf courses and driving ranges. The municipal links are Ala Wai and Pali (both 18 holes), Kahuku (9 holes)—and by mid-1970, Waipio at Waipahu (18 holes). Other public or semi-private courses where visitors can play are: Bay View Golf Center, Kaneohe (18 holes, lighted); Fort Shafter Golf Course (9 holes); Hawaii Country Club, Kunia Road (18 holes); Hawaii-Kai Golf Course (18 holes); Mid-Pacific Country Club, Lanikai (18 holes); Moanalua, near Tripler Army Medical Center (9 holes); Makaha East (18 holes) and Makaha West (18 holes), Makaha Inn golf courses; Mililani Golf Club, near Wahiawa (18 holes); Francis H. Ii Brown Golf and Country Club, Pearl Harbor (18 holes); Olomana Golf Links, Waimanalo (18

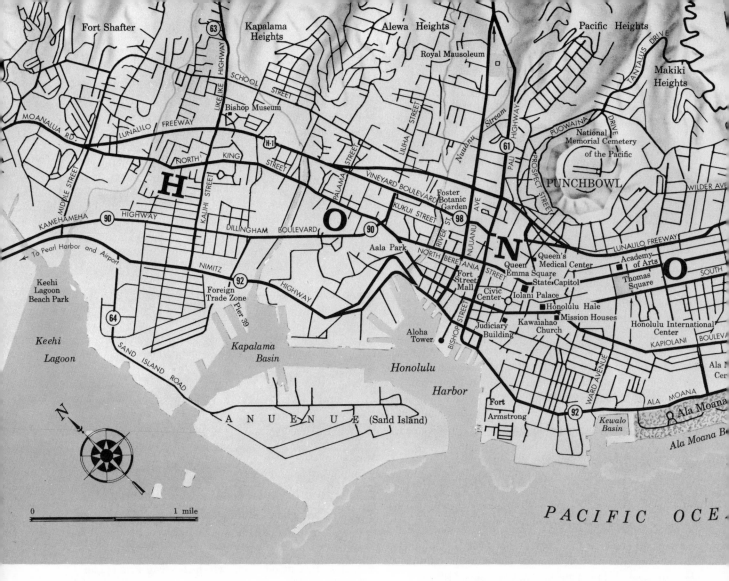

holes); Leilehua Golf Club, Wahiawa (18 holes). You can play at Oahu Country Club and Waialae Country Club, both 18-hole courses, if you are with a member or have a guest card. Kapiolani Park and Bay View Golf Center have lighted driving ranges.

Tennis

You'll find public court complexes at Kapiolani, Ala Moana, and Keehi Lagoon parks, Wahiawa Recreation Center, and Kailua Field, and one or two courts at various playgrounds. Some have lights. Waikiki Tennis Center at 3908 Paki Avenue in Kapiolani Park is open to the public (fee charged), and rackets can be rented there or at private clubs. Military families including reserves can use the lighted court at Fort DeRussy.

Hunting

Wild boar inhabit both the Koolau and Waianae mountains and there are a few goats in the Waianaes. They can be hunted in certain forest reserves all year, but go with

a guide—the country is rugged (see Outdoor Fun, page 12). During bird season (November 1 through mid-January, weekends and holidays), public shooting areas are opened for dove hunting. Consult the Fish and Game Division for locations. Buy licenses at its office or sporting goods stores.

Archery

There is a public target range in Kapiolani Park. The Pacific Bowman's Club (1826 Pali Paa Place, Honolulu) and the Hawaii Kyudo-Kai Archery Club (1405 South King Street, Honolulu), which practices Japanese-style archery, meet Sundays at Kapiolani, often for tournaments, and are good sources of information on bow-and-arrow hunting.

Spectator Sports

Honolulu has all the sporting events you would expect in any major city and college center—baseball, football, track, boxing, wrestling, swimming meets—but there are

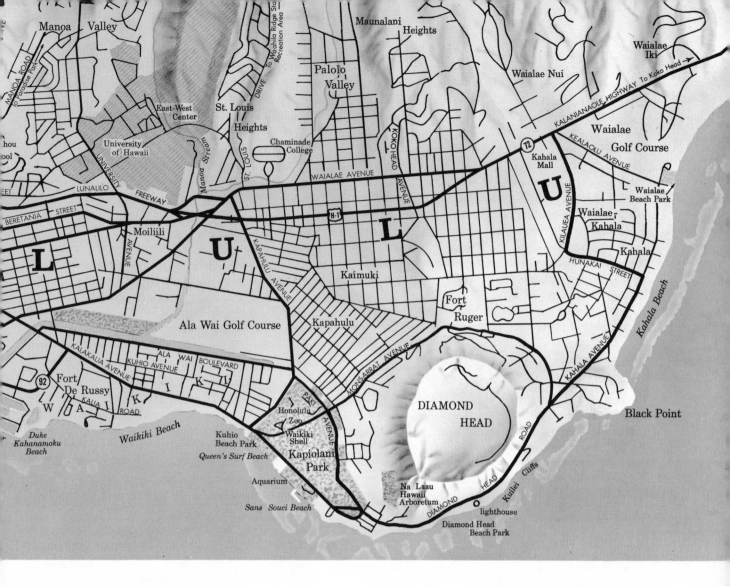

also a number of not-so-ordinary spectator sports which are especially fascinating to visitors.

Outrigger canoe racing. On the Ala Wai Canal, off Waikiki, and in various protected bays around the Island (see page 14).

Japanese archery. See Archery, above.

Japanese martial arts. You can make arrangements to watch *karate* classes and practice sessions (every day) and occasional tournaments at the Karate Association of Hawaii, 1502 South King Street, and Oahu YMCA's. International and state tournaments are held at Honolulu International Center and Civic Auditorium. Watch *aikido* (non-aggressive physical culture) classes at Aikido Hawaii, 3224 Waialae Avenue (gallery for visitors), and the Young Buddhist Association, 1710 Pali Highway. Get information on *judo* classes, practices, and tournaments of Oahu's dozens of *judo* clubs from the Young Buddhist Association and Oahu YMCA's. *Kendo* (fencing) classes and practices are held at Ainakoa Playground Pavilion, 1331 Ainakoa Avenue (Wed., Fri. 7 P.M.), and Kotohira Jinsha Temple, 1045 Kama Lane (Mon. 7 P.M.).

Rugby Union football. Local teams, including champion Church College of Hawaii team, play Saturdays Oct.-Jan. at Keehi Lagoon Park and Church College of Hawaii at Laie. Check Church College Athletic Department for schedules. Free.

Polo. Sundays at 2:30, March to September, at Mokuleia Polo Club (adm. fee). See page 45. Scrimmages Wednesdays. Call Waikikian hotel for details.

Cricket. Honolulu Cricket Club (c/o 64 Nawiliwili St., Honolulu) plays in Kapiolani Park Saturday or Sunday at 1:30 P.M. Free.

Honolulu

This fascinating city of 350,000 is at once South Seas, Orient, and modern U.S.A. It suffers from the same growth problems that plague every American city: choking auto traffic; freeways a-building but incomplete; sprawling new subdivisions; redevelopment of old districts. Cranes hover like praying mantises over newly-rising towers, some of them condominiums, the new vertical settlements springing up all over this land-scarce community. But happily, much still remains of bygone days: New England-style churches, wooden box temples furnished with shrines of bronze and gold-leaf, and government buildings straight from 18th century Europe; Chinatown, crowded with chop suey houses, noodle factories, bakeries, and open-front markets where smelly foods lie alongside a jumble of chinaware; small frame shacks, each with a little garden, huddled together along alleys and lanes; gracious homes with expansive gardens; precarious-looking houses on the steep hillsides, their understructures hidden by delicate wooden lattices; walking vendors with *leis* or pastries, others on wheels with local lunch favorites or a complete line of groceries; *limu* (seaweed) gatherers, elders in old-country dress, lady barbers who give neck rubs, and people everywhere costumed colorfully and comfortably down to their *zori*-clad —or bare—feet.

Honolulu sprawls over 25 miles of Oahu's leeward shore (from Hickam Air Force Base to Makapuu Lighthouse ridge). From water's edge, its ridges and valleys stretch up to cloud-topped peaks, and at night, houses on the heights become patchwork patterns of light. Residential sections also extend from Diamond Head all the way to Koko Head. Waikiki and business and industrial sections cover the central waterfront.

It won't help you much in Honolulu to know which way is east or west. You'll have to pick up the local directions: *mauka,* toward the mountains; *makai,* toward the sea; *Ewa* (eva), toward the Ewa Plantation (beyond Pearl Harbor); and *Waikiki* or *Diamond Head* (and beyond Diamond Head, *Koko Head*). You'll hear someone say, "Go two blocks *Diamond Head* on Kalakaua, then *mauka* on Kaiulani."

On the following pages we describe the city's places to visit by area so you can see what "discoveries" are near main attractions already on most tourist itineraries. With a city map you can plot some worthwhile excursions.

Drive these roads, and explore these districts for panoramic views, fine homes, gardens, and trees: Alewa, Pacific, Tantalus, Round Top, Makiki, St. Louis, Maunalani heights drives; Paki Avenue; Noela Drive; Diamond Head Road; Makalei Place; Nuuanu, Manoa, Fort Ruger, Black Point, Kahala, Waialae-Kahala, Waialae Golf Course, Waialae Iki, Wailupe, Niu districts; Portlock Road on to Koko Kai. From the heights at night the city is a dazzling spectacle of lights beneath a fog-free sky.

Noteworthy landscapes are the Board of Water Supply's park-like pumping stations and reservoirs (such as Makiki and Nuuanu) and Pali Highway poinsettia hedge that blooms from December to March.

At many new office buildings, hotels, churches, shopping centers, and isolated studios and stores, you can see work by Hawaii's top artists, designers, and craftsmen. We have singled out some. You'll discover others and can get help on where to find certain kinds of work from the State Foundation on Culture and the Arts.

Waikiki

Visitor headquarters is a 1/2 - by - 2 1/2 - mile peninsula bounded by the sea, Ala Wai Canal, and Diamond Head. Once a swamp with taro patches and duck ponds, Waikiki is a city within a city. It has the beach, hotels, apartments, houses, restaurants, shops, theaters, offices, travel agencies, parks, and tall palms. It's crowded, colorful, delightfully wacky. It is also noisy: You hear wind, surf, traffic, music, mynah birds, voices, jet planes, and—in daytime—the tractors, jackhammers, and power saws that accompany the rise of more skyscrapers.

You soon learn that Waikiki is not one continuous crescent, but a series of beaches (some natural, some man-made). Each beach has its own flavor and habitués, but the people-watching is good at all of them, and you can walk the shore, partly along sea walls, the entire length. The water temperature is in the 70's; the reef a half mile offshore protects you from strong currents and unwelcome fish, and waves break far out, giving surfers a long ride.

In the daytime, beach boys at stands between Duke Kahanamoku Beach and the Outrigger Canoe Club will introduce you to surfing, outrigger canoe-paddling, and the swift-sailing catamarans. You can take hula lessons, watch demonstrations of Hawaiian or Japanese flower arranging and coconut hat weaving, see Island fashions modeled during luncheon, go to the "Hawaii Calls" broadcast, the Saturday Art Mart, or the Sunday band concert, visit the reef fish and turtles at the Aquarium and the rare tropical birds at the Zoo. At night there's music of some description everywhere, from impromptu ukulele-playing on the beach in front of the Reef Hotel to the smooth dance orchestra at the Royal Hawaiian. You can get involved in duplicate bridge or try one of the party "packages"—a *lu'au,* supper sail, Chinese or Filipino dinner and show. (See Night Life, page 11, and Events, pages 20-22.)

Day or night you can shop (many stores stay open until 9 or after). You can dine or have cocktails at spots that range from the gracious outdoor terraces of the Royal, Halekulani, or Kaimana (the last two have cocktail time Hawaiian entertainment) to vantage points in the sky; one (Top of Waikiki) revolves, another (Top of the Ilikai) is reached by a glass-walled elevator up the 30-story face of the hotel, and a discotheque atop the Outrigger Hotel is called The Moon.

A few experiences you should not overlook: Visit the beach early or late in the day when it's as uncrowded as the travel folders show it. Go out at night for a moonlight swim or to see lights of sampans and torch fishermen out on the reef beyond white ribbons of surf, and the shadow of Diamond Head looming above shore lights. View a flaming tropical sunset; the most colorful usually occur in winter months. Walk out on the Kuhio Beach pier to watch boys surf with *paipo* boards, catch local teen-agers' lingo and observe their fads in beach costume. Kibitz on chess and checkers games played under the Kuhio arbors. Stroll Kalakaua Avenue; you get an eyeful at any busy time—*malihinis* venturing out in flamboyant new outfits; people gathered around a portrait painter, buying seed and shell trinkets at thatched huts, or listening (free) to the music emanating from an International Market Place night spot; cars backed up from cross-walks occupied by surfers, shoppers, and beachgoers. Explore Kapiolani Park; joggers of all ages go around it; residents exercise their dogs and wash cars in the shadow of posh hotels and apartments.

Ala Wai Canal, built in 1922 to drain swamps, is now a scenic waterway lined with golf course, palm trees, apartments. Shell and outrigger canoe crews race and practice in it; mullet fishermen sit for hours atop the walls or in now-rickety chairs rigged along the sides; a few houseboats are moored in the harbor at the ocean end. You can rent battery-powered U-Drive boats at McCully St. boathouse (6 P.M.-midnight; from 11 A.M. all school holidays).

Ala Wai Boat Harbor is the moorage for most private craft, headquarters for the Waikiki and Hawaii yacht clubs.

Duke Kahanamoku Beach and Lagoon are examples of man-made additions to the Waikiki crescent; they were built by industrialist Henry J. Kaiser in the late 1950's, named for Hawaii's famous Olympic swimming champion (1912 and 1920) who died in 1968.

Ilikai, 1777 Ala Moana, Western International complex at gateway to Waikiki, with 1,100 hotel rooms and suites and several hundred condominium apartments (1,000 units under one roof); Pacific Ballroom to seat 2,000 or divide into smaller rooms; restaurants; shops; night spots. From glass-walled elevator to topside restaurant you view yacht harbor, terrace with colored fountains where torchlighting ceremony and Hawaiian entertainment are held during cocktail hour.

The Waikikian, 1811 Ala Moana. Its lobby, a hyperbolic paraboloid constructed of wood, takes its shape from a South Seas spirit house. Hawaiian in feeling; lush plant material.

Hilton Hawaiian Village, 2005 Kalia Rd., is growing combine of towers, restaurants, shops. Landmarks are Rainbow Tower with 30-story-high rainbow murals, designed by Millard Sheets, on ocean and mountain ends (16,000 pieces of ceramic tile almost 1 foot square—in 17 colors and with special textures and glazes to make them non-reflective; lighted at night); first aluminum geodesic dome—an auditorium; Coral Ballroom that holds 3,500. Note Jean Charlot frescoes in Kona Koffee Shop.

Fort DeRussy. Recreation base for all branches of the service —lockers, overnight accommodations, restaurants, long stretch of beach, parade ground. High-rise hotel will go up at Diamond Head end. Remains of 1911 coastal defense battery will be used in its beach and social centers.

Huinakolu Kai (YWCA Beach Club), 2161 Kalia Rd., occupies first two floors of Waikiki Shore, is open to all YWCA

In this comic hula, *dancers shake feather gourd rattles, tie sashes around mu'umu'us to emphasize hip movement.*

members who pay club fees and to others (men and women) on daily fee basis. Tourist memberships are available. Facilities include dressing rooms, lockers, surfboard racks, lanai, reserved beach, kitchen, grills, picnic tables, a range of classes.

Halekulani Hotel, 2199 Kalia Rd., has been several times enlarged and remodeled since its beginning in 1917 as a small family-owned inn, but retains its old-fashioned charm, is an oasis amid concrete towers. Cocktails with a Hawaiian serenade on *kiawe* terrace, meals in lava-pillared dining room or ancient *hau* tree arbor where Jack London rested and wrote, and the Monday and Thursday night (9 P.M.) Polynesian show on oceanfront lawn are Waikiki traditions. Main building with high-pitched roof is the work of Architect C. W. Dickey, dates from 1931. "House Without a Key" lanai was made famous in Earl Derr Biggers' Charlie Chan "Who-done-its."

Canlis', 2100 Kalakaua Ave. Stunning lava rock restaurant with copper roof, interior waterfall, sculpture, aviary.

Waikiki Branch, First National Bank, Kalakaua at Lewers, has 100-foot Jean Charlot fresco showing Hawaii's first contacts with outside world.

Old Gump Building, 2200 Kalakaua Ave., handsome blue-tile-roofed structure by Architect Hart Wood opened in 1929 to house S. and G. Gump Collection of art treasures, now has offices, Heidelberg restaurant. Its exterior details include stained Burmese teak woodwork, verde antique copper gutters.

Prince of Peace Lutheran Church, 333 Lewers St., is view penthouse of 12-story Laniolu, a retirement home topped by cathedral façade with masonry cross.

Bank of Hawaii Building, 2222 Kalakaua Ave. Tower with grill of concrete arches includes **Waikiki branch bank** with E. M. Brownlee brass-and-bronze sculpture of stylized canoe prow beneath rain clouds, and Ruthadell Anderson tapestry from dried twigs, grasses, seaweed, coral; **Grossman-Moody, Ltd.** (Mon.-Fri. 8:30-5) with Oriental antiques and jewelry; a fancy **Woolworth's,** with popular restaurant.

Sheraton Hotel complex, from central Kalakaua to beach, includes: **Royal Hawaiian**, the "Pink Palace," built in 1927 as successor to old Royal on present site of Armed Services YMCA downtown. New York architects adapted Spanish Baroque design to Hawaii's climate; contemporary tower blends with it. Part of original foliage garden remains, even coconuts on the land when Kamehameha V built his beach home in 1870's. Stunning, mirror-backed floral arrangement, lighted for photography, is at end of lobby just outside elegant Monarch Room where dinner dancing can be out-of-doors. Also in hotel: **Royal Hawaiian Art Gallery** (local art); **The Lacquer Shop** (Japanese antiques). In street arcade: **Hawaii Visitors Bureau Information Center**. The **Moana**, Waikiki's first large tourist hotel, has famous Banyan Court where dining, dancing, concerts, hula shows take place under immense, 85-year-old Indian banyan. Hotel includes 1901 frame structure and concrete wings added in 1918 (with high ceilings, spacious rooms), and former Surfrider, 1952 prototype of most Waikiki high-rises. **Princess Kaiulani**, notable for undulating balconies and pitched-roof street-front shops. **Surfrider**, 1969 tower with balconies angled to give ocean views from most rooms and regal ballroom that divides into meeting rooms named for four Kamehamehas. Going up on beach is **Sheraton-Waikiki**, to be Sheraton's largest hotel anywhere when it opens in 1971, with 31 stories, 1,800 rooms, 3,500-seat ballroom.

International Market Place, 2330 Kalakaua Ave. More than 50 open-front shops, vendors' carts, restaurants, night clubs with an emphasis on the Pacific are set in a tropical garden with banyans. You can watch craftsmen making seed *leis*, clothes, jewelry and sandals, blowing and etching glass, weaving coconut hats, painting portraits. New tiers of shops will open at Kuhio Ave. entrance by spring, 1970. Market Place hours are 9 A.M.-10 P.M.; some places open at 7; night spots stay open until 3 A.M.

Teele Gallery, 405 Nohonani St. (Mon.-Sat. 9-5; free), has paintings for rent and sale, some by local artists.

Honolulu Zoo, *just a short walk from most Waikiki hotels, has typical zoo animals as well as unusual ones.*

Hawaiian Wax Museum, 2340 Kalakaua Ave. (Mon.-Sat. 9:30 A.M.-10:30 P.M.; Sun. 10-10; adm. fee). Lifelike wax figures of personalities in Hawaii's history are arranged in 18 scenes that illustrate major chapters, from arrival of first settlers to annexation. Royal gowns, medals, coins, documents on display.

Kuhio Beach Park extends from Moana to concrete pier at end of Kapahulu Ave. Popular with board and body surfers, surfer watchers; includes arbors with chess and checkers tables, bathhouse, benches, telescope. Its "**Wizard Stones of Kapaemahu**" are four legendary boulders, the largest weighing about 8 tons, said to have the powers of four soothsayers who came to Oahu from Tahiti before the 16th century.

St. Augustine's Church, 2512 Kalakaua Ave. Massive, symmetrical concrete church with verdigris roof has 200-year-old tapestry, baptismal font, and two statues from the delicate, open-sided frame chapel it replaced.

Kapiolani Park, a sweep of 140 acres from Kapahulu Ave. to Diamond Head, contains ironwood and monkeypod-lined drives, Waikiki Shell (outdoor amphitheater), bandstand, zoo, aquarium, flower garden, tennis courts, archery and golf driving ranges, picnic tables, beaches (Queen's Surf, Sans Souci), bathhouses, snack bars. Note 1929 **War Memorial Natatorium; Queen's Surf**, oceanfront mansion where President Roosevelt conferred with Admiral Nimitz and General MacArthur during World War II, turned into restaurant, night clubs, *lu'au* spot; and **Louise Dillingham Memorial Fountain**, Italianate, cast limestone, with jets of water that shoot up and inward from circular base and center tiers, in action from about 7 A.M. to 10 P.M. and illuminated at night.

Honolulu Zoo, 151 Kapahulu Ave. (daily 9-5; free). Some 1,650 mammals, birds, reptiles, amphibians, and fish representing almost 350 species live comfortably out of doors in 40-acre tropical botanic garden. Bird collection outstanding for 50 kinds of waterfowl (most in lagoons) including native Koloa duck and Laysan teal, the *nene* (state bird), birds of paradise, cockatoos, cranes, hundreds of unrestrained pigeons children are encouraged to feed. Among the animals are descendants of original Hawaiian cattle, sheep, pigs, and their Egyptian-like Indo-China dog without a bark. Also, "Animalanai" where animals are exhibited in replicas of natural habitat; touch-and-learn children's zoo (domestic animals) by 1970; snack bar; picnic grounds.

Kapiolani Flower Garden (entrance at 3625 Leahi Ave.; daily 9-3; free) has beds of anthuriums, vanda orchids, bird-of-paradise, gardenias, perennials.

Daisy, 463 Kapahulu Ave. (Mon.-Sat. 10-5:30). Quality weaving, jewelry, ceramics, other articles by Hawaii craftsmen.

Waikiki Aquarium, 2777 Kalakaua Ave. (Tues.-Sat. 10-5; Sun. 1-5; adult adm. fee). Beautifully-colored fish, corals, and other marine life from mid-Pacific waters displayed in sun-lit tanks; outdoor pool has tortoises and entertaining seals which visiting children help to feed.

Outrigger Canoe Club, 2909 Kalakaua Ave. Private beach club with dining areas, locker rooms, volleyball courts; offers 2-week guest privileges to members of affiliated Mainland clubs and visitors sponsored by a member.

Elks Club, 2933 Kalakaua Ave. Visiting Elks are welcome at waterfront clubhouse with beach, pool, dining room. Meetings are Mondays, 7:30 P.M.

Hawaii School for Girls, upper end of Poni Moi Rd., occupies La Pietra, the Diamond Head estate of the late Mr. and Mrs. Walter F. Dillingham, leaders in Island business, philanthropy, and society for half a century. The two-story pink stucco, tile-roofed mansion was built in 1921 around a court with arcades; it is modeled after several villas near Florence, Italy, including one in which the Dillinghams were married.

Diamond Head. Craggy profile of this ancient crater is as familiar as Gilbraltar. Once it was coast defense fort, bristling with guns poking through its high walls. Hawaiians knew it as Leahi (place of fire); it got its present name in the 19th century when visiting sailors scooped up volcanic crystals and mistook them for diamonds. Crater is National Natural Landmark and State Monument. Its slopes have private homes nestled in girdle of trees, 9-acre botanic garden, old gun emplacements stepping down 760-foot face. When firing ranges in vast, desolate interior are not in use you can drive in through a tunnel off Diamond Head Rd. in Fort Ruger and hike to the seaward rim—along a gently-graded trail, up 99 steps, through a tunnel, up spiral stairways and ladder of the gun emplacements, and out onto an exciting, top-of-the-world perch (call Hawaii National Guard Diamond Head range officer for permission, directions). Also inside are Federal Aviation Agency air traffic control and Pacific communication centers (call ahead to visit).

Na Laau Hawaii Arboretum, on slope of Diamond Head, reached by marked, ¾-mile trail from Makalei Pl. Replanting of native dryland plants (with name tags) was work of Garden Club of Honolulu and late naturalist, George C. Munro. From terrace overlooking Waikiki, trail continues through 9-acre preserve.

Diamond Head Road between Kapiolani Park and Kahala is a scenic drive past fine homes. It crosses Kuilei Cliffs, Diamond Head's drop into the sea, passes Diamond Head lighthouse and a monument to Amelia Earhart, famous aviatrix lost in the Pacific while making a round-the-world flight. The panorama from the bluff takes in residential Honolulu the length of Maunalua Bay, from Black Point (look for the columns of Doris Duke's "Shangri-La") to Koko Head and Koko Crater.

Diamond Head Beach Park, beneath the cliffs and reached by a spur road, is popular with fishermen and surfers. At low tide you can walk the shore to Black Point, on sand and lava, through tide pools, past oceanfront homes and Kaalawai Beach (safe swimming).

Civic Center

The Civic Center includes government buildings, new ones and old, and other early structures from the waterfront to the freeway, and from downtown to South and Alapai streets. Its master plan calls for a "great park" from mountains to the sea. Even today the central section, with the historic treasures, is park-like and just the right size for walking. Pick up a copy of the state's map folder, *Monarchy Promenade* (free at Waikiki travel counters, the Mission Houses, or Palace), and take a turn through the last century, from the houses of the first missionaries to the old royal residence to the fine cathedrals near the contemporary Capitol. You'll see a number of National Historic Landmarks: the Palace, Barracks, and Bandstand; Kawaiahao Church and Lunalilo's Tomb; the Mission Houses and Adobe School House. We give visiting times for buildings that have guides. At others, you're welcome inside at reasonable hours. Drive through the center at night; several landmarks are illuminated; the Capitol is dramatic.

Hawaii State Capitol, Hotel St. This tropical state's capitol has an open crown, and from the open-ended central court you look up five levels to the sky. The monumental building, its shape a little like the long-gone first (1845) Iolani Palace, was designed by architects John Carl Warnecke and Associates and Honolulu's Belt, Lemmon, and Lo. It has reflecting pools on two sides, surrounding columns (60 feet, fluted, like stylized royal palms) that rise to grills wrapped around the upper levels of

Contemporary state capitol *contrasts with old Palace (right) and Iolani Barracks (left), both being restored.*

offices. Below, flanking the court, are cone-shaped legislative chambers extending from underground to first-floor spectator galleries. The volcano-shaped crown is formed by 36 cantilevered concrete ribs arching from the roof, with glass mosaic tiles between. Note the volcanic rock and cast stone on outside walls; interior paneling, doors, stairways, desks, and trim of Big Island *koa*; Molokai sand in court paving; draperies and rugs influenced by *tapa* designs; Marisol's bronze sculpture of Father Damien (duplicate of statue in U. S. Capitol) in rotunda.

Iolani Palace, King and Richards Sts. (Guide in Throne Room Mon.-Fri. 8-12, 1-4; Sat. 8-12). The ornate, concrete-faced brick building, with colonnaded lanais, was finished in 1882 for King Kalakaua, later was the home of his sister, Queen Liliuokalani, until the monarchy was deposed in 1893, and was her prison for nine months in 1895 following an uprising aimed at restoring her to the throne. It was the seat of Hawaii's government until 1969. On the first floor are the former state dining and reception room and Throne Room (recently Senate and House of Representatives chambers); upstairs are former living suites which became executive offices. The Palace is being restored to its 1880's appearance, to become a living museum in which a royal family might still be in residence. Visitors may watch the work in progress.

Bandstand, on Palace grounds, is octagonal pavilion built for King Kalakaua's coronation in 1883, later moved to present site and used for concerts. Foundation and pillars (they represent the eight islands) were rebuilt in 1919-20, but copper-roofed dome is original and has Hawaiian coat-of-arms inside. Most shields on exterior are designs based on various flags. Royal Hawaiian Band performs Friday noons.

Iolani Barracks, on Palace grounds, is being restored after its move to make way for new capitol. Built of coral block in 1870-71 to house Royal Household Guards, the barracks has been used by National Guard of the Republic, U.S. Army, a service club, Hawaii National Guard, and has been a state office building. Next it will be a military museum and headquarters for present-day ceremonial Royal Guard.

Kawaiahao Church is occasional setting for pageantry when Hawaiian societies honor certain royal birthdays.

Kekauluohi Building (Archives of Hawaii), Palace grounds (Mon.-Fri. 7:45-4:30; Sat. 8-12 Sept.-June), was built in 1953 to house nation's most complete Hawaiiana collection.

Kanaina Building (Attorney General's), Palace grounds, was built in 1906 to house pre-annexation Hawaiian government records, was changed to office building in 1954. Oahu's only Captain Cook memorial (1928) is on 7-ton boulder out front along with an ancient sacred lava rock.

Hawaii State Library, 478 South King St. (Mon.-Fri. 9-9; Sat. 9-5; Sun. 1-5). Columned 1913 structure framed by spreading trees was designed by brother-in-law of Andrew Carnegie who gave some of the building funds; side wings added in 1929. Open-air patio has art shows (circulated to branches), inviting spots for reading. Library has excellent Hawaiian-Pacific Room, Mainland newspapers on file.

Honolulu Hale, King and Punchbowl Sts. City Hall (built 1929; wings added 1951) has a Mediterranean look; a patio, open to the sky and with a great staircase, is surrounded by city-county offices. Out front are a pool with fountain, pagoda given by "sister" city, Hiroshima.

Mission Memorial Buildings, City Hall grounds, built in 1915-16 of red brick in New England style as memorials to first missionaries, were headquarters of Congregational churches until 1947, then made city-county offices.

Mission Historical Library, 560 Kawaiahao St., built in 1950 to house libraries of Hawaiian Historical Society and Hawaiian Mission Children's Society (descendants of missionaries, popularly called Cousins' Society), which maintains Mission Houses and cemetery.

Mission Houses Museum, 553 S. King St. (Mon.-Sat. 9-4; Sun. 12-4; adm. fee), includes: Hawaii's oldest frame house, built in 1821 of timbers cut and fitted in Boston, sent around the Horn, and used as mission center, home, school for more than a century; coral block printing house with working replica of original Ramage press brought to Hawaii in 1820 aboard brig *Thaddeus*; two-story coral house that was mission storehouse and home of Levi Chamberlain, mission business agent. Buildings are being totally restored.

Kawaiahao Church, 957 Punchbowl St., is Honolulu's oldest church (1842). It is of Greek Revival style and made of timber from Hawaiian and West Coast forests and coral blocks cut on the reef. The church, which was preceded by four thatch structures, stands on the site of Hawaii's first mission (1820) and near an ancient sacred spring (the church name means "the fresh water pool of Ha'o"). Scene of royal inaugurations, weddings, christenings, and funerals, Kawaiahao still knows pageantry when Hawaiian societies turn out in regalia to honor royal forebears. Sunday service (10:30) is given in Hawaiian and English, features Hawaiian hymns by excellent choir, is followed by tour. In front is **King Lunalilo's Tomb,** Gothic, finished in 1876. Mission cemetery is on Kawaiahao St. side; congregation cemetery extends to Queen St.

Adobe School House, behind church, is city's oldest (1835) and perhaps only adobe building; its lime mortar was made from burned coral. Now used by church and for 1969-70 Hawaiian Mission Sesquicentennial Center.

Old Brewery, 553 Queen St. A favorite with artists and many Honoluluans, this 1900 red brick relic with tall, narrow façade was designed by a New York architect experienced in brewery construction, housed equipment shipped in a chartered schooner, made Primo, then Royal beer (except during Prohibition) until closed in 1960.

Kapuaiwa Building, Queen and Punchbowl Sts., was the third structure of Kamehameha V's planned civic center, still houses government offices. Of blocks set in mortar, its Ewa wing dates from 1884, the Waikiki addition, 1930.

World War II Memorial, Kekuanaoa (State Office) Building, King and Punchbowl Sts. On tablets set into base of 18-foot shaft built in 1944 are names of Hawaii's 528 World War II casualties. Building (465 S. King) dates from 1926, still carries designation, "Territorial Office Building."

Aliiolani Hale (Judiciary Building), King and Mililani Sts. European-style structure, oldest in Civic Center and a State Historic Site, is palace-like because it was first designed to be one. Plans were changed and it was completed in 1874 as parliament building of the kingdom, but King Kalakaua also used it for dances and receptions. It became the judiciary building in 1893 when Iolani Palace was converted to executive building.

Kamehameha the Great Statue, in front of Judiciary Building, made of gilt and bronze in Florence, Italy, is duplicate of original which stands at Kapaau on Hawaii island (page 88). Replica, ordered when original was temporarily lost at sea, was unveiled during Kalakaua's coronation in 1883. A copy of this replica is first statue of a king in U. S. Capitol—one of 50th state's two representative figures.

Federal Building, King and Richards Sts., housing main Post Office, Federal Court, is a Mediterranean adaptation with courtyard, verandas with graceful arches. New York architects built it in 1922 and a few years later, a companion, the **Hawaiian Electric Building** across the street.

Other government buildings, built from 1934 to 1959 and most named for *alii* (royalty), lie *makai* of Queen St. The U. S. Immigration Office with Spanish tile roof is oldest. It's at 595 Ala Moana near the Ala Moana, Kakaako, Richards block where a new Federal complex is going up.

The Falls of Clyde, Pier 5 (daily 10-5; adm. fee). Square-rigger is world's only remaining 4-masted ship, and only liner to have flown the Hawaiian flag. In service in the Pacific from 1898 to 1959, it is now a floating maritime museum, restored and operated by Bishop Museum.

YWCA, 1040 Richards St. Designed and landscaped by women architects in 1927, the 3-story Italianate headquarters wraps around an open-air court, divided for swimming, dining—a new wing will go up on patio's open side. The Y offers inexpensive courses lasting 5 to 10 weeks in such subjects as hula, ukulele, Oriental cooking, languages, flower arranging. Patio dining room, handcrafts shop open to public.

Armed Services YMCA, 250 S. Hotel St. U-shaped, Latin-style building on site of old Royal Hawaiian Hotel has 372 rooms for servicemen, plus swimming pool, recreational facilities, information counter; dining room is open to public.

St. Andrew's Cathedral, Beretania and Queen Emma Sts. Headquarters of Hawaii's Episcopal diocese was founded by Kamehameha IV and Queen Emma who had plans drawn in England. Building, using some cut stone sent from England, was started in 1867, complete enough for first service in 1886, finished inside in 1902. Additions since include 24 by 55-foot, stained-glass front wall; pool and fountain with 10-foot bronze statue of St. Andrew by Ivan Mestrovic. Next door is a century-old girls' school, **St. Andrew's Priory;** and just up Queen Emma St., at 1317, pretty **St. Peter's Episcopal Church.** It was built in 1914 by a rector from China, has *koa* wood interior carving with a Chinese motif. Congregation is mostly Chinese.

Washington Place, 320 S. Beretania St. Governor's home, oldest continuously occupied residence in Honolulu, is a white colonial building dating from 1846. It was built by Captain John Dominis of coral blocks and wood. His daughter-in-law, who became Queen Liliuokalani, lived in it after the overthrow of the monarchy until her death in 1917. The government bought it and opened it as executive mansion in 1922, added lanai in 1954. Not open to public, but easy to see.

Board of Water Supply Public Service Building, 630 S. Beretania St. Façade of vertical aluminum sun control fins is patterned after grill on imperial palace in Peking. Poinsettia hedge puts on winter show. Note water theme fresco inside, bas-relief sculpture on older Alapai St. building.

Queen's Medical Center, 1301 Punchbowl St., founded in 1859 by Kamehameha IV and Queen Emma, has buildings ranging in age from pre-1900 to the present, but no original structures. Historical exhibit room (weekdays 10-4) has changing displays. Grounds abound in fine ornamentals including rare bombax trees that have bloomed in February or March for 70 years. Close by and also just *mauka* of Beretania are **Hawaii Medical Library** with Prometheus sculpture by E. M. Brownlee; **Mable L. Smyth Memorial Auditorium** (honoring a part-Hawaiian public health nurse); and more contemporary government buildings.

Downtown Honolulu

For walk-about sightseeing, we divide downtown into two parts: the Bishop and Fort financial and shopping region, and the old-style Oriental shopping district from Nuuanu to Liliha, much of it called Chinatown.

Aloha Tower, at foot of Fort St. (daily 8 A.M.-9 P.M.). Ride elevator to observation balcony on 10th floor to view downtown buildings and harbor's liners, freighters, quaint sampans, pole fishermen. A landmark since 1926, the tower is 184 feet, has four identical sides with clock face and "aloha" engraved in balcony, contains offices, is lookout for controlling ship movements.

Terminal and piers, built around Aloha Tower. Passenger liners usually dock at Piers 8, 9, 10, and 11. Outdoor escalator connects terminal's passenger deck with Irwin Park which has a fountain, shade trees, *lei* sellers on "boat day." To tour a liner in port, call the steamship line—generally Matson, P & O, or American President Lines.

Bishop Street. Broad avenue with palms, graceful early buildings, is changing to canyon of new towers. Some buildings are headquarters of "Big Five" sugar factors. They no longer control Island business, but have branched into new fields and around the world. Note the arcaded Italian Renaissance **Dillingham Building** (1930) and **Theo H. Davies Block** (1921), the latter to make way for twin towers; distinguished **Alexander & Baldwin** (1929), an East-West amalgam, with overhanging tile roof, by architects C. W. Dickey and Hart Wood; the **Alexander Young,** a grand 1903 hotel, now mostly offices, stores. A twin of Amfac's 20-story glass-and-marble tower will replace its 1901 domed, native stone building on the Fort Street side of its block. **Financial Plaza of the Pacific** (Architects Leo Wou, Victor Gruen Associates) is a redeveloped block with striking 1968 buildings of volcanic aggregate, tinted bronze glass, and sculptural detailing linked by a promenade overlooking a corner plaza with fountains, trees. Its giant is 22 stories, houses **Castle & Cooke,** Hawaii's largest corporation, on its top three; lobby of 12-story **American Savings & Loan** tower has Florentine-made mosaic mural symbolizing Islands' volcanic origin; **Bank of Hawaii** is 6 stories with massive columns and cornice.

Union Street Mall, *mauka* of Hotel St., between Bishop and Fort. First narrow downtown street to be turned over to walkers is also rest and picnic stop for weary shoppers.

Fort Street Mall. Most of Honolulu's long-time main shopping street, named for a fort that stood about on the Amfac site from 1817 to 1857, is a new, lively, pedestrian way. Along more than ¼ mile, from Queen to Beretania, are pools, fountains, a waterfall, benches, trees, vine-covered archways, refurbished store fronts, poles flying banners, overhead lights with speakers for music, and two plazas, King Street, and Damien, at Beretania. A mural in the King Street underpass has crushed *pahoehoe* panels with petroglyphs executed by contemporary artist Edward Stasack.

Pier area *is viewed from corner of Bethel and Merchant streets. At right: old police station, now traffic court.*

Our Lady of Peace Cathedral, Damien Plaza. When dedicated in 1843 on site of Hawaii's first Roman Catholic chapel, this headquarters of the Honolulu diocese was a coral block rectangle with steeple. It has been enhanced over the years with a raised ceiling, balconies, tile roof, front columns. Tower's bells and clock were made in Paris in 1825. A plaque in yard marks where Hawaii's parent *kiawe* grew—starting from seed in 1828.

C. Brewer Building, 827 Fort Street Mall. Hawaii's oldest corporation has a handsome 1930 tile-roofed home of textured concrete and cut stone, with two-story lobby rotunda and walled garden court.

Hawaiian Savings Gallery, 830 Fort Street Mall (Mon.-Thurs. 8-8:30; Fri. 8-6; free), has exhibits by Island artists, new show every 2 months.

Old Downtown. Along and just off Merchant St., from Fort to Nuuanu, are the oldest (pre-1910) commercial buildings the city has left. They're in office use, or derelicts, but some may have façade and cornice detailing restored, enjoy new life as restaurant, boutique, antique shop, artist or architect studio in planned Merchant Square development. On Merchant between Bishop and Bethel look for: 1899-1901 **Stangenwald Building,** at 119; **Bishop Estate's** original (1896) lava stone office, 71-77; the 1877 **Bishop Bank,** 63; 1881 home of an early newspaper, **Hawaiian Gazette,** 76-84; **Melchers,** oldest (1853-4) of the lot, 51; **Kamehameha V's 1870 Post Office,** city's first all-concrete structure, at Merchant-Bethel corner, along with 1909 **Yokohama Specie Bank** and 1931 **Police Station,** now Traffic Court. Up Bethel is tiny **Friend Building,** an 1887 publishing plant, at 926; and the high-rise (for 1906) **McCandless Building,** 925. At Merchant and Nuuanu: the **Royal Saloon** (1890) and **Foster Building** (1891) with tiny brick warehouse behind. Up Nuuanu at Hotel: **Perry Building** (1888) that survived 1900 Chinatown fire.

Oriental Shopping District—Chinatown

Time is almost up for "Old Honolulu," settled in turn-of-the-century years by Oriental immigrants and more recently shared by Hawaiians, Filipinos, and servicemen on liberty. *Ewa* of Nuuanu Stream, it's lost to redevelopment. Chinatown is due for renewal, too—some buildings, some character may be saved—and new concrete buildings have pushed up against its Victorian relics of wood and brick. Happily, many have the district's traditional occupants—chop suey houses, herb shops, noodle factories, import stores, confectioners, and people who may still wear the dress of their homeland and gossip in native tongue. You still see open-front shops with wares bursting out the door beneath decorative cornices a story or so above.

Chinatown, bounded by Nuuanu Ave., Beretania and River Sts., Nimitz Hwy. Import shops carry hardware, basketry, dishes, pottery, jewelry, fabrics, home furnishings. Markets have many strange foods—fresh, dried, packaged, tinned. Noodle factories, bakeries, restaurants also sell food to take out. (See What to Eat, pages 11 and 12.) Maunakea St. is mostly Chinese, has **Wo Fat** restaurant (an institution), and *lei* vendors; Japanese places are scattered, but generally closer to Nuuanu Stream. Don't miss **Ozaki Hardware,** 209 N. King St., for fine cutlery; or an herb shop to see the raw materials of centuries-old Chinese medicines. (See Chinatown tours, page 21).

Hotel Street—on and just off—has Chinatown's honkey-tonk collection of bars, night clubs, tattoo parlors, pool rooms, penny arcades, fortune tellers—something to see, but not alone.

Fish markets, King and Kekaulike Sts. (daily)—one old, open-sided; the other glassed in, air-conditioned—have local fish, meats, produce, foods from *poi* to *kim chee*.

Fish auctions, Pier 15 and Market Place, 218 N. Nimitz Hwy. At Pier 15, sampans unload tuna, *mahimahi*, other fish in their catch from 5:30 A.M. until 6:45 when bidding (conducted in local lingo) starts. When all fish are sold auction moves to Market Place, about 7:30 A.M.

Chinese societies. District, surname, secret, or trade groups founded by Chinese immigrants for mutual aid are now institutions (with meeting rooms, ornate shrines) to carry on socio-religious customs. Here are a few to visit: **Chee Kung Tong,** 357 N. Kukui St.; **See Dai Doo,** 1300 Pali Hwy.; **Ket On,** 1123 Maunakea St.; **Lung Doo Chung Sin Tong,** 159 N. Hotel St.; **Kwong Chau,** 184 N. King St.; **Lum Sai Ho Tong,** 1315 River St. (red and gold, lively, Taoist family temple of Lum, Lam, Lim, and Lin clans).

New Oriental Town. Blocks between Beretania, River, Kukui Sts., Nuuanu Ave. are being rebuilt with shopping complexes, one of Japanese inspiration, another Chinese that will include apartments, Chinese societies, language school.

Nuuanu Stream bisects old town. Fishermen moor small boats under bridges that connect River St. with College Walk. All of College Walk and part of River between Beretania and Vineyard are being transformed into pedestrian malls, segments of a planned Nuuanu Stream and Valley linear park and greenbelt. Kukui and Kauluwela districts from College Walk to Liliha have modestly-priced townhouses and apartments, headquarters of voluntary health and welfare agencies.

Izumo Taishakyo Mission, 215 N. Kukui St. Temple built without nails in 1923 by carpenter from Japan was moved to *Ewa* bank of stream, rebuilt on podium, still has some original timbers and striking roof silhouette with clusters of three protruding horns, barrel-shaped member atop ridge, authentic Shinto symbols.

Toyo Theater, 1230 College Walk. Distinguished old Japanese cinema with tile roof, courtyard.

Aala Park, *Ewa* bank of stream, *mauka* of King. Gathering place of neighborhood is partly old and shaded with monkeypods and banyans, partly new with sophisticated landscaping, fountain, pavilion, bandstand.

Old Oahu Railway & Land Co. Terminal, 325 N. King St. From Architect Bertram Goodhue's sprawling 1925 Spanish Mission-style depot with tile roof, arches, and patios, passenger trains ran part way around the island to Kahuku, through 1947. A few freight cars still move over narrow-gauge track to pineapple canneries. Depot now has offices, bus terminal.

Wholesale produce markets, behind old railroad depot. Truckloads of fruits, vegetables grown on Neighbor Islands and in rural Oahu are brought here for distribution. Most action takes place early in the morning.

"Ewa" Side of City

Dole Company, 650 Iwilei Rd., the cannery topped by the pineapple-shaped water tower, offers conducted tours (and pineapple juice from a fountain) when cannery is operating. Call for schedule; busy season is summer. Adm. fee.

Foreign Trade Zone, Pier 39. Nation's 9th duty-free zone for importing, processing, re-exporting foreign merchandise.

Anuenue (Sand Island). Man-made protection for Honolulu Harbor has industrial yards, Coast Guard bases, unoccupied oceanfront popular for camping, fishing. People water ski in Keehi Lagoon, fish from Honolulu Harbor banks. Drive Sand Island Road to Diamond Head end for a fine view of city waterfront, skyline, harbor activity, Aloha Tower.

Airport region. Blocks *Waikiki* of airport, *makai* of Nimitz and *mauka* of Kamehameha Hwys. are mushrooming with busi-

Ancient Hawaiian dwelling is displayed in Bishop Museum. Gourds above platform were for water storage.

Thrones of Kalakaua and Liliuokalani, last king and queen of Hawaii, are now housed in Bishop Museum.

ness and industrial plants, hotels, restaurants, some quite extravagant, many well-landscaped. **First Hawaiian Bank's Moanalua Branch,** 1000 Mapunapuna St., built of precast and finished marble aggregate, features native woods and a bronze-and-steel E. M. Brownlee relief mural, "Metropolis." **Keehi Lagoon Beach Park,** off Lagoon Dr., has picnic area, views of boating, aircraft take-offs, adjacent Disabled American Veterans memorial obelisk, illuminated at night.

Honolulu International Airport, a Pacific crossroads, has one of the world's most colorful and exciting terminals, now expanding to accommodate more and bigger planes and planeloads. No transpacific flight arrives or departs without a crowd of *lei*-bearers at the gate, and hostesses in Hawaiian garb treat many an incoming passenger to pineapple juice. Approach-road *lei* stands, most staffed by Hawaiian ladies, are open around the clock. From main building—with most eating spots, shops—you overlook Chinese, Japanese, Hawaiian gardens.

Fort Kamehameha. Established in 1909, now a housing area for army families.

Hickam Air Force Base. Chief military field in Pacific, headquarters for the U.S. Pacific Air Force, and a stopover for most military flights between Mainland and Asia.

Salt Lake, once salt water, then drained and used as freshwater reservoir, is being filled in for homes, apartments, a golf course with ponds and waterways for hazards.

Tripler General Hospital. World's largest military hospital (1,500 beds), built by the Army in 1948 and used by all services. Main 5-story building with roof garden is mountainside landmark, commands fine city view.

Moanalua Gardens along Moanalua Rd. Private estate with magnificent trees, meandering stream, open to public for strolling, picnicking. Note two historic buildings: **Kamehameha V's Summer Cottage** (1860's) with delicately-carved lanai balustrades; and **Chinese Hall** (1905) with upturned eaves, carved roof details, wall paneling, all sent from China.

Fort Shafter. Headquarters for U.S. Army of the Pacific. Established in 1907, it was hub of army activities for Pacific Theater during World War II.

Bishop Museum, 1355 Kalihi St. (Mon.-Sat. 9-4:30, Sun. 1-5; adm. fee). Exhibits in three main buildings, Museum Hall (1889), Bishop Hall (1891), Hawaiian Hall (1903)—handsome edifices of cut stone with koa wood interiors—portray cultural and natural history of Hawaii and other parts of the Pacific basin. Look for a model *heiau,* feather capes and *kahilis,* costumes, ancient tools, sculpture, tapa, surfboards. Book store is stocked with works on Hawaiian, Pacific history, flora, fauna, and unique gift articles at all prices. Reference library has thousands of volumes. An outdoor exhibit of old railroad cars and plantation machinery illustrates the history of industry in the Islands. The planetarium has permanent exhibits in astronomy, morning and afternoon shows, and evening shows Fri. and Sat. The Museum was founded by Charles Reed Bishop in memory of his wife, Princess Bernice Pauahi.

Kamehameha Schools, Kapalama Heights. A 618-acre campus with schools for 2,500 boys and girls with Hawaiian blood, founded in 1887 as sole beneficiary of estate of Princess Bernice Pauahi Bishop, last member of Kamehameha dynasty. (Bishop Estate is Hawaii's largest private landholder with 9 per cent of state's land, worth more than $300,000,000.) You can drive through the campus any day; various music programs are fun to attend (see pages 13-14).

St. Theresa's Church, 712 N. School St., a 1963 sanctuary, has stained-glass window depicting St. Theresa, patron saint of missionaries, marble altar with mosaic background for crucifix, tower with 4 bells, lighted clock. Most worshippers are Filipino.

Kaumakapili Church, 766 N. King St., an imposing 1911 edifice, with Romanesque and Gothic features, also has unusual curved, graduated seating; services, singing in Hawaiian, English.

Tamashiro Market, 802 N. King St., noted for seafood: live local and imported crabs, lobsters; live Mainland clams, oysters, periwinkles; fresh fish, as many as 80 species at a time.

Old Palama Fire Station, 879 N. King St. Picturesque brick landmark with tile roof, brick relief trim, balcony, equipment-cleaning tower; dates from 1901, is now retired.

Continental Sausage Co., 1157 N. King St. Makes and sells a wide variety of European-style sausages.

Leap from cliffside *into Kapena pool in Nuuanu Stream.
You reach this spot by trail from Nuuanu Memorial Park.*

Four temples: Jikoen Buddhist, 1534 Kalihi St., is recent, Okinawan, a branch of Honpa Hongwanji founded in 1938; grounds contain memorial hall with shrine above, inscribed boulder commemorating leader of some 19,000 Okinawan immigrants to Hawaii starting in 1900. **Kotohira Jinsha,** 1045 Kama Ln., is Shinto, its architecture and appointments nearly authentic; note roof details, *torii* (entrance gate), and symbols of spiritual cleansing (outdoor washing place, cloth or paper strips that flap in the breeze); mission dates from 1920. **Koboji Shingon,** 1223-B N. School St., and **Higashi Hongwanji,** 1128 Banyan St., both with roofs characteristic of Hawaii's Japanese Buddhist architecture.

Nuuanu Valley

This valley you drive through on the way to Nuuanu Pali and Windward Oahu has some fine homes, large old trees, splendid mountain views. It is also a "church row." Some two dozen churches, temples, and related institutions lie on or just off Nuuanu Avenue and Pali Highway. We list those with unusual features.

Queen Emma Redevelopment Area, 75 acres bounded roughly by Kukui, Queen Emma, School Sts., Nuuanu Stream. New buildings include Queen Emma Gardens (high-rise apartments designed by Minoru Yamasaki), Harris Memorial Church (Methodist), Nuuanu YMCA (full athletic facilities, meeting rooms). See Dai Doo Chinese Society, Kwan Yin Temple.

Kwan Yin Temple, 170 N. Vineyard Blvd. Flamboyant temple with green tile roof and red trim has both Buddhist and Taoist deities but is presided over by 10-foot gold statue of Kwan Yin, goddess of mercy. Ceiling panels, altars, other statuary also imported from China. Worshippers come and go daily, consult fortune teller, light joss sticks at altars, burn heavenly money, symbolic paper clothing in incinerators on terrace.

Foster Botanic Garden, 180 N. Vineyard Blvd. (daily 9-4; free). A 20-acre tropical botanic garden with rare exotic plants and trees; comprises a prehistoric garden, economic garden, cathedral-like grove of giant kapoks and earpods; outstanding orchid, bromeliad, and palm collections. Free self-guiding tour map at office.

Liliuokalani Gardens, Waikahalulu Lane off School St. A 5-acre natural park, to be connected by footpath under freeway to Foster Garden, includes Waikahalulu Falls which drop to form swimming hole in Nuuanu Stream. Picnicking permitted.

Pacific Club, 1451 Queen Emma St. Businessmen's Club organized in 1851. Building is new and handsome.

Honpa Hongwanji Mission, 1727 Pali Hwy. Largest Buddhist mission, headquarters for 35 temples in state, has Indian-style temple built in 1918 to commemorate 700th anniversary of founding of Shin sect, 1963 hall of Japanese design.

Hawaii Chinese Buddhist Society, 1612 Nuuanu Ave. Tan Wah Temple is remodeled church furnished with Hong Kong imports. Members organized in 1955 to re-establish orthodox Buddhism; special services first, fifteenth days of lunar month.

Soto Mission of Hawaii, 1708 Nuuanu Ave. Zen Buddhist temple resembles Indian structure. Interior appointments are Japanese and surroundings include *bonsai* plants. Each weekday morning a priest explains Buddhist fundamentals in English.

Japanese Consulate, 1742 Nuuanu Ave. Modern building designed in Japan has national Japanese emblem at entrance, water garden in rear.

Ishii Garden, 1720 Huna Ln. Tea house restaurant on Nuuanu Stream began as private home (1914-18) and Japanese garden of Yukichi Ishii, still has "old country" character.

Korean Christian Church, 1832 Liliha St. Founded in 1918 by Korea's late Dr. Syngman Rhee, who worshipped here during long years of exile in Hawaii. Handsome façade of 1938 church is replica of a gate in Seoul. Congregation is mostly Korean.

St. Francis Hospital, 2260 Liliha St., has outstanding interior design, chapel, art works: E. M. Brownlee entrance statue of St. Francis in wrought iron, ceramic, mosaic; outdoor metal sculpture by Martin Newman; inside frescoes, mosaic, ceramic murals and sculpture; gallery of paintings by Jean Charlot, other noted Hawaii artists.

Honolulu Myohoji Temple, 2003 Nuuanu Ave. Japanese shrine with striking "peace tower" in serene setting off street. Entrance doors flank larger-than-life-size Buddha statue.

St. Luke's Church, 45 Judd St. Red-trimmed Episcopal church of Korean architecture for a mostly-Korean congregation.

Hawaii Conference of the United Church of Christ, 2103 Nuuanu Ave. Colonnaded structure built around courtyard is headquarters for association of early missions and allied churches.

Kyoto Gardens (Honolulu Memorial Park), 22 Craigside Pl., has replicas of two of Japan's treasures: Kyoto Kinkaku-ji (Golden Pavilion) with gilded Phoenix atop copper-shingled roof; three-tiered Sanju Pagoda of Nara; visible from Pali Hwy. scenic stop.

Nuuanu petroglyphs area. Go through Nuuanu Memorial Park, take trail up Nuuanu Stream past three pools fed by falls (Alekoko, Alapena, Kapena), caves with petroglyphs, picnic spots. Kapena is fine swimming hole with cliffs to jump off. Downstream (you beat your way through tangle on either bank) are remnants of corrals and road Kamehameha the Great used when he forced Oahu warriors over the Pali and took the island.

Royal Mausoleum, 2261 Nuuanu Ave. (Mon.-Fri. 8-4; Sat. 8-12:30), is burial ground of Kamehameha and Kalakaua dynasties. Original mausoleum, a Gothic Revival in Latin cross shape, was finished in 1865, and remains of royalty interred in tomb on Iolani Palace grounds were transferred. It was made a chapel in 1922 after bodies were moved, most to family crypts, some with taboo markers (*pulo'ulo'u*).

Chinese Buddhist Assn. of Hawaii, 42 Kawananakoa Pl., imposing, bright-colored Chinese temple with gilded Buddhas and Kwan Yin. On grounds: aged monkeypod, sacred Bo or

Bodhi trees (*Ficus religiosa*), meditation tree of Buddha.

Community Church of Honolulu, 2345 Nuuanu Ave. At modern quarters of predominately Chinese United Church of Christ congregation, walk to entry in lava rock façade bridges carp pool. Behind is turn-of-the-century Victorian house with Georgian features, home of Hawaii Loa College until fall 1970.

Philippine Consulate, 2433 Pali Hwy. White house with veranda was built before World War I, probably as German consulate.

Unitarian Church Gallery, 2500 Pali Hwy. (weekdays 9-3; weekends 9-12). One-man and group shows, some of local artists.

Temple Emanu-El, 2250 Pali Hwy., is successful blend of Jewish symbolism and contemporary architecture. Ark (with sacred scriptures) has teakwood grilles 25 feet high, doors with symbolic tablets of teak. Wing-shaped bronze lamp with "Eternal Light" flame is suspended from ceiling above.

Nuuanu Congregational Church, 2651 Pali Hwy. Lava rock wall and foliage hide all but white angled roof and steeple of church serving primarily Japanese congregation.

Todaiji Temple, Jack Lane off Nuuanu Ave. Only temple of Kegon sect of Buddhism outside Japan is coral color of Kyoto temples, presided over by world's only female Buddhist bishop (call ahead to visit). On July 16 Todaiji members set offerings, lighted candles a-sail (see Bon Dances, page 14).

Nichiren Shoshu of America Headquarters, 2729 Pali Hwy. Hawaii center of Japan-based religion that has main temple on Mt. Fuji, and Soka Gakkai, a lay organization that is better known.

St. Stephen's Church, 2747 Pali Hwy. Bold gray concrete structure rises from ground level to 30-foot-high peak at one end, accented by 70-foot-high bell tower at other end.

Chinese Consulate, 2746 Pali Hwy. Striking building with contemporary adaptations of Chinese concave roof and gateway features—inside or out—glazed tiles and terra cottas, superbly carved woods and ivories, richly painted woodwork. Courtyard separates consular and memorial hall pavilions.

Korean Consulate, 2756 Pali Hwy., occupies spacious white house separated from street by lawns and big shade trees.

Queen Emma Summer Palace, 2913 Pali Hwy. (Mon.-Fri. 9-4; Sat. 9-noon; adm. fee). Hanaiakamalama, now a museum, was summer retreat of Kamehameha IV and Queen Emma, built about 1847. Classic white frame house, maintained by Daughters of Hawaii (members are guides), contains furnishings, personal belongings of the queen. Garden has original trees, plants.

Tenrikyo Temple, 2920 Pali Hwy., is recent, of Japanese design, and for a mystical faith (neither Buddhism nor Shintoism) started in Japan in 1838 that has 3,000 Hawaii adherents.

Daijingu Temple of Hawaii, 61 Puiwa Rd. Shinto shrine in converted home honors sun goddess; stone lions at entrance.

Oahu Country Club, off Pali Hwy. Hillside golf course hemmed in by green mountain walls has sweeping view to harbor, new clubhouse (by early 1970), outstanding jade vines.

Church of World Messianity, 3510 Nuuanu Pali Dr. Modern Japanese white concrete structure has wing-like entrance canopy symbolizing spiritual uplift, 14 pillars representing order in teachings of religion founded in Atami, Japan, in 1931. Front garden has 1,000 azaleas; Japanese dry garden behind.

The Plain Between Downtown and Waikiki

Two boulevards—Ala Moana and Kapiolani—run from the downtown area out to Waikiki. Two parallel streets —King and Beretania—meet Kapiolani downtown and Kalakaua Avenue near Waikiki. Places we point out in this section lie along or just off these main roads or crosstown connecting streets, *makai* of Lunalilo Freeway.

Kakaako District, between Ala Moana, Kapiolani, out to Piikoi. Along mostly narrow, clogged streets, amid old shacks, corner stores, family factories, and new business, industrial, and office plants from concrete boxes to spreads with arches · and courtyards, are art displays, antique and import shops, art-craft workshops, and unusual factories and mercantile establishments worth a visit:

Art displays: Contemporary Arts Center of Hawaii, News Building, 605 Kapiolani Blvd. (Mon.-Fri. 8-6; Sat. 8-3); one-man, two-man, group shows, often tied to community cultural festivals. **Davis Gallery,** 910 Ala Moana (Mon.-Sat. 8-5); Leeteg of Tahiti black velvet paintings; local, Mainland, European oils, watercolors, and prints.

Artists and craftsmen at work: The Foundry, 899 Waimanu St., (Mon.-Sat. 9:30-5); artists and craftsmen glass blowing, making metal jewelry, casting in bronze and aluminum, firing in Raku ceramics kiln, in restored, brick-floored old foundry with gallery. **Ceramics Hawaii,** 629C-Cooke St. (Mon.-Fri. 8:30-4:30); good original pieces, most for commercial use. **Kawa'u Kilns,** 650 Ala Moana (7 days, 10-12, 1-3); hand-thrown and molded, Hawaiian design originals—lamp bases, wedding plates, mugs. **Kamaka Hawaii, Inc.,** 550 South St., (Mon.-Fri. 7:30-4, tours by arrangement); Hawaii's only ukulele factory, some guitars, lutes. **Woodworking factories,** see page 21.

Antiques, imports: Ansteth Limited, 1020 Auahi St. (Mon.-Fri. 9-5); costly Oriental antiques and art objects, fine home furnishings. **Cost-Less Imports,** 929 Auahi St. (weekdays 9-9, Sat. 9-5, Sun. 10-5); modern or ancient, hand or machine-made, cheap or costly imports from Orient, South Seas, "Down Under." **Carriage House Antiques,** 217 Ward Ave. (Mon.-Fri. 9:30-4:30); Hawaiian and Oriental antiques and art objects (branch at 410 Nahua St., Waikiki.)

Unusual businesses: Ala Moana Farmers Market, 1020 Auahi St. (daily 7:30-5:30); more than a dozen stores with Oriental foods, Hawaiian favorites, fresh seafoods, Island produce. **Kanai Nissei Shokai,** 515 Ward Ave. (daily 7-11:30); Japanese *tofu* (soybean curd) ready before 7:30, *aburage* (fried *tofu*) later. **Fishing supply stores** and a few **kamaboko** (fish-cake) **factories.** (See Oahu Telephone Directory Yellow Pages).

Kewalo Basin, between Ward Ave., Ala Moana Park, is home of sport-fishing craft, Pearl Harbor and other cruise boats (kids may dive for coins when they depart), sampan fleet, tuna cannery, two restaurants (**Fisherman's Wharf** for seafood; **Sampan Inn** for hearty low-priced fare). Most sampans unload catches in early morning (around 5:30), a few in late afternoon or evening. University of Hawaii's Look Laboratory studies in ocean engineering include tsunami and wind wave research.

Ala Moana Park. On 76 acres between Ala Moana and the sea are grass, fine trees, *hau* arbors, ponds, bridges, picnic tables, softball fields, lawn bowling, tennis courts, food stands, dressing pavilions, long sand beach bordering swimming lagoon. Good surfing grounds offshore. Handsome pavilion with banyan court contains **Children's Museum** (Mon.-Fri. 9-4; Sat. 9-12; free) with outstanding shell collection, children's art, Hawaiian artifacts.

Magic Island, 35-acre peninsula off Ala Moana Park, is completed step in planned reclamation of 85 acres of reefs for beaches, recreation space, perhaps hotels, apartments. Kewalo peninsula, center island to come.

Central YMCA, 401 Atkinson Dr. Rooms, athletic facilities, swimming pool.

ILWU Memorial Association, 451 Atkinson Dr. (Mon.-Fri. 8-4). Interior has fresco by Mexican artist Pablo O'Higgins.

Ala Moana Center, between Kapiolani, Ala Moana, Piikoi, Atkinson (Mon.-Fri. 9-9, Sat. 9-5:30; most stores open several hours on Sunday). Several-level shopping "city" has some 155 stores and services from specialty shops to department stores; malls, fountains, pools, aviary, plantings, outdoor escalators,

In Ala Moana Center, *you can browse through import stores, specialty shops, department stores, food markets.*

parking (almost 8,000 stalls); art works (E. M. Brownlee's fanciful children's sculptures; fountains with Ceramics Hawaii's whimsical figures, Bumpei Akaji's mosaics and bronze birds, George Tsutakawa's 2-ton bronze abstract); activity area; Oriental and Occidental foods in 30 shops and restaurants; **Gima's Art Gallery** (one-man shows by Island artists); **Great Things** (selected contemporary household objects by best designers). **La-Ronde restaurant** atop 25-story Ala Moana Building revolves once an hour.

Kapiolani Business District, between Ala Moana Center, King, Kalakaua. Partly old, mostly new complex of apartments, hotels, office towers, banks, shops, art galleries. On Kapiolani look for: **Gallery Asian** at 1216—near Pensacola (Mon.-Fri. 9-4, Sat. 9-12); antiques. **C. S. Wo & Sons Ltd.** at 1504; furniture store with continuing exhibit of Island art, ceramics. **First Hawaiian Bank** at 1585; Ben Norris abstract collage murals inside. **American Savings & Loan** at 1600; Juliette May Fraser fresco of Tahitians' voyage to Hawaii, Ken Shutt sculpture of birds, arts shows. **Toho Theatre** at 1646; Japanese films.

Other places: Brighter Days, 612 Sheridan St. (Mon.-Fri. 9-5); local crafts, especially ceramics. **Boyer's,** 830 Keeaumoku St. (Mon.-Sat. 8-5); hand-wrought jewelry. **Yasumi's Art Studio,** 914 Keeaumoku St. (7 days, 8-7); Oriental antiques, Japanese prints; **Olde Harbour Forge,** 1349 Kamaile St. (Mon.-Sat. 10-4); ornamental blacksmith specializing in chandeliers, whale craft. **The Lantern Shop,** 1631 Kalakaua Ave. (Mon.-Fri. 10-4:30, Sat. 10-2:30); Oriental antiques. **Saints Peter and Paul Church,** 800 Kaheka St.; 24-sided building with crown-shaped, tiered roof, bronze spire and cross, unusual carved altar section and baptistery. **Pagoda Floating Restaurant,** 1525 Rycroft St.; carp are fed at 8, 12, and 6 while diners watch.

Ke Alaula O Ka Malamalama Church, 910 Cooke St. Plastered frame building with wooden steeple serves 400 Hawaiian, Japanese, Filipino, Korean members of Protestant Hoomana Naauao O Hawaii; they spill out the door at services, which are in Hawaiian, with 15 minutes in English. Choir sings some member-composed hymns. Church is similar to 1897 landmark it replaced (like Hilo relative, page 72), has same bell, Victorian pulpit, choir loft railing, 14 pews (rear ones once for royalty).

Old Catholic Cemetery, King St. just *Ewa* of Ward Ave., was in use as early as 1860.

Honolulu International Center, Kapiolani, King, Ward. Air-conditioned complex in former estate-coconut grove, "Old Plantation," comprises Honolulu Concert Hall, Arena, and between, Exhibition Hall with meeting rooms, Assembly Hall. Arena, for sports events, big-crowd shows, holds 8,400, is surrounded by moat with hundreds of carp given by Japanese government. Concert Hall (holds 2,158) is architectural landmark, blending massive angular sections of white concrete with soft circular arches. Note Bumpei Akaji metal mural in lobby, Hawaiian-motif door decoration throughout center.

Thomas Square, bounded by Beretania, Victoria, King Sts., Ward Ave. Park linking Concert Hall and Academy of Arts has pool and fountain encircled by aged banyans. Square was named for British Admiral Richard Thomas who restored Hawaii's independence in 1843 after Kamehameha III had been forced to cede the Islands to Great Britain.

Honolulu Academy of Arts, 900 S. Beretania St. (Tues.-Sat. 10-4:30; Sun. 2-5; free). A masterwork of Architect Bertram Goodhue (started in 1927) has overhanging tile roof, galleries around five open courts, central atrium. Contains world-recognized Oriental art, masterpieces from Kress collection of Italian Renaissance paintings, modern European paintings. Exhibits local work, traveling contemporary shows. Has unusual Hawaiian plant arrangements, art school, shop (art books, museum reproductions), garden cafe for light lunch.

First Methodist Church, 1020 S. Beretania St. Award-winner by Architect Alfred Preis; of masonry with imbedded lava, partly screened side walls, sculpture by Jerry Aidlin.

Toad Hall, 1048 S. Beretania St. (Tues.-Sat. 10:00-8:30, free), features work by University students.

Pacific Gallery, 1098 S. Beretania St. (Mon.-Sat. 9:30-5; free), has work of the best Island artists.

McKinley High School, 1039 S. King St. Oahu's oldest public high school celebrated its centennial in 1965.

First Chinese Church of Christ, 1054 S. King St. Fine Chinese building with pagoda, patterned tile façade trim, opened in 1929, 50 years after church founding by immigrant converts.

Makiki Christian Church, 829 Pensacola St. Member of United Church of Christ, with large Japanese congregation. This landmark, completed in 1932, is modeled after a Japanese castle that was considered by the founding pastor to be a place of refuge and grandeur.

Shingon Temple, 915 Sheridan St. Fine example of Japanese Buddhist architecture; 1917 work of priest from Japan.

Joji's, 1259 S. Beretania St. (Mon.-Sat. 8:30-5). Japanese folk art; occasional one-man shows by famous potters.

Jodo Mission of Hawaii, 1429 Makiki St. Japanese Buddhist temple (1932) of Indian style—pink with gold domes, arches.

Mormon Tabernacle, 1560 S. Beretania St. Giant banyans frame formal entry pool and mural lighted at night. Visitor Center in foyer (Mon.-Sat. 8-5; Sun. 1-5) has paintings. After 11 a guide shows you about, explains Mormonism.

Central Union Church, 1660 S. Beretania St., has Hawaii's largest United Church of Christ membership. Colonial church built in 1923, matching chapel, on 8-acre lawn with monkeypods.

Punchbowl to Palolo

Here are some things to see on heights and in valleys—Punchbowl, Tantalus, Makiki, Manoa, St. Louis, Palolo—back of the central city, *mauka* of Lunalilo Freeway.

Tennent Art Foundation, 201-203 Prospect St. (Tues. 10-12; Fri. and Sun. 3-5; free). Noted local artist Madge Tennent's prized paintings and drawings of the Hawaiian people.

National Memorial Cemetery of the Pacific, Puowaina Dr. (daily 8-5), in vast bowl of Punchbowl Crater Hawaiians called Puowaina (Hill of Sacrifice). Tablets in seemingly endless rows mark 21,000 graves of war dead (World Wars I and II, Korean, Vietnam). Massive monument, "Gardens of the Missing," has names of 26,000 missing servicemen on marble slabs leading up to statue of Columbia, a chapel, and portico with 10 Pacific war map murals. From crater rim, you overlook city center, view sweep from Diamond Head to Waianaes.

Tantalus is city's highest, coolest residential section (summit, 2,013 feet) with houses all but hidden in magnificent rain forest. See it on a loop starting on Tantalus Dr. up through **Papakolea,** picturesque Hawaiian Homestead settlement, or Round Top Dr. just past the Board of Water Supply's splendid **Makiki Pumping Station**—a fine Hart Wood building in a landscaped park. The road climbs to 1,600 feet, has view turnouts, gives access to several easy hiking trails.

Puu Ualakaa State Park, off Round Top Dr., has picnic grounds, short wilderness walks, spectacular views to head of Manoa Valley, into Punchbowl, over much of Leeward Oahu.

Makiki Nursery, 2179 Makiki Heights Dr. (Mon.-Fri. 8-5). Hawaii's biggest commercial nursery for tropical ornamentals.

First Presbyterian Church, 1822 Keeaumoku St. First church of this last-to-arrive (1961) Protestant group.

Fernhurst, 1566 Wilder Ave. YWCA residence hall.

Arcadia, 1434 Punahou St. Tall, elegant retirement home.

First Church of Christ Scientist, 1508 Punahou St. Distinguished 1923 lava rock structure by Hart Wood, with steep shingled roof, Gothic entrance, wall opening to garden.

Punahou School, 1601 Punahou St., founded in 1841 for children of missionaries, now one of nation's largest preparatory schools. Buildings range from coral stone Old School Hall (1851) to contemporary chapel Architect Vladimir Ossipoff, built out over lily pond—with Erica Karawina abstracts in stained glass.

College Hill, 2234 Kamehameha Ave. University of Hawaii president's home is 1902 Victorian with fine Georgian trim.

Manoa Valley (Congregational) Church, 2728 Huapala St., built (1967) mostly by pastor-contractor, skilled members, has steel ribbing, 38-foot-high Karawina stained-glass mural.

Salvation Army Girls Home, 3016 Oahu Ave., shares Manoa hillside garden with **Waioli Tea Room** (luncheon; tea by reservation), **Bakery** and **Gift Shop** (Mon.-Sat. 7-4); a **grass house** where Robert Louis Stevenson wrote—when it stood in Waikiki; and diminutive **Waioli Children's Chapel** with appropriate stained-glass designs by Erica Karawina.

Paradise Park, 3737 Manoa Rd. (daily 9:30-5:30; closed Wed. Oct.-May; adm. fee). Lush 15-acre garden deep in valley has one of world's largest free-flight aviaries—you walk down ramp past scores of exotic birds; unique *hau* forest, bamboo jungle walks; other aviaries, some with native birds; flamingo pond; continuous trained bird show; gift shop; restaurant (dinner, too; *lu'au* Tues.). For tours, see page 21.

Harold L. Lyon Arboretum, 3860 Manoa Rd., 124 acres of tropical trees and shrubs (1,000 species), is University of Hawaii teaching-research ground. Visits by arrangement.

Manoa Falls. From end of Manoa Rd., walk up mile-long, always-muddy trail to falls and splash pool in jungle.

Manoa Chinese Cemetery, 3355 E. Manoa Rd. Interesting markers cover green hillside. Pavilion (key at house next door) has Tseng Yu-ho frescoes illustrating Chinese legends.

Mid-Pacific Institute, 2445 Kaala St. On preparatory school campus overlooking university, note original building of local lava stone, Juliette May Fraser's 92-foot mosaic mural on auditorium façade, outstanding rainbow shower tree.

University of Hawaii, lower Manoa, has some 18,000 students, faculty of 2,000, excels in geophysics, tropical agriculture, ocean engineering, Asian and Pacific studies, travel industry management, biomedical sciences, sociology, art. **Hawaii Hall** was first (1911) of "old campus" buildings with entrance columns, red tile roofs. Most new ones have good architectural art. **George Hall Art Gallery** (Mon.-Fri. 8-4:30) features faculty, student work. A map-guide (available at Office of University Relations, Bachman Hall) identifies campus trees and plants. For tours, see page 21.

East-West Center, 1776 East-West Rd. National educational institution established in 1960 to promote cultural and technical interchange among peoples of Asia, Pacific, and U.S., has students from 25 countries, outstanding I. M. Pei architecture and Japanese garden, shares university campus (note connecting Mall). **John F. Kennedy Theatre** is designed for Japanese Kabuki. **Jefferson Hall** has Art Gallery (Mon.-Fri. 8-4:30) with periodic exhibits by Asian, local artists, photographers; the cafeteria is an interesting place for lunch. Four tours, see page 21.

Chaminade College, 3140 Waialae Ave. Society of Mary liberal arts college (St. Louis High School for boys adjoins) has 900 students, stresses business, science, social science. Buildings are modified Spanish except modern circular chapel.

Waahila Ridge State Recreation Area, end of Ruth Pl. atop St. Louis Heights. Park in Norfolk pine forest has trails, picnic tables, group camp shelters, views of Manoa, Palolo.

Palolo Higashi Hongwanji Mission, 1641 Palolo Ave. Modern temple borrows from both Japanese, Indian traditions.

Palolo United Community Methodist Church, 2106 Palolo Ave. "The Church that Junk Built"—member-constructed with donated materials—has Erica Karawina leaded glass cross in Sunday School.

McCully to Koko Head

Old districts *mauka* of Ala Wai Canal, extending eastward to a crest back of Diamond Head (McCully, Moiliili,

East-West Center *students lunch beside Manoa Stream. In Jefferson Hall are cafeteria, lounge, offices, gallery.*

Nuuanu Pali Drive *twists through jungle of eucalyptus, ginger, hau, philodendron. Planting began in 1890's.*

Kapahulu, Kaimuki), have small homes and gardens (with mangoes), commercial sprawl along main streets (harboring good drygoods stores, Oriental and *saimin* cafes), Japanese language schools, new apartments. East of Kaimuki and Diamond Head, Honolulu's nicest recent subdivisions (pages 28, 40) merge with old, lushly grown expensive Kahala along the shore. They cover ridges, valleys, and peninsulas off Kalanianaole Highway all the way to Koko Head.

Japanese Shinto temples: Hawaii Ishizuchi Jinsha Shrine, 2020 S. King St., is authentic structure built with wooden pegs and wedges in 1963 by carpenters from Japan. **Inari Jinsha Shrine,** 2132 S. King St., is old (1914), painted bright red, has statues in front denoting its patron, the fox.

The Willows, 901 Hausten St. (luncheon, dinner, except Sunday). Thatched dining pavilions are set over lighted spring-fed lily pond stocked with huge carp, croaking bullfrogs. Tropical shrubbery, willow and plumeria trees are outstanding.

Japanese Chamber of Commerce, 2454 S. Beretania St. (Mon.-Fri. 8-4). Modern building adjoins authentic Japanese tea house and garden. For summer cultural show, see page 20.

Crossroads Ceramic Center, 1212 University Ave. (Mon.-Sat. 9-3), part of handsome Church of the Crossroads complex. Craftsmen use Shimpo wheels, Raku kiln for experimental glaze work. Some classes in pottery, serigraphy, fine arts.

Moiliili Nishi Hongwanji Temple, 902 University Ave., is topped by a steeple with 9 tiers, signifying 9 re-births necessary to reach Nirvana. Steps to temple symbolize man's difficulties.

Iolani School, 563 Kamoku St. Campus of modern build-

ings across Ala Wai Canal from Waikiki is independent, Episcopal-related boys' prep school founded more than a century ago.

Scattered churches: Episcopal **Church of the Epiphany,** 1041 Tenth Ave., a tiny lava rock "Hawaiian Gothic" half a century old, has recent Erica Karawina stained-glass windows, one with Hawaiian figures. **Wesley Methodist Church,** 1350 Hunakai St., features 30-foot-high Karawina "Tree of Life" faceted in cement. Episcopal **Church of the Holy Nativity,** 5286 Kalanianaole Hwy., has award for design using lava rock walls, sheltering roof. **Kilohana Methodist Church,** 5829 Mahimahi St., is very modern, has daring roof design.

Kahala Mall, Waialae Ave. between Hunakai, Kilauea. More than 60 stores open to Hawaii's only enclosed, air-conditioned mall. It's a park with sculptural fountain, Florentine glass chandeliers, activities (hula lessons, wine tasting, fashion shows, art exhibits, cultural programs), restaurants, snack shops, boutiques, gourmet market.

Kahala Hilton, 5000 Kahala Ave. Bougainvillea climbs balcony trellises of stunning 10-story hotel on beach next to Waialae Country Club. Stop in to see lagoon with porpoises, turtles, fish; three lobby chandeliers containing 28,000 pieces of colored glass; orchid displays; local art.

Co-op Gallery, Niu Shopping Center (daily 9-5; Fri. until 9; Sun. sidewalk shows). Outlet for group of local artists.

Hawaii-Kai, development started by late Henry J. Kaiser on 6,000 acres comprising Koko Head, Koko Crater slopes, adjacent valleys, and Kuapa Pond (ancient fishpond of 523 acres with one 5,000-foot wall, now Hawaii-Kai Marina). Of 3,000 units built (10,500 single and multi-family dwellings projected), some are houses or townhouse clusters on the water; their residents water ski, cruise to ocean or shopping center. Hawaii-Kai also has tree nurseries and a planting program; golf course; recreation center; luxury homes on Koko Head (Koko Kai) including pink buildings of Kaiser estate. Queen's Beach resort is in planning stage.

Oahu Circle Trip

The trip across the island to the windward side, then north around the Koolaus, is an all-day outing.

Take Pali Highway (route 61) or Nuuanu Pali Drive (both described below) to visit Nuuanu Pali, famous Windward Oahu overlook and break in the *pali* of the Koolaus, the northwest-southeast spine of Oahu. Here is one of the few places where you can drive into the midst of a *pali*—a line of nearly vertical cliffs at the head of ranks of valleys, the work of centuries of shaping by wind and water of the volcanoes that rose out of the sea.

Scenic Likelike Highway (route 63) from Honolulu's Kalihi Valley to Kaneohe travels Wilson Tunnel, then descends through banana farms at the very base of the *pali*. Before it quite reaches Kamehameha Highway, Kahekili Highway turns off northward to Ahuimanu Road (which meets Kamehameha at Kahaluu), giving the easiest access to Haiku and Ahuimanu valleys and a close look at the dramatic cliffs, remains of the ancient elongated Koolau dome that collapsed, then was battered by sea and gouged by rain.

To Nuuanu Pali and Kailua

Nuuanu Pali Lookout was the high point of the cross-island route used until 1961 when the freeway that tun-

Nuuanu Pali Lookout *is crowded briefly when tour buses arrive. Lookout's northwest corner is least windswept.*

From Wilson Tunnel *Likelike Highway descends along the base of green cliffs seen from Nuuanu Pali Lookout.*

nels beneath was completed. Now the lookout is the center of Nuuanu Pali Natural Park, a greenbelt at present, with new terraces and trails in the making.

The fastest way to reach the lookout (on a spur, 7 miles from downtown) is via Pali Highway. But for a more intimate view of the rain forest that protects and nourishes Honolulu's Nuuanu Valley watershed, turn off on old two-lane, winding Nuuanu Pali Drive (it's well marked, crosses the highway a couple of times). You drive through a luxuriant forest of eucalyptus, *hau*, bamboo, *ti*, ginger, and philodendron. Look for the short path (lower exit of Judd Trail) to Jackass Ginger swimming hole, about 150 yards below a reservoir spillway where you can park. The reservoir water aerator station has lily ponds and waterfalls.

A marker on Pali Highway points to Upside Down Falls on the valley's northwest bluff—a temperamental performer, but if the wind is strong and it has rained recently, you can observe the falling water being blown upward into a mist. Nuuanu Pali Drive brings you closer.

At the lookout a breathtaking view confronts you—and usually great blasts of chilly wind that lift skirts, take hats, spoil hairdos. From the 1,186-foot-high terrace, your eye follows the fluted palisades several miles northwest to Mokolii Island, then travels back to Mokapu

Peninsula at the opposite end of Kaneohe Bay. Surrounding peaks are 2,000 to 3,000 feet high. Below are green pastures, farms, golf course, cemetery, undulating hills—and some urban encroachment. Morning is the most predictable time for clear skies, good light for photographs —and tour buses.

After lookout improvements are completed (among them: separating automobiles and people, giving pedestrians viewing preference), the abandoned old Pali road will be made a promenade with rest shelters and surface treatment to illustrate its history: a Hawaiian footpath, improved for a horse trail in 1845, later widened for carriages, then for cars. If you walk down now, you can see sections of concrete and cobblestones that predate the modern asphalt, and can enjoy unduplicated views—out of the wind. A footpath goes underneath the highway to Auloa Road, more of the old cross-island route now a hiker's domain. From Kamehameha Highway below you can drive up Auloa or Kionaole Road to where they intersect, then walk.

The descent from the Pali opens up new vistas, including a view of 1,643-foot Olomana Peak (a green Matterhorn), highest point on the ridge between Maunawili and Waimanalo. From Castle Junction, you can continue straight through Maunawili Valley to Kailua, and follow Kailua and Kaneohe bays around to Kaneohe. You can meander through Maunawili—past new homes and a few remaining farms—on Auloa Road which rejoins Kailua Road (route 61) farther down; or go *mauka* on Auloa, then take Kionaole back to Kahehameha Highway. Kamehameha Highway (route 83) goes directly to Kaneohe, past Pali Golf Course and the beginnings of Hawaii Loa College's campus on 150 acres just opposite.

Along Kailua Road's "church row," turn into the Windward YMCA parking area and visit Ulu Po Heiau, the highest-ranking kind of temple kings used and a State Historic Site. It was probably built by captured warriors but legend attributes it to *Menehune,* the construction-minded dwarfs, who passed stones hand over hand for 6 miles. Walk a stone path across the huge platform and down the far side to a rock well at the edge of Kawainui Swamp, a moist green bowl of 750 acres to be dredged and made a park with a lake.

Windward Oahu

Several miles of sandy beach from Lanikai to Mokapu Peninsula are lined with homes. Frequent rights of way provide beach access. Off Lanikai are the Mokulua Islands; the one shaped like a camel's back has a fine beach. Kailua Beach Park is splendid, has Popoia ("Pancake") Island offshore and a pond running inland fringed with homes. Breakers in the Kalama section are gentle enough for novice board and body surfers. Mokapu is occupied by Kaneohe Marine Corps Air Station; off its Ulupau Crater tip is Moku Manu (Bird Island), a refuge for terns, boobies, and man-of-war birds.

Windward Oahu *offers easy cycling. Nearly level road passes scenic cliffs, beaches. This is near Kualoa Point.*

Inland are the business districts of Kailua and Kaneohe, Hawaii's second and third-ranking cities which serve a suburban population pushing 100,000. They have high-rises, and more and more stores and restaurants. Kailua's biggest church, St. Anthony's (114 Makawoa St.) seats 1,000. It's shaped like a cross, has four patios, massive tile roof, and impressive handwork—from pews made by Trappist monks to Erica Karawina's stained glass abstracts.

From Kailua's beach road, Kalaheo Avenue, you cross Mokapu Peninsula, follow Kaneohe Bay Drive (route 63) to Kamehameha Highway. Huge Kaneohe Bay has coral gardens (and glass-bottom boat, page 21), Kaneohe Yacht Club (class boats), Coconut Island with private resort and the University of Hawaii's Hawaii Institute for Marine Biology, and old royal fishponds (some filled for home sites).

You can see Heeia Fishpond (88 acres, 5,000-foot wall) from the high ground of Ulu Mau Village at Heeia (daily 9:30-5; adm. fee). Here you'll find a replica of a Hawaiian chief's village with thatch houses, workshops, gift shop (village handcrafts), restaurant (lunch daily; dinner and Hawaiian show, Fri., Sat.), and a stage, in a coconut grove, with almost-continuous 45-minute shows. You can watch *poi*-pounding, *lei*-making, *lauhala* weaving, hulas, and chanting, and have old Hawaiian life explained. For tours, see page 21.

Inland, (best approached from Kahekili Highway) are Haiku Gardens on Haiku Road, a jungled estate with restaurant overlooking grass houses, lily ponds, and bamboo groves; and Valley of the Temples in Ahuimanu Valley, a memorial park (daily 9-5) with a remarkable likeness—in concrete—of Kyoto's classic Byodo-in Temple. The temple is set between a reflecting lake with hundreds of carp and the majestic *pali* and is flanked by a ceremonial tea house and a 3-ton brass bell you can ring. In Ahuimanu, you can see a fence that outlines part of an old *ahupua'a*—the early Hawaiian land division which, typically, followed a valley out to sea in a widening "V" (fishermen and upland farmers pooled their resources—with some going as tax to the chief).

Kamehameha Highway through Kahaluu passes various establishments with amusing names: Hygienic Store (groceries), where the Kahekili-Ahuimanu route comes out, and Antiques & Junque (Oriental objects of quality; many temple dogs). Some days at Maikai Poi Factory (between 5-7 P.M.), you can watch taro roots emerge from machines as a mush which workers then mix with water and bag. Oahu's best—but shrinking—taro crop comes from here in Waiahole Valley. Drive in a way—it's still a bucolic spot. Waiahole also has one of the last old wooden open-front fruit and vegetable markets that used to sprinkle the highway.

Center's replica *of Tongan queen's home has coconut sennit binding, cushiony floor of mats on palm fronds.*

Polynesian Cultural Center lagoon. *Tahitian huts at left, Fijian, right; 57-foot Maori war canoe beyond outrigger.*

Kaneohe Bay ends at Kualoa Point where a large beach park is in the making; it will include Mokolii, or Chinaman's Hat, Island offshore, and eventually nearby Molii Fishpond, only Oahu pond still in commercial use. You'll pass ruins of a sugar mill that ground its last crop a century ago. Today this land is devoted to stock and cattle raising.

The rock formation on the cliff north of Kaaawa Beach Park is known as the Crouching Lion. It was once a fishing shrine and inspired the name of the restaurant in the big rock house beneath the crest.

The road swings inland around magnificent Kahana Bay at the mouth of a tropical valley with fruit trees left by early settlers. From the beach park (and boat ramp), shaded with *kamani* and ironwoods, you can look across the water to the overgrown stone wall of Huilua, Oahu's oldest fishpond and a National Historic Landmark, beneath pandanus-laden cliffs. The whole valley is to become a park.

All the way to Kahuku you notice fishermen out in small boats or swimming with spears over the reefs. You'll pass a string of beach parks (crowded on weekends); beach cottages; modest motels or cottage resorts; tour-stop restaurants like Coco Joe's (with shop featuring its lava products) and Pat's at Punaluu. Punaluu also boasts Hunnicutt Art Gallery (Tues.-Sun., 10-6) with a good selection of local work.

At Hauula, a marker points the way to Sacred Falls, an 80-foot drop into a 50-foot-wide gorge at the head of Kaliuwaa Valley. The falls form a deep, crisp swimming hole, but it's a muddy mile's walk from a cane field road. Notice Hauula's old court house and expansive beach park, and visit Hauula Congregational Christian Church—not only the charming wooden structure but, on its scenic hillside, ruins of large Lanakila Church which earliest members finished in 1862 using local coral and timber. North of Hauula take the spur out to windswept, sea-battered Laie Point, to look up and down the coast and at the ocean surging through a hole in an offshore islet.

Laie is largely a settlement of Hawaiian and Samoan Mormons. About 6,000 mountain-to-sea acres have been a Church development project since 1864. They include the town, Polynesian Cultural Center, a motel and restaurant (and shopping and resort centers to come), Church College of Hawaii (interesting murals), and the landmark Mormon Temple, built in 1919 in the form of a Greek cross, decorated with friezes, and set off by a formal garden. You can walk the grounds, attend narrated theater presentations (daily 10-5) on Mormonism and the colony.

Polynesian Cultural Center condenses the vast span of Polynesia into walking distance between replicas of villages of Samoa, Tonga, Old Hawaii, Tahiti, Fiji, and Maori New Zealand, with small huts and huge meeting

At Waimea Falls *you can ride this train for the 1-mile trip to the falls and pool. Some visitors prefer to hike in,* *then ride back. A swim and a picnic lunch at the park is a good way to break the round-the-island drive.*

houses. They're along banks of a lagoon where water pageants occur each afternoon. At each compound, natives of the particular islands (many are Church College students) tell you about the dwellings and their culture, demonstrate crafts, perform songs and dances. Touring the villages (Mon.-Sat. 11-5; adm. fee) takes 1½ hours. Evenings you can dine at a Polynesian buffet (from 5:30), watch a Polynesian revue (by reservation) on an open-air stage with cliff backdrop and fountains for a curtain. There's also a snack bar and shop with locally-created and imported crafts. For tours, see page 21.

The North Shore

Kahuku—both fertile, sugar-growing plain across Oahu's north tip and close-knit town with mill and company houses—is in the midst of change. The plantation will shut down in 1971 and the region will have turned tourist destination: first a hotel and golf course on Kuilima Point; ultimately a spread over land seaward of the highway from Kahuku town to west of sheltered Kawela Bay. Visit Kahuku's pretty golf course, between town and beach; its first-in-the-nation community-school library, with all communications media from books to closed-circuit TV; and the Methodist Church built by its members.

The coast from Kawela to Waimea Bay has the big-rolling winter surf (page 23). Just to look at waves along Sunset Beach when they run up to 30 feet is a thrill. In the Paumalu section you'll see Comsat, largest, most versatile station on earth for commercial satellite communications—television, telephone, telegraph (call a day ahead to visit—weekdays); one dish antenna is 10 stories tall. A marker points to a cliff-formation likeness of George Washington's head; legend says a prince turned to stone while chasing a lover to whom he had been unfaithful.

Turn up Pupukea Road, then a spur, to Puu-o-Mahuka Heiau, Oahu's largest ancient temple (its three walls run to 520 feet), a National Historic Landmark and State Historic Park—with descriptive plaque. It was a place of human sacrifices and where a famous priest forecast the Islands would be overrun by strangers from a far-off land. The view extends from Waimea Bay and Stream far below all the way to Kaena Point.

At Waimea Falls (daily 10-6; adm. fee), a half-mile inland from the highway, you can ride the "Menehune Train" (a narrated tour) or walk along a trail to a natural pool and waterfall for a swim and picnic. Other trails burrow deep into an unspoiled valley with *koa*, guava, and orange trees, and fern grottos. You'll find a snack bar and small children's zoo near the park entrance.

From Waimea Bay (beautiful sand, hazardous current) to Haleiwa you travel drier country, feast on more views of the unprotected coast, see attractive beach homes around Kawailoa and a modern dairy farm which has provided a thatch-roofed picnic shelter and children's "animal farm" for the public. Go 2 miles up Kawailoa

Drive to one of few remaining plantation camps, a hillside village with quaint temple and church amid waving cane.

Explore Haleiwa, a mix of old plantation and fishing village—grown a little Bohemian—that lost out as the Waialua District's main settlement when newer Waialua grew up around the mill. Haleiwa was where missionaries built the North Shore's first church, Queen Liliuokalani vacationed, and Oahu's first rural resort hotel opened in 1899 (it's gone, but new ones are coming).

The highway skirts Haleiwa Beach Park with generous expanses of grass, sand, and palms, fringing the head of Waialua Bay and facing the Mokuleia shore and the head of the rugged Waianaes. It crosses the narrow arched bridge over Anahulu Stream—look inland upon a few small boats at rest under a cover of trees, or outward on many craft moored in the boat harbor. It passes the only real restaurants—Haleiwa Sands (inexpensive buffet lunch) and Sea View Inn (fresh seafood)—pint-size bank, old wooden court house, big concrete theater, and archaic buildings that house pool halls, surfboards, souvenirs, and small markets that do a whopping business on "shave ice." One relic is Fettig Art Galley (daily 10-4), headquarters for North Shore Artists who display Sunday afternoons on the fence of Cannon's Pony Farm, at the Kahuku edge of town and open weekends for youngsters' pony and carnival rides. Visit Liliuokalani Church, the fourth (1961) sanctuary on the old mission site. It is steeple style, has the ancient bell, a memorial archway, and the clock the queen presented in 1890 on which the hours are the 12 letters of her name. Adjacent gravestones date from the 1830's.

Turn off and make a loop along Haleiwa Beach Road, then Paalaa Road. A spur at the end of the boat harbor leads to Alii Beach at one end of a long, broad ribbon of sand bordering winter surf grounds, and to Waialua Bay's 800-foot rock breakwater popular with surfer-watchers and fishermen. Summer seas are calm at Alii and farther along at Army and Jodo Mission beaches. On Haleiwa Road look for the Jodo Temple and Japanese language school, graceful fire station and elementary school, little Hawaiian Protestant church; and on Paalaa, taro patches, banana groves, and the Shingon Mission—with Japanese roof and jalousies.

Take Haleiwa Beach Road or the main route 83 to Waialua Beach Road (route 82), then turn off up to the mill almost in Waialua's tree-shaded center with handsome early bank and an old cane haul railroad engine. Nearby housing camps have interesting temples and churches—ask your way—and going out to Farrington Highway (route 99), you pass St. Michael's imposing church and school.

Farrington goes west to Mokuleia Polo Club and vacation house colony (page 27), Dillingham Field (private planes, soaring—page 24), a beach park for camping, organization camps, then becomes the dirt road around Kaena Point (page 50). Farrington goes east to Thompson Corner where routes 99 and 83 join. On route 83 (toward Haleiwa), look out in a cane field for the stack of the old mill of 1880's vintage; a Chinese banyan grows on top. Continue south on a cane road from the end of route 83 and look in another field for ruins of a large Catholic church, and graves marked with crosses or Oriental characters.

Inland to Honolulu

To reach the cool, 1,000-foot Leilehua Plateau, take either Kamehameha Highway (route 82) from Weed Junction at Haleiwa's edge, or take older, prettier Kaukonahua Road (route 99) from Thompson Corner. Kaukonahua Road bears the name of the state's longest stream which meanders 33 miles to Waialua from its source in the Koolaus. The routes join after climbs through cane, then pineapple. Both provide good views of 4,040-foot Kaala, Oahu's highest peak (a restricted road goes up to a FAA-National Guard radar facility on top), Kolekole Pass (only break in the Waianae *pali*), and the more distant Koolaus.

Drum Drive is a narrow, restricted-access military road that goes from route 82 along the plateau to Pupukea. It travels through pineapple fields, then forest, passes streams, dips into scenic valleys, gives access to trails, and connects with several unimproved roads (also restricted) running uphill from the North Shore. Call

Along banks *of Haleiwa's Anahulu Stream, small boats tie up beneath overhanging trees. View is from bridge.*

Waialua Sugar Co. to check road conditions and ask permission to go in. Usually all but the Helemano-Opaeula section requires a 4-wheel-drive vehicle.

Wahiawa is shopping center for 45,000—pineapple hands, suburbanites, Schofield and Wheeler service families. Stop in at 50-year-old Kemoo Farm Restaurant on route 99 for a free descriptive map folder, *Discover Historic Hawaii*; places of interest in these parts lie along a confusing labyrinth of roads. Kemoo has an exhibit of tropical plants, and from its patio you view Lake Wilson, Wahiawa's fish-stocked reservoir, framed by eucalyptus.

You can get a pineapple education on the north and east outskirts of town: Dole Pineapple Pavilion has freshly-picked pineapples and a display tracing the history of the industry in Hawaii. Dole's Hay Plant takes its name from the dairy-cow fodder made from the leaf of the pineapple plant. Dole's plantation community is Whitmore Village. Del Monte's Variety Garden exhibits plant varieties and explains pineapple culture.

Wahiawa Botanic Garden, 1396 California Avenue (daily 9-4; free; picnicking), is devoted to plants that thrive in cool, wet regions—endemic plants brought down from the mountains and fine collections of aroids and ferns. Wahiawa has a fine anthurium nursery, too—Rusty's, 1238 Kaala Avenue (Mon.-Fri. 8-4:30; Sat. until noon), and a representative Buddhist temple—Wahiawa Hongwanji Mission, 1067 California Avenue. Ask directions to the Kukaniloko Birth Stones, one of two sacred places for royal birth in Old Hawaii, reached by a dirt road off Kamehameha Highway.

Schofield Barracks, home of the 25th Infantry Division, began in 1909 as a cavalry base and island fortification center and was the Army's largest post until World War II. Drive in Macomb Gate to tour. Look for the 7-foot dragon statue, emblematic of the 14th Infantry's Peking assault during the 1900 Boxer Rebellion; two soldiers made the dragon with kitchen tools. Army Museum (Fri., Sat., Sun. afternoons; free) has historical relics going back to the War of 1812 as well as exhibits on current military efforts. Any day you can drive up to—but not over—Kolekole Pass (page 50).

Wheeler Air Force Base is shared by Army and Navy and preserved in its park-like pre-World War II form. In front of Headquarters (get visitors' pass at gate) stands a replica of a P-40, the aircraft at Wheeler on December 7, 1941, when Japanese planes flew through Kolekole Pass and bombed Wheeler and Schofield en route to Pearl Harbor.

Kamehameha Highway (route 99) on to Honolulu cuts through forested hills and bridges deep Kipapa Gulch before reaching sprawling residential and commercial outskirts. Near Wahiawa it passes between Mililani Golf Club and Mililani Town, a "new town"

gradually taking over 3,000 acres of pineapple fields (target population: 25,000 by 1977). Visit the sales pavilion, a contemporary landmark with observation deck and a garden of the cool-country plants being used in the town landscaping. Look at homes, garden townhouses, low-profile apartments, two public parks (one with swimming-recreation center), the town walkway system, and a shopping center with hidden parking, sheltering roof, garden malls.

You'll have Pearl Harbor in view on the long downhill drive, and the highway passes part of its huge Navy base, the only one in the country designated a National Historic landmark. The Arizona Memorial by Architect Alfred Preis is a bridge of white concrete spanning the hulk in which 1,102 men are entombed. The Navy's free shuttle boats to it leave Halawa Landing (for schedule, and tours of harbor, see page 21).

Hawaiians believed that Pearl Harbor was the home of the beneficent shark queen whose shark people protected them by killing man-eating shark intruders. They further believed the first dredging of the harbor channel occurred without mishap, despite destruction of a fishpond and fish god shrine, because Navy workers ceremoniously buried the image stones. When the foundation of the almost-completed first-dry dock collapsed in 1913, the Hawaiians believed it was because the dock was built over the home of the shark queen's son and angered sharks pulled it down.

Before reaching Halawa Gate, you drive through such towns as Pearl City—its corner landmark, Pearl City Tavern, has a huge menu (Japanese, seafood), monkey zoo, weekend outdoor art shows—and Aiea. Look for Sumida Watercress Farm, a welcome green space in the congested urban scene. The owner's Watercress of Hawaii produces almost all of Hawaii's delicious watercress, most of it here on 11 acres of semi-swamp along Pearl Harbor's rim. The picking is done in the morning.

Drive uphill on Aiea Heights Road, past Hawaii's only sugar refinery which processes all Island-grown sugar consumed locally (all other raw sugar goes to the large refinery at Crockett, California). At the top, about 3 miles up, is a pleasant state park with the ruins of Keaiwa Heiau, an ancient medicinal temple, and plantings of all the things the early Hawaiians used for medicines. The park has picnic and camp grounds and lies at the start of some easy forested hiking trails.

To get into Honolulu from Aiea, stay on Kamehameha Highway (route 90 after Farrington Highway joins it) to pass Pearl Harbor's gates. Or take Moanalua Road (route 72) which joins Lunalilo (H-1) Freeway; it crosses roads up hillsides to Camp H. M. Smith and Tripler Army Medical Center, skirts Moanalua Gardens, goes through Fort Shafter (page 35). Camp Smith,

World War II's heavily-used Aiea Naval Hospital, is headquarters for the Pacific Command that embraces all services and all bases from the West Coast to and including the Far East, and for Fleet Marine Force Pacific.

The Koko Head-Waimanalo Loop

From Waikiki to Koko Head, around the east end of the island, and back through Nuuanu Pali's tunnels (routes 72, 61) is a 35-mile drive you can do leisurely in a few hours. Combine it with a visit to Sea Life Park (about half-way along), or take all day and linger at one of the fine beaches the route passes.

To get from Waikiki to Kalanianaole Highway (route 72) the prettiest way, drive out Kalakaua Avenue and Diamond Head Road (page 31), then tree-shaded Kahala Avenue, either continuing to Kealaolu Avenue and following it out along the edge of Waialae Country Club's hibiscus-bordered links, or turning off through Waialae-Kahala (perhaps on Elepaio, then Hunakai or Kilauea) and passing Kahala Mall (page 40).

It's city all the way to Koko Head and Koko Crater, which rise at the end of Maunalua Bay. Nice districts lie off both sides of the highway. Koko Head (642 feet) and Koko Crater (1,208 feet) are centers of a 1,260-acre regional park that comprises natural areas, Hanauma and Sandy Beach parks, scenic lookouts, a botanic garden, rifle range, and other parts to be developed for recreation. According to legend, the two landmarks resulted from last attempts of the volcano goddess, Pele, to make a home for herself on this island before giving up and moving to others. Eventually Koko Crater's high rim will have a lookout and a means of access (trail or tramway) easier than the climb up its rocky open slope.

Along the highway pass between Koko Head and Koko Crater, you'll find a lookout over Kuapa Pond (Hawaii-Kai Marina), the road into a Job Corps Center, and another down to the parking area above Hanauma Bay and a view over a palm-fringed lagoon of inspiring beauty and such clarity it has been made a marine preserve. The bay is one in a line of craters formed during Oahu's last eruption. Over centuries, the elements have opened it to the sea. Men have blasted sandy swimming channels out of its coral bottom, a favorite haunt of snorkelers. Note the coloring: emerald green in channels, purplish over coral, deep blue beyond the reef.

Paths wind down to a beach park (crowded on weekends). Trails along rock ledges about a foot above the sea go from the wide beach along both sides of the bay almost to the headlands, past tide pools and fantastic rock formations. On the east shore, you can scramble through an arch eroded by sea and wind in an old lava flow. Hanauma's western backdrop is Koko Head.

From Koko Crater *climbers view Hanauma Bay, Koko Head, Hawaii-Kai. Ascent is steep but up open slope.*

Between Koko Head and Halona Blow Hole, the road snakes through a series of stratified cliffs of volcanic tuff—hardened remains of explosive showers of ash and mud once thrown out by Koko Crater and smaller vents. You pass a lookout to Lanai island and a road to the rifle range (in a crater). You look over seaside bluffs such as Bamboo Ridge, occupied by fishermen, and will see a roadside monument to fishermen who have been swept off rocks out to sea. Turn into the lookout terrace above the Blow Hole. When waves are big, a geyser shoots up through a hole in the ceiling of a submerged lava tube. From the opposite side of the parking area, you look down upon Halona Cove, a narrow turbulent inlet between sheer cliffs, but with beach nicely sheltered for a picnic.

You can walk the shoreline between the Blow Hole and Hanauma to get a close look at the region's rock structure—grotesque pinnacles, bold cliffs with undulant faces—enjoy the rugged seascapes, visit with fishermen out on those points. But go at low tide, watch the sea, stay on dry rocks where possible, and cross wet places between waves. Rocks are step-like and make it easy to escape to higher ground—even up to the highway.

The grassy slope above the highway has a natural rock bridge that's a challenge to climb; try shoes that grip, bare feet, or "all fours"—it's almost vertical. Walk up (quite a way) from the highway, starting at a point about a turn toward Honolulu from the Blow Hole parking

Porpoises and whales *perform in the Hawaiian Sea Pageant at Whaler's Cove alongside replica of* Essex.

area, opposite the fishermen's memorial, and you'll probably spot it—along the Koko Crater summit trail.

Koko Head Sandy Beach is a popular spot for camping, picnics, and body surfing for those who can handle strong breakers and currents. A road opposite goes to Koko Crater Botanic Garden, 200 acres of dry land plants (cactus, succulents, hybrid plumerias in color groupings). You can arrange a tour with the Botanic Gardens Division of the Department of Parks and Recreation. Another side road goes into Hawaii-Kai Golf Course, a green valley in a landscape of scrub grass and rock (clubhouse dining room open to public).

To drive the winding spur to Makapuu Lighthouse up on the black headland that is Oahu's eastern tip, get a permit from the Commander, 14th Coast Guard District, 677 Ala Moana. The effort is worthwhile as the long view up the Windward Coast from an observation station above the tower is splendid. Morning light throws the Koolau *pali* into sharp relief, turns inshore waters to emerald. The cliff has a face-like formation Hawaiians say is the demi-goddess Malei, guardian of the seaways.

The highway passes a fine windward overlook, too, above Makapuu Beach Park, famous for its body surfing. If you're not equal to Makapuu's mighty breakers, go on to sheltered Kaupo Cove, or sandy, calmer shores in Waimanalo. Offshore is Manana (Rabbit) Island where a few rabbits—descendants of European hares taken there

by a sugar planter in the 1880's, live compatibly with shearwaters, noddies, and terns.

A metal sculpture of a porpoise on the highway opposite Makapuu directs you into Sea Life Park (Tues.-Sun. 10-6; adm. fee), home of one of the greatest varieties of marine life on exhibit and trained porpoises and whales with a wider range of activities than any others in captivity. From 10:30 two shows alternate: a sea pageant at Whaler's Cove; behavioral experiments in Ocean Science Theatre in which men and porpoises train for ocean assignments. Permanent exhibits include: the Hawaiian Reef, a 300,000-gallon glass tank with living coral reef and more than 100 species of marine animals which you see as you walk down a spiral ramp from the rim to its floor; Leeward Islands Pool, like a coral atoll, with turtles, seals, sea birds; and Kaupo, an old Hawaiian fishing village rebuilt on its site, with fishpond, taro patch, exhibits on ancient fishing techniques and lore. There is a restaurant and a gift shop. For information about tours and bus service to the park, see page 21.

Sharing the 65-acre site with Sea Life Park are the Oceanic Institute—one of its research projects is learning how to extract protein from the sea (note its fish farms on Molokai, page 117); and Makai Undersea Test Range, operating from a pier ½ mile toward Waimanalo and visible, where scientists and engineers operate habitats and submersibles to test men and materials at various depths—their activity eventually will be observed in the park over television.

The Waimanalo plain is guarded by a fortress-like *pali*, its unusual fluting owing to streams that cut the outer soft lava rock back to the harder strata of the Koolau Range. The coastline here is flat, with rocky points fishermen like, in-between strips of sand, a dandy beach park, and houses strung out over several miles.

Waimanalo was mostly sugar cane until 1947. In Waimanalo town, you'll find the old stone plantation office remodeled as the Old Plantation—gift shop, snack bar, *lu'aus*, art displays, typical Hawaiian country garden. Much of the land is still cultivated with fruit, vegetables, and flowers; various tropical varieties are under study at the University of Hawaii's nearby experiment station (call Horticulture Department to arrange visit). Ask your way to Yokooji Anthurium Farm (41-759 Kaulukanu Street), a one-acre carpet of red and green tucked away at the foot of the mountain wall—plus a half acre of vanda orchids and some beds of bird-of-paradise. Waimanalo's modern lava and sandstone Catholic church has a mosaic of its patron, St. George, over the door and sculptures, mural, and frescoes, mostly by Waimanalo people, inside.

Bellows Air Force Station opposite town has a grand beach park open weekends and holidays for camping and swimming—46 acres of coral sand with ironwoods and palms for shade. The road on to Pali-Kailua Highway (route 61) junction cuts through verdant foothills popular with horesback riders (signs point out stables), passes Olomana Golf Club (with public dining) and new housing tracts with fine views of Olomana Peak.

Leeward Oahu and the Waianaes

Honolulu is in the lee of mountains, but when Islanders speak of Leeward Oahu they mean the island's big western portion, the Waianae Mountains and their coastal fringe, the driest of all regions. The high mountains are outdoorsmen's territory; the few roads that climb them are restricted (private or military). The southern coral plain has Barbers Point Naval Air Station, two sugar plantations, and some of Oahu's fastest-growing communities. The Waianae Coast has superb beaches, swimming, surfing, fishing, and camp sites—and no rain. Long favored by local people it has now come in for resort development. Farrington Highway (route 90), the coastal road, is paved to Makua, about 40 miles from Honolulu, where most people turn around. It takes a 4-wheel-drive to make it on around Kaena Point to Mokuleia in order to return up through the center of the island.

Through Waipahu and Ewa to Makua

On route 90 out of Pearl City, watch for access to H-1 Freeway if you want to go straight to the coast; it rides high, gives a sweeping view of plains and mountains. To visit cane-country Waipahu and Ewa on the way, stay on route 90, the left fork, at the Ewa-Wahiawa junction which comes a little after the freeway-Wahiawa divide. On the *makai* hillside is Leeward Community College which opened in January, 1969, to serve all the new suburbs.

Along Farrington Highway, Waipahu is all clutter, but turn up Waipahu Depot Road to the mill that presides over the old town center like the castle of a medieval village. The concrete emplacement in the bank at its foot (at the head of Depot Road) is the old fire station, with buckets inside. The 1897 factory still has a fire lookout on top (no longer used). Drive old Waipahu Street past tree-shaded bungalows and some flavorful buildings like Marigold Bar that began life in 1898 as a plantation dispensary, was a USO club during World War II. A town fixture is Arakawas, a modern department store grown from a tailor shop started in 1909. Going out of town over Farrington Highway bridge, look back across the picturesque hollow of taro and bananas with the mill as its backdrop.

Farrington passes Kunia Road (route 75) going north. At Ewa-Waianae Junction, Fort Weaver Road (route 76) heads south—a worthwhile side trip—to

bustling Ewa Beach and its military neighbor, Iroquois Point, and sends off a spur to Ewa, as compact and pretty a plantation town as you'll find. You first pass a handful of false-front buildings—one the general store, Honouliuli Shokai—all of them commercial vestiges of old, still lively Honouliuli. Honouliuli's community association fosters such beautification projects as the growing of Oahu's official flower, the *ilima*—plants are around the homes along dirt roads leading toward Pearl Harbor. Note the plaque along the main road where Oahu's first successful well was drilled, in 1879—the event that sparked sugar-growing on this fertile, but dry, land.

Ewa's graceful frame buildings (most from the 1930's), overhung by trees, are near the mill (see page 21 for tours). Note the company office, plantation locomotive used until 1947, plantation store turned supermarket, manager's home, pretty churches and temples, and school with its notable bronze Lincoln, the result of a small bequest left by a devoted principal and a sculptor (Dr. Avard Fairbanks) who donated the rest of its cost. Ewa Beach has a seismic wave warning center, a beach park favored by *limu* (seaweed) pickers, and Shiro's Huli Huli Drive Inn with an amusing menu.

West of the Ewa turnoff, Farrington passes a narrow, paved side road up the mountain to Palehua, a splendid forest with a few private cabins perched on the ridge for views down over the Waianae Coast or east all the way to Pearl Harbor and Diamond Head. The turnoff is marked "to Timberline Camp." It's in sky country just below the locked reserve (telephone ahead to visit). At summer sessions children ride, hike, swim, learn crafts.

Rounding the south slope of the mountains, you pass turnoffs to Makakilo, Barbers Point, and landscaped Campbell Industrial Park (oil refinery, cement plant,

Spreading kiawe trees *shade white sand of Waianae Coast beach. Landmark is Mauna Lahilahi at Makaha.*

auto racing course). You reach the sea at Kahe Point, where you'll find the first in a chain of parks along the coast to the north, most with comfort stations, camp sites, grills, tables, and water. Kahe has a coastline view. Others—including Kahe Beach just beyond (privately maintained, but for the public)—have fine sandy beaches. Several offer good swimming—sometimes (get advice from residents). This coast is subject to wave lashings, currents, disappearing sands.

The highway travels the coastal strip at the mouth of big valleys hemmed in by parched cliffs, their lowlands scrubby with lantana, cactus, koa haole, kiawe—the Koolaus cut off much of the trade-wind rainfall from the Waianaes. Once this was sugar land, and before that many self-sufficient Hawaiians grew taro, rice, and vegetables, pastured cattle, and fished. The district still has lots of Hawaiians, but today you see small farms and home sites radiating from four towns (Nanakuli, Maili, Waianae, Makaha), and a roadside hodgepodge of quonset huts, tumble-down shacks, neat box dwellings and business establishments, cafes, markets, filling stations, high-rise apartments, and narrow-gauge railroad tracks. A Navy Pearl Harbor-to-Lualualei train still rolls over them occasionally, and restoration of the old passenger train—for scenic rides—is planned.

Drive side roads into lower reaches of Lualualei and Waianae valleys to see dairy and truck farms, mango orchards, wild cotton along roadsides, bits of cane field flumes still used for irrigation. Notice Waianae's frontier-town buildings, modern library and Buddhist temple, and Pokai Bay which has a fine strip of sand and a breakwater that protects the many fishing boats and makes swimming always safe.

The scene is different where Makaha Valley breaks into the mountains. Along the shore are two beach parks, Mauna Lahilahi, and Makaha, the great winter surfing mecca that was once a fishpond; attractive homes; apartments and a shopping center. Inland is Oahu's largest tourist and residential development outside Waikiki, with two 18-hole golf courses, dining rooms, 200-room cottage hotel, heliport, a tree nursery, and a tower hotel and condominiums abuilding. Five more hotels, many more apartments and townhouses are planned for eventual accommodation of 23,000. Makaha's deeper recesses are being left in natural state for hiking and riding, and the Makaha Historical Society and Bishop Museum are taking care of historic sites. Ask permission at Makaha Inn to visit well-preserved Kaneaki Heiau or to join the hotel's valley tour—you hike through remains of villages, taro patches, coffee farms.

Makua is the place Hollywood turned into 19th-century Lahaina to film "Hawaii." It has a great beach and swimming in summer, and Kaneana Cave—Hawaiians of long ago believed its inner reaches, now blocked by cave-ins, led to spirit dwellings of dead chiefs. Just beyond is a quaint cemetery.

Kaena Point Road

Two-thirds of a 9-mile, coral-and-gravel road that follows the old railroad bed around Kaena Point is not too bad going. But the narrow, rocky, 3-mile stretch around the tip is tough to negotiate even in a 4-wheel-drive vehicle.

For 2 miles (paved), you skirt a military firing range in Makua Valley. If there's action, signs are posted, but always stay out of the country above—there may be unexploded shells around. The entire rocky shore is fishermen's territory; their favorite spot is the moi hole—an underground cave about opposite the spur road uphill to a missile tracking station. On the 3 miles from moi hole to the automatic lighthouse out on the point, you pass large Keawaula Beach at Yokohama Bay where surfers go, and the views of the whole Waianae Coast and its vertical backdrop are unsurpassed.

On the windward side you face 4½ miles of rough going—but a good North Shore view—to Dillingham Field where the road meets the paved Farrington Highway (see page 45).

Kolekole Pass Road

Kolekole Pass is 1,700 feet high and shadowed by peaks that rise another 1,000 feet or more. Kolekole Pass Road lies entirely within military reservations—Schofield Barracks to the east; Lualualei Naval Ammunition Depot to the west. It is open to the public only once or twice a year (such days are announced in newspapers).

Drive from Schofield to Lualualei for the better view. You can ask permission at Schofield Macomb Gate to drive up to the pass any day, over a serpentine road through luxuriant forest. (You'll need proof of automobile insurance covering public liability and personal indemnity, will be told not to smoke or take pictures at the pass or on the Lualualei side except at a designated lookout.)

From the high point, impressive views lie to the east and west. Ask at the gate house if you can drive the spur to Kolekole Rock—oldtimers say it represents the pass's lady guardian, Kolekole. Driving down into Lualualei Valley, you drop fast, around hairpin turns, and go from rain forest to brush-covered slopes.

Kunia Road

Kunia Road (route 75) connects Schofield Barracks with H-1 Freeway and Farrington Highway. From north to south it descends through pineapple fields, then sugar cane, affords a look at the forested windward side of the Waianaes, the high point, Kaala, and the Kolekole gap.

Ever-changing colors *of Waimea Canyon walls, enhanced by shifting shadows, make view from lookout spectacular.*

KAUAI...the Garden Island

Kauai is called the Garden Island, and a look at the lush, green vegetation that covers almost its entire mass tells you why.

Volcanic activity stopped first on Kauai, and over thousands of years the forces of nature have altered this land. Kauai was built up by an ancient volcano, Waiale-ale, which is 5,243 feet in elevation at its highest peak, Kawaikini. Aided by strong winds, the torrential rains of 400 to 600 inches a year which fall on Waialeale have eroded gorges up to 3,000 feet deep along its flanks and have sent streams large enough to be called rivers flowing down to the sea.

Rain, wind, and powerful wave action have made Kauai's northwest coast a series of bold precipices which drop off steeply to the sea and into verdant valleys worn between them. The deep gulches of this Na Pali Coast and Waimea Canyon surround the Kokee Plateau (3,000 to 4,000 feet high) and its huge Alakai Swamp—so nearly level that heavy rains drain off slowly, but in high waterfalls over the tableland cliffs. This vast, nearly

inviolate region, some of it state park, comprises most of the land that would be protected in a proposed Kauai National Park.

You can rarely see Waialeale's summit because of the low-hanging clouds that surround it, but you can see the scenic wonderland that extends downward from the wet, forested slopes and valleys to a broad, fertile, agricultural plain to white sand beaches shaded by tropical growth. Just as striking are the contrasts you see by following the shore of this small (553 square miles) circular island, Hawaii's fourth in size. The long stretch of windward coast from Na Pali around to Wailua is damper, cooler, and greener than the lee side from Koloa to Polihale. Rainfall varies from 100 inches a year on the north shore to around 20 at Kekaha in the southwest.

The waves of Polynesian immigrants came early to Kauai, and Kauai was the first island visited by Captain Cook in 1778. This was the only one of the islands not conquered by King Kamehameha. After Kamehameha's two attempts to reach the island had been thwarted,

Kauai's King Kaumualii voluntarily submitted to the all-island rule in 1810. A few years later, a Russian emissary almost got him to break away from Kamehameha and put his island under Russian protection. The remains of the Russian Fort at Waimea Bay are a reminder of the 19th-century rivalry between the United States, Great Britain, France, and Russia for control of the Islands—a rivalry that was largely responsible for Hawaii's remaining independent until 1898.

According to legend, Pele, the fire goddess, tried first to make a home on this island for herself and her lover, Lohiau, then king of Kauai; but after several unsuccessful attempts to dig a dry pit where she could start her fire, she continued south to the other islands, finally stopping on Hawaii where she still lives in Kilauea Volcano.

Everywhere on Kauai you will hear tales of the *Menehune*. Whatever early storytellers could not explain, they attributed to the legendary *Menehune* — said to be elves, or an early race of small, broad, muscular people. The island has many *heiaus,* dams, ditches, and trails supposedly built by *Menehune*, who finished each job in a single night or never returned to it.

Hawaii's first successful sugar plantation was started at Koloa in 1835, and sugar is still Kauai's biggest interest. Pineapple, bananas, papayas, and more than half of the state's crop of taro are grown here, too, and cattle roam several large ranches and many tiny ones. This little island plays a prominent role in scientific research and exploration. A tracking station at Kokee keeps tabs on our men in space; and Barking Sands is headquarters for an underwater test range devoted mostly to anti-submarine warfare. Kauai's population, pushing 33,000, is concentrated in farm towns of 4,500 and less that still have charming lanes of false-front buildings. Hotel rooms now number some 2,000, mostly in expanding resort clusters.

Festivals

Perhaps one of these special Kauai events will be going on during your stay:

Prince Kuhio Festival (March); Kauai goes all out for this statewide tribute to Kauai's native son on the weekend closest to his March 26 birth date; memorial ceremony at Prince Kuhio Park, his birthplace; pageant and "Hawaii Calls" broadcast in Lihue. **West Kauai Saddle Club Rodeo** (June); Kekaha. **Cherry Blossom Festival** (June); Eleele; bonsai show, Japanese and other ethnic dances. **Farmers Fair** (June); Kapaa. **"Little Transpac"** (July); biennial race from Honolulu to Hanalei Bay following Transpacific Yacht Race. **Hanalei Art Festival** (July or August); Hanalei; juried show of paintings from all islands; craft demonstrations; *lu'au*; Holoku Ball. **Kauai Annual Invitational Golf Tournament** (November); Wailua Golf Course.

How to Get There

Kauai lies 72 miles northwest of Oahu. Aloha Airlines and Hawaiian Airlines make the 20-minute trip between Honolulu and Lihue airports about two dozen times a day. Air Hawaii operates daily commuter flights over the route; Royal Hawaiian Air Service offers charters to Lihue or its Poipu Airstrip at Koloa. The air taxis and two Kauai-based helicopter firms specialize in air sightseeing (see page 53). Matson liners call at Nawiliwili on inter-island cruises.

Where to Stay

How you will spend your time is the big factor in choosing where to stay on Kauai. All four major resort regions have luxury hotels and medium-priced and budget accommodations. Close to the airport, and convenient bases for sightseeing, are the Lihue-Nawiliwili and Wailua-Waipouli areas. Kauai Surf Resort, the island's giant, is spread around Nawiliwili Bay, with almost 500 rooms in tall buildings and cottages, golf course, fine swimming beach (Kalapaki), and several restaurants. The largest of Lihue's raft of small places is the Tip Top Motel (34 rooms)—it grew from a bakery-cafe that is a town institution. Coco Palms, opposite Wailua Bay, is noted for its lagoon and coconut grove, native-inspired pageantry, architecture, and furnishings. To the south are Kauai Resort Hotel, overlooking Lydgate Park, and other hotels now going up. North of Wailua Bay are Kauai Sands, Castaways, and several hotels being built in the 80-acre Coconut Plantation development.

The Poipu beaches, on the leeward coast about 15 miles from Lihue, have a number of hotels, notably Waiohai whose cottages are styled from two gracious old homes made a part of the complex, and Sheraton-Kauai, a low-profile hotel built of natural materials. On the north shore, about 30 miles from Lihue, the famous hotel is Hanalei Plantation, built on the estate used for filming the movie "South Pacific" and planned by the movie set designer. Guests ride a jitney to cottages strung down the bluff to open ocean and a funicular to Hanalei River which they ford by boat to Hanalei Beach. From Hanalei to Haena, there are a growing number of apartments and cottages for rent (write Hawaii Visitors Bureau, Lihue).

Luxurious camping is available at 250-acre Kahili Mountain Park, situated at 700 feet a few miles north of Koloa, inland from route 50. You sleep on hotel beds but in cabins or tents with outdoor cooking counters (you provide only food). The camp has a lodge with snack bar, a lake, community *furo,* horses to ride, trails to hike. Write Kahili Mountain Park, Inc., Box 122, Koloa.

In Kokee State Park (page 62), Kokee Lodge rents furnished cabins and partially-furnished dormitories. To arrange off-season use of YWCA and Methodist Church camps, write organization headquarters in Lihue.

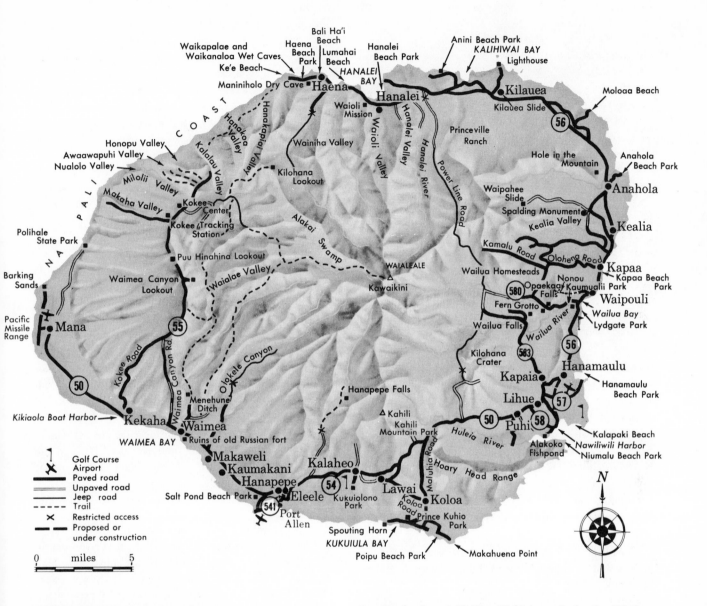

Getting Around on the Island

At Lihue Airport's transportation booths, you can rent a car or buy 1 or 2-day tours. You can't drive completely around this island: formidable cliffs (Na Pali) stand in the way. Instead you make two separate excursions: (1) Kaumualii Highway (route 50), then Kokee Road (route 55) to Kokee and lookouts into Waimea Canyon and Kalalau Valley, 100 miles round trip from Lihue; and (2) Kuhio Highway (route 56) to Hanalei and Haena and a Na Pali Coast view, 80 miles round trip from Lihue. Plan a day for each drive to give yourself time to stop often, to tour a garden or museum, have a swim and picnic, and to take side trips—to Koloa and Poipu, Bark-

ing Sands, Lawai Valley, Kukiolono Park, the Wailua Homestead country, Waipahee Slide, or the Wailua River boat trip to the Fern Grotto.

Visiting remote country by helicopter is a Kauai specialty. Garden Island Helicopters and Kauai Helicopters offer several scenic tours at per person rates, other tours by charter, and taxi service (many of the hotels have heliports). You can skim the razor-sharp Na Pali ridges and land in an uninhabited valley to picnic beside falls; fly into Waikoko Crater and up to its high, boggy rim, Waialeale; hover over Waimea Canyon. One Air Hawaii tour leaves Lihue Airport on a circle of the island; another, day-long and from Honolulu, features air and

Beachcombers *will enjoy this cove at Port Allen; glass dumped nearby is smoothed by waves, washed ashore here.*

ground sightseeing of Kauai; both fly you over Niihau. Kauai Guides (Box 122, Koloa), using helicopter, boat, or 4-wheel drive, will help you to a back-country adventure of your choosing: a hike on Kokee trails; camping in Na Pali with all equipment supplied; or a truck ride and walk to the Hoea Valley *heiau* above Kekaha. Kokua Malihini (R.R.1, Box 255-N, Kapaa) arranges special interest tours.

Smith's buses ply between Nawiliwili and Kealia, stopping at hotels, visitor attractions, or wherever flagged down.

You'll find a State Visitor Information counter at the airport and a Hawaii Visitors Bureau office in Lihue Shopping Center.

Recreation on Kauai

Camping and Picnicking

Camping and picnicking are popular at Kauai's fine beach parks. Get a permit (small fee) from Kauai County Department of Parks and Recreation, Lihue, to camp at Haena, Hanalei, Anini, Anahola, Kapaa, Hanamaulu, Niumalu, Poipu, Hanapepe, and Salt Pond. They have pavilions, showers, rest rooms, fresh water, and grills.

To camp in Lydgate and Polihale parks (fully-equipped) or Na Pali's Milolii and Nualolo Kai valleys, get a permit from the State Parks office, Lihue. You don't need a permit for Na Pali's Hanakoa and Hanakapiai. To camp in Kalalau Valley, get permission from Makaweli Ranch. All the big valleys but Kalalau have primitive shelters; Milolii and Nualolo Kai have rest rooms, and Milolii has water. Besides beaches, several have streams and waterfall-fed pools that make idyllic camp settings (boil water to drink). For agencies that rent campers, see page 12. You can use them at Haena, Kapaa, Hanamaulu, Niumalu, and Polihale.

For a picnic, note Kaumualii Park, a coconut grove beside the Wailua River, and Kukuiolono Park, with a rolling green lawn and long view to sea. Kokee and Waimea Canyon parks (page 62) abound in picnic spots, and you can camp at Kokee's center and off remote roads. Check in at Kokee Park Headquarters (7-6, summer; 7-3:30, off season). See also: Kokee, Kahili Mountain Park, page 52.

Swimming, Surfing, Beachcombing

Swimming. For year-round safe ocean swimming, note these beaches: Salt Pond, Kukuiula, Poipu, Kalapaki, Hanamaulu, Lydgate (in man-made ocean pool), Wailua (at Kapaa end), Anahola (by pavilion), Anini, Hanalei (at pier), and Ke'e. Others may be hazardous. Look for posted warnings; ask residents before venturing in.

There are notable fresh-water swimming spots: Kokee's Kawaikoi Stream; Hanakoa Valley pool; Limahuli pool; Haena wet caves; Wainiha intake; Kilauea and Waipahee slides; Wailua Falls pool; Wailua River.

Surfing. Favored board surfing sites are Nawiliwili (Kalapaki Beach), Wailua, and Hanalei bays, and the Poipu shore (with one cove for body surfing, too). There's big surf at Pakala (paddle a mile east from Waimea Bay). Some beach hotels rent boards and offer lessons.

Beachcombing. Any seldom-trod sands have rewards, but here are a few tips: Wailua Beach, near river mouth, for glass fishing floats; Anini shoals and "Bali Ha'i Beach," for shells; Lumahai for olivines in the sand; Port Allen's beach below the Japanese cemetery for beach glass.

Fishing

You can troll for all the tropical big game fish from charter boats based at several harbors: Port Allen (write Duarte's U-Drive and Tours, Ltd., Kalaheo); Nawiliwili (Aloha Kai Sportfishing, R.R.1, Box 322-P, Kapaa); and Hanalei (Hanalei Kai Beach Service, Hanalei Plantation Hotel)—with charters also for *'o'io* (bonefish) fishing. Or write Pacific Game Fishing Unlimited, 1777 Ala Moana, Honolulu.

You can arrange spear fishing, diving, or snorkeling jaunts through your hotel or with Kauai Skin Diving Company, Koloa. Reefs off Poipu and Kukuiula, Nualolo and Milolii valleys, and from Hanalei to Kalihiwai yield colorful small fish, lobsters, turtles, and squid. Surf casting for *ulua*, *'o'io*, and *moi* is good all around the island, and *moi* can be caught in throw nets off Na Pali. Pole fishermen—and women and children—line harbor piers to catch red *'aweoweo* during their late-summer run. Impromptu *hukilaus* (group seine fishing), commercial or for fun, are held at Nawiliwili, Hanamaulu, Wailua, Kalihiwai, Hanalei, and Wainiha.

You can cast for rainbow trout during season (generally August-September) in Kokee's 15 miles of streams and ditches and 15-acre Puu Lua Reservoir. Many ponds and reservoirs have bass, bluegills, tilapia, catfish, carp, and *'o'opu*, but the only public area is Wailua's 30-acre reservoir. You can fish some streams for mullet, tilapia, and *'o'opu*, and gather *opae* and *hihiwai*. Wailua River tributaries have smallmouth bass. Buy your annual freshwater fishing license — and get more information — at the State Fish and Game Division in Lihue, or Honolulu. Kokee trout fishing requires an additional permit (free) which you pick up at Kokee Park Headquarters.

Boating, Water Sports

At Kauai Surf Resort you can ride waves in an outrigger, sail a Sunfish, or cruise by catamaran—around Nawiliwili Bay or up the Huleia River to water ski, fish, and picnic. Hanalei Kai Beach Service offers water skiing, river boating, Na Pali Coast cruising (any fishing boat can be chartered for this). River boat trips from Wailua Marina to the Fern Grotto are frequent, delightful, and on most everyone's itinerary (page 57).

Hiking, Horseback Riding

Kauai has a real hiking and horseback riding center in its Kokee and Waimea Canyon state parks (see page 62). Trails go down into Waimea Canyon, across Alakai Swamp, and along the ridges that separate the deep Na Pali valleys. They range from short nature walks like Iliau Loop to longer but still easy hikes such as Awaawapuhi Ridge Trail, to tough overnight pack trips.

The Na Pali Coast (page 60), despite helicopter landings, is still a world for travelers on foot or horseback. The trail into Hanakapiai and a loop trail in the valley are easy. To hike on to Hanakoa or all the way to Kalalau requires stamina and equipment for camping—you can have it packed in by horse or helicopter.

Trails go up to a shelter on the chest of the 1,241-foot Sleeping Giant—Nonou Mountain. To climb the east side, 2 miles, start from a marker on the upper end of Haleilio Road through Wailua Houselots from route 56. The west side trail starts from Kinalu Road off Kamalu Road in Wailua Homesteads and after 1½ miles joins the other trail ½ mile from the top.

Hanakapiai Valley, *an easy 2-mile hike from Haena, is but one of the lovely jungled valleys of Na Pali Coast.*

The State Forestry office in Lihue has published information on most trails open to hiking. Some other rewarding trails—Hanapepe Valley, Olokele Canyon, Wainiha Ditch (a jeep road), and Power Line (a Wailua-Hanalei jeep road)—cross private land; but Kauai's Hawaii Visitors Bureau may be able to help you obtain permission to hike them. Also see Kauai Guides, page 54.

You can hire horses and guides from Garden Island Riding Academy, near Wailua Golf Course; Kahili Mountain Park; Thomas Chandler at Hanalei (he conducts Kalalau pack trips and pig hunts in Hanalei Valley); and usually from Kokee Lodge.

Hunting

Pheasants, Japanese and California quail, lace-necked and barred doves, and chukar and Francolin partridges may be taken on weekends and holidays during season (generally November 1 to mid-January) in four public areas: Puu Ka Pele and Kekaha (most of West Kauai), and the Wailua and Kalepa grounds near Lihue.

Hunters go into most of the island's forest reserves for pigs and goats, but Na Pali ridges and valleys and the upper and back slopes of Waimea Canyon are favored. Pigs can be taken all year but only in the canyon area; goats are hunted there and at Na Pali during seasons. A limited season on blacktail deer is held in November. Write the Fish and Game office in Lihue for other regulations and help in arranging trips.

Golf

Wailua Golf Course is a challenging, 18-hole, oceanside spread with clubhouse popular for dining. The Kauai Surf course above Nawiliwili Bay has 9 holes but with two tees. You play Kukuiolono's 9 holes for $1, payable on the honor system—just drop your money in a box. Waiohai has a 9-hole short Par-3 course for hotel guests.

Bicycling

Several hotels and Kawamoto's in Kapaa have bicycles for rent.

Lihue and Nawiliwili

Lihue is the seat of Kauai County, which includes the privately-owned island of Niihau off Kauai's southwest coast. Nawiliwili Harbor, downhill a mile, is Kauai's chief port. Down in a gulley in another direction is the Lihue Plantation Company mill, one of the state's largest sugar mills; tours are conducted several mornings and evenings a week. Little Lihue has had a face-lift: new houses, hotels, motels, cafes, banks, library, museum, government buildings, shopping center, convention hall, industrial park; more of the same will gradually fill the long slope to Nawiliwili Light.

Visit Lihue Shopping Center, with a mall, Japanese gardens, carp pond, eating spots, and Kauai Stores—an outgrowth of Lihue Store founded by the plantation in 1850 (it still displays the old mascot—a carved wooden figure of a man with a spyglass). The Haleko Shops section across Rice Street is comprised of four two-story, concrete plantation duplexes built between 1910 and 1918 in a German style unique in Hawaii (the plantation was German-owned until World War I). The buildings have been restored and now house gift shops, an art gallery, and popular JJ's Broiler. Plants in the surrounding botanic garden are labeled to tell their traditional uses and which of Hawaii's ethnic groups introduced them. Also in the garden are shrines and sculpture—including the Lihue Horse Trough, a marble fountain bought in Italy and shipped around Cape Horn in 1909 by Pastor Hans Isenberg, a German immigrant and brother of a plantation founder.

The Kauai Museum has a permanent collection of Hawaiiana, changing exhibits, and a gift shop with outstanding imports from Oceania (some collector's items) as well as Kauai handcrafts. Also on Rice Street are the shops of designer Guadalupe and Kay O'Kauai, Hawaiian-wear manufacturer who also makes outfits to order.

Lihue Cemetery's rows of simple tombstones, on a hill overlooking the mill, contrast sharply with a stately white marble monument erected in 1911 in honor of the Rice family, island pioneers. The monument was exhibited at Bremen and Paris art galleries before it was shipped around Cape Horn to Kauai. Back of nearby Lihue Union Church is a quaint little Hawaiian cemetery nestled in a grove of plumeria trees. On a neighboring hill sits Lihue Lutheran Church, built in 1883, with an ornate altar and high pulpit like a church of old Germany.

Nawiliwili Harbor is dominated by the sprawling Kauai Surf complex, which looks out over Kalapaki Beach and the bay to the Hoary Head Mountains and their green-clad peak, Haupu, and by a bulk sugar plant (you can watch the raw sugar being loaded by conveyor right into a freighter's hold). Look for the fascinating old building remodeled for Kawakami Shoten (one of a string of Kawakami stores) which sells everything from ice cream to Japanese imports. Club Jetty is a night spot famous for local color. At Menehune Garden (daily, 8:30-4:30; adm. fee), Sarah Kailikea takes you through a splendid old estate of 6½ acres with aged coconuts, a giant weeping banyan, and tropical plants and herbs (labeled), tells you the historic use of each plant, dances, chants, demonstrates Hawaiian instruments, and gives you sugar cane to chew.

Drive route 51 past the route 58 junction, industrial works, and small boat moorage, and continue uphill to Niumalu, a Hawaiian settlement and park with fine harbor view, and the lookout over serene Alakoko Fishpond in Huleia River at the foot of the jungled Hoary Head Mountains. According to legend, the pond was built by *Menehune* for a princess and her brother under their usual conditions—that no mortals watch them, and that they complete the wall in a single night. But the royal pair could not restrain their curiosity. By the light of the moon, they watched the little people, lined up in a double row for as far as they could see, passing rocks from hand to hand to workers at the dam. They watched a little too long, however, and were discovered by the *Menehune* who turned them into the twin pillars of stone you see on the mountainside above. And the *Menehune*, having used up their time, had to leave two gaps in the wall. Chinese mullet raisers later filled these in, and the pond is still in use.

Lihue to Haena

From Lihue to Haena is only 40 miles—on route 56; but inviting side roads start before you're even out of town. Route 57 goes to Lihue Airport (2 miles), but continue another mile to Ahukini Landing to look into calm Hanamaulu Bay and up the windswept coast. At Kapaia, on Lihue's edge, look for picturesque plantation houses; Ka-luna Hawaii Sportswear in the old Kapaia store (branch in Tahiti Longhouse, Kukuiula); a modern Hongwanji Buddhist temple; and Spanish-like Immaculate Conception, Kauai's largest Catholic church.

Wailua Region

Turn inland at Kapaia and drive several miles to Wailua Falls where about a half dozen white ribbons of water plunge over a high canyon wall in the river's upper reaches. Usually the pool below has enough water for swimming; a trail descends the steep bank.

Hanamaulu, another plantation village, has false-front classics in its post office and market, and a popular cafe with a Japanese garden and dining rooms specializing in Chinese food. Turn seaward to the beach park on the bay, with coconut grove, lily pond, and graceful ironwoods.

Between Hanamaulu and the Wailua River watch for: Kauai Hardwood (bowls, trays, and carvings made to order); the mast of a grounded freighter (distant view); Wailua Golf Course; a budding resort area; ruins of Malae Heiau (inland, above the river, on a cane field knoll), which plantation workers cultivate around, fearing bad luck if they disturb an ancient shrine; and Lydgate Park, one of several recreational and historic areas (a National Historic Landmark complex) that comprise Wailua River State Park. Tahitian peoples landed in this region 1,000 years ago. Once there were seven temples spaced at intervals from the Wailua River mouth to its source, Waialeale. Lydgate has picnic and camp grounds, beach, lava-rimmed ocean pool, a view of Wailua Bay, and remains of a temple of refuge that once sheltered people escaping from battle or crime (like the Honaunau Refuge, page 83). Shore boulders with petroglyphs are sometimes exposed on the ocean side of the highway bridge.

A side road inland along the river's south bank takes you to Wailua Marina, with docks for the Fern Grotto river boats, a restaurant, and shops; and on to 22-acre Kauai Tropical Gardens (adm. fee), with all that its name suggests plus Japanese landscapes, lagoons with tropical fish, and places to shop and eat.

Boats leave the Marina all during the day (there are night excursions with dinner and special pageantry) for a landing upstream, start of a short trail through dense jungle to the Fern Grotto, a damp cave draped with lush ferns. River banks are covered with pandanus and *hau*, and rare *pili* grass once used for houses. Caves in the bluffs were royal burial grounds. The boat captains tell legends, and a Hawaiian chorus serenades you from the grotto—an amphitheater with fine acoustics.

Coco Palms Hotel occupies grounds just north of the river that include the century-old lagoon of Kauai's last

Popular Kauai excursion *is launch trip up Wailua River to Fern Grotto. The 3-mile trip takes about 1½ hours.*

queen and an 1896 coconut forest, setting for evening torchlight pageantry. Visit its museum and library (daily, 9-5) to see some fine Victorian furnishings. On the bluff above Wailua Beach is the Sea Shell (meals, drinks, shop, bakery).

Drive route 580 inland on the north side of Wailua River, over the ancient Highway of the Kings. Commoners were forbidden to use this route, and rulers had to be carried—their feet were considered too sacred to touch the ground. Opposite Coco Palms are Rehabilitation Unlimited, Kauai (handcrafts made and sold), and Kaumualii Park (with picnic tables in a riverside coconut grove).

In the Poliahu area of Wailua River State Park, you'll find Kauai's oldest *heiau*, Holo-Holo-Ku, remarkably like Tahitian temples. Partially restored, it contains reproductions of idols and a priest's grass house, a sacrificial rock, and royal birthstones. At the top of the hill, stop at the site of Poliahu Heiau and the king's home, an inspiring place from which to view the river far below. A trail goes down to the Bell Stone which resounds musically when struck with a rock. Once it was used to signal Malae Heiau and to herald the birth of royal children. Cross the road to view Opaekaa Falls, another magnificent cascade.

The road continues into Wailua Homesteads—small farms, ranches, fruit and macadamia nut orchards. Stop

You'll recognize this scene *if you saw the movie "South Pacific." It's picturesque "Bali Ha'i Beach" at Haena.*

at Alexander's Nursery, a mile from the falls—a fascinating, disorganized collection of about everything that grows in Kauai's home gardens; and the University of Hawaii Agricultural Experiment Station (call ahead to visit), with early Hawaiian medicinal plants. The road crosses a reservoir and soon becomes the 4-wheel-drive Power Line route to Princeville Ranch (see Hiking, page 55). Before driving it, check conditions with the State Highway Division in Lihue; through the wettest high country the going is tough—maybe impossible.

Roads criss-cross these hills back of Kapaa and Kealia—past streams with swimming holes. Instead of reversing course you can follow one of these roads and rejoin highway 56 at Kapaa or Kealia.

The highway between Wailua River and Kapaa skirts usually-turbulent Wailua Bay and bisects a large coconut grove in the midst of new hotels. An art gallery occupies a ramshackle building opposite the Castaways. But first turn inland just north of Coco Palms and drive a mile (the last ¼ mile on dirt) to the Rice Production Training Center to see "miracle rice" in all stages of growth. Every two weeks, agricultural trainees, who will later go to Asia, plant a little of the fast-growing, high-yield new variety that can mean self-sufficiency for many rice-eating populations.

Look along the mountain top for the outline of Nonou, the Sleeping Giant (see Hiking, page 55). Ha-

waiians tell you he was a sleepyhead, but also a painstaking worker. Once, when he had worked extra hard to help build a *heiau* in honor of a god, he was rewarded with a *lu'au*. But he ate so much and was so tired from his labor that he settled down for a nap on a comfortable hill and never awakened.

Kapaa to Anahola

Kapaa is home to a pineapple cannery, papaya plant, balconied stores (and modern ones), and these churches and temples worth notice: the Episcopal; Seventh-Day Adventist; Mormon (especially the adjoining structure with veranda); and wooden Buddhist temple and youth hall.

From Kapaa to Anahola, the countryside is pineapple, planted in unbelievably straight rows through gray-blue mulch paper spread over the soil to hold in moisture and prevent weed growth. The highway bypasses wonderful scenery traveled by stretches of the old winding road, spurs down to the sea, and several roads which branch west from Kapaa and Kealia.

Take the road uphill south of Kapaa Stream bridge to St. Catherine's Catholic Church, a square structure with ceramic murals and frescoes by Jean Charlot, Tseng Yuho, and Juliette May Fraser. The view back, of Kealia camp stretched along the stream, is fine picture material.

You can continue from the church into Wailua Homesteads, or turn right just past the building to go down into Kealia Valley and follow the stream — and perhaps picnic on its bank under a monkeypod tree. The rough road ends at the Spalding Monument at an intersection that is the gateway to Waipahee Slide.

For the easier way to Waipahee (usually marked), take Kealia Road from route 56 for 2½ miles to Spalding Monument, through the plantation camp with post office (keep left where the road forks). Then take a marked, 3¼-mile cane road (negotiable in a passenger car unless it's muddy) that ends in an area abundant with guavas and the similar *wai-a-wi*. A ⅓-mile trail, bordered by Japanese cedar, *ti*, and ginger, leads down to the stream, where you can ride a waterfall down a natural rock slide into a crisp pool. You can walk rocks down the right-hand side about ¼ mile to a larger swimming hole.

Anahola is a Hawaiian homestead area. Look for the pretty red-roofed church on the hillside and a roadside fruit and juice stand in a thatched hut; drive down to the tree-lined bay (pavilion, swimming) through the picturesque settlement where people still gossip and snooze on front porches.

Anahola to Hanalei

Beyond Anahola you glimpse the "hole in the mountain" which a legend says was made when a giant hurled his spear with such force it pierced the rocky cliff. The old road winds down through Moloaa Valley, and from it a turnoff goes to the remains of a little village virtually wiped out in the 1946 tidal wave.

At Kilauea, ask in the town how to get down to the swimming hole in Kilauea Stream (below the highway) which the "South Pacific" movie people made famous. You can dive from cliffs, or zip down a man-made slide over the falls into a large, deep pool rimmed with ginger. Kilauea also has two interesting churches: St. Sylvester's Catholic Church, an octagon with an interior designed as a "church in the round" and containing more fine Jean Charlot frescoes; and quaint Christ Memorial Church, of stone with a craggy rock façade and fine stained glass windows. The side road to the mill ends at a lighthouse set on a peninsular bluff high above the sea and commanding rugged seascape views in both directions. The tower (weekdays, 12-4; weekends, 8-4) on the state's northernmost point contains the light first sighted by ships from the Orient, and its clamshell lens is the largest of its type in the world. The peninsula is a nesting place for red-footed booby birds in spring and summer. They are very amusing and quite unafraid of people, so you can photograph at close range.

To reach Kalihiwai Bay and Anini Beach, turn back onto the old road after you cross the new highway bridge across Kalihiwai Valley; stop on the Kilauea side for a valley view that takes in some sparkling waterfalls.

Anini, down a side road from the old coastal route, is a long ribbon of sand with a backdrop of cliffs festooned with mangoes, *hau,* pandanus, palms, bamboo, and parasitic vines. It's a little like Tahiti, even the houses (tumble-down shacks and comfortable summer cottages). The water is shallow out to a protecting reef popular for torch fishing, usually safe (sometimes discolored from cane wash), and there are shells and a small beach park. Kalihiwai Bay has a calm, peaceful look but winter tides can be treacherous and the little village now clustered along the shore has sprung back after two tidal waves that carried houses out to sea.

The highway crosses Princeville Ranch which, along with Anini below, is becoming a resort region.

Hanalei to Haena

From a roadside lookout you gaze over Hanalei Valley, checkered with flooded taro patches (and a little rice), bisected by the silvery Hanalei River, rimmed with precipitous green mountains. The backdrop of neighboring Waioli Valley is often laced with waterfalls. From the highway as it starts its winding descent, or part way along the road into Hanalei Plantation, you will get a different view—across the valley to crescent-shaped Hanalei Bay, bounded by a green headland. The hotel (page 52) en-

joys splendid views. Its Country Store is an old estate home that was turned into the plantation house for "South Pacific."

From the bridge where the highway reaches the valley floor, you can follow a spur road several miles into the valley along the river bank where yellow ginger, purple ground orchids, guavas, and pomelo now abound in an area once cultivated for oranges.

Hanalei has humble bungalows, comfortable summer homes, some tourist apartments, a court house, post office, liquor store, restaurants (the Rice Mill, Hanalei Taro Inn), Tahiti Nui (for night life), two general stores (Ching Young, Ching Ma Leong), a photogenic lily pond, museum, and five churches.

Notice Waioli Social Hall, the original mission church, built in 1841 (present Waioli Hui'ia Church next door dates from 1912). Its thatchlike sloping roof and wide eaves have influenced much Hawaiian architecture. Behind is the mission home (two stories with verandas, built in 1836), restored, with many original furnishings. Usually the caretaker will take you inside. Modern St. William's Catholic Church across the road has a Hawaiian longhouse shape, and tile murals by Jean Charlot. Hanalei Museum in a plantation cottage (daily in summer; check hours other seasons) features turn-of-the century furniture, agricultural tools, artifacts of various ethnic groups, and a snack bar with tropical fruit juices and ice creams.

Hanalei also has a splendid beach, but swim only by the pier, past the beach park near the end of the shore road across from Hanalei Plantation bluff.

Perhaps the most photographed small bay in the Islands is Waikoko at the eastern end of the Lumahai shore. From the marked viewpoint on the highway, a trail descends the pandanus-laden cliffs to a small rock-edged cove where you can picnic — and swim when the blue sea is calm. The Lumahai sands (which contain olivines) stretch west a long way, but offshore current makes swimming dangerous. At Wainiha Bay take the macadamized road which climbs above the river to the powerhouse for a sampling of this heavily-wooded valley with its perpetual waterfalls that rise in Alakai Swamp. You can hike or drive on up a 5-mile jeep road to the intake for a swim if you make arrangements with Kauai Electric Company. Wainiha's Sea Runner Art Gallery (on the highway) has batiks by Jerome Wallace, whose reputation extends far beyond his Kauai home.

The peaceful Haena region, once heavily settled, is now sprinkled thinly with ramshackle homes of old-timers and vacationers' cottages—old and new. Every rock, cave, and cliff speaks a legend; beaches are little roamed; mountain peaks are jagged, yet clothed in foliage and softly overhung with clouds. Stop in at Ha'i O Kauai cottage colony on green cliff-backed "Bali Ha'i Beach" (with shells for the gathering) of "South Pacific" fame.

You will come to Maniniholo Dry Cave which legend says was made by *Menehune* as they dug for a supernatural being who had stolen their fish; and to the Waikapalae and Waikanaloa Wet Caves said to have been dug by the fire goddess, Pele, while she was trying to find herself a home. Youngsters at least will enjoy dips into their spooky dark, cold water.

It is not usually safe to swim off Haena Beach Park, but idyllic Ke'e Beach at the end of the road is placid the year round; just east you'll find the tiny roadside "wash-off" pool in Limahuli Stream. At low tide you can walk the mile from Haena Park to Ke'e along the sandy shore (take shoes for a few rocky spots) and explore fascinating tidepools. Ke'e's backdrop is the triangular Fire Cliff. From its summit, stalwarts once hurled blazing logs to be caught by wind currents and carried far out to sea, for a fireworks spectacle.

Na Pali Coast

You can glimpse the spectacular Na Pali Coast from the northern end of Ke'e Beach. Ridges of cliffs rising 2,000 to 3,000 feet from the sea embrace a series of deep, jungled valleys from here all the way to Barking Sands.

Until helicopter excursions began (page 53), few people had set foot in these uninhabited valleys, some accessible only from the sea in fair weather. The flights and landings are exciting, but only a sampling of what this country holds for outdoorsmen—even those who start a camp-out with a helicopter landing—in any valley from Hanakapiai down to Milolii.

You can view Na Pali from a boat any time the weather is favorable. Landing on this coast is usually impossible in winter as sandy beaches disappear when the big swells pound the shore. But in summer you can often go in to swim, camp, hunt, and fish. (See Boating, page 55.)

A few valleys are accessible by hiking or riding horseback over the 11-mile Kalalau Trail (page 55). Hanakapiai, the first, is a steep but easy 2-mile walk, and if you go just ¼ mile along the trail that starts from the end of route 56, you will be rewarded with a splendid view back down upon Ke'e Beach and the Haena reefs. The trail on to Hanakapiai is resplendent with pandanus, *ti*, *kukui*, guavas, and wild orchids, has spectacular Na Pali overlooks, and reaches a broad beach. You can picnic, dunk in small pools in the stream, or in the ocean when summer sands are in, and explore a shelter cave. A 1¼-mile loop, a spur off the main trail, goes into the valley across ancient taro terraces, through a mango grove, and past ruins of a coffee mill where there's a shelter.

Out of Hanakapiai the trail climbs steeply and does not drop to sea level again until it reaches Kalalau Beach. Footing is good, but the going is either up or down (no level places to ease leg work) and the weather is hot. About 6 miles along is Hanakoa, a good rest stop or a destination in itself. A path leads from a rustic cabin to a wonderful swimming pool with waterfall in Hanakoa Stream. From across the stream, a ⅓-mile spur goes up to Hanakoa Falls, a cascade at the rear of a fork of the valley.

From Hanakoa on, the country gets drier. You encounter sisal, lantana, and cattle. The trail enters Kalalau, the largest valley (about 2 miles wide and 3 miles deep), near the main stream, more than a mile from the favored campsite on its mile-long beach—near a small stream with waterfall "shower" and bathing pool. As you cross the valley, note the branch trail that climbs inland near Kalalau Stream and offers good valley exploring. You can follow the main stream all the way to Davis Falls. Some like the beach dry caves for sleeping. Everyone wades and splashes in the wet caves. In summer, you can partly swim, partly wade to neighboring Honopu, the legendary "Valley of the Lost Tribe," where remains have been found of an ancient Polynesian settlement that unaccountably vanished. Kalalau was the hideout of notorious Koolau the Leper, who refused to be moved to the Molokai settlement and shot several pursuers so he could remain here until he died—several years later.

Along the South Shore

You leave Lihue on Route 50 for Waimea Canyon and Kokee, or Barking Sands; but you can detour to Koloa (Maluhia Road) and the Poipu-Kukuiula coast and return to the main road on Koloa Road from Koloa through Lawai Valley.

Within the first 8 miles look for: the marvelous old post office-store at Puhi, and a new Kay O' Kauai shop; the turnoff to Kipu Ranch at the foot of Haupu peak; Halfway Bridge over the Huleia River (take a short spur to the right to a swimming hole and waterfall); Knudsen Gap between the Hoary Heads and Kahili, end of the island's central mountain mass; roadside ginger.

Koloa and Poipu

Maluhia Road starts off through a grove of eucalyptus to Koloa (3 miles), a historic town with big trees and charming wooden buildings. You can see the stone mill stack of Hawaii's first bona fide plantation—a National Historic Landmark to be restored and made the focus of a sugar industry museum. Ask the way to three quaint-but-thriving temples—the Hongwanji, Jodo, and Odaishi (Shingon); the restored colonial church of Koloa Mission, started in 1834; and St. Raphael's south of town, Kauai's oldest Catholic mission (1841), with impressive 1856 masonry church, coral stone houses, graveyard, outdoor altar, and a tiny lava rock chapel that seats eight.

As you drive downhill to the sunny coast, you encounter confusing road forks. Turn left to Poipu Beach Hotel and resorts and beaches east of it; go straight to Koloa Landing, then left to Plantation Gardens and Sheraton-Kauai; veer right for the Kukuiula shore and Spouting Horn.

Whalers, as many as 50 at a time, used to winter at Koloa Landing where hotel buildings now sit upon the cove's west bluff. Plantation (formerly Moir's) Gardens (daily 8:30-5; adm. fee; restaurant; shop) has some 4,000 plant varieties including one of the world's great cactus and succulent collections, water lilies, and tropical trees. A Hawaiian *tutu* (grandma) who knows botany and local lore shows you the 6½-acre estate.

At Poipu Beach Park you'll find a shallow cove with gentle body-surfing waves for youngsters. Beyond and west, in front of several hotels, there's smooth water for swimmers and surf suitable for boards. To the east is Brennecke's Beach where experts body surf. The Poipu road ends above Makahuena Point, at the crater where Kauai's last eruption occurred. You can walk down to sand dunes—an old Hawaiian burial ground—and rocks with petroglyphs visible at low tide.

The road to Kukuiula Bay, South Kauai's pretty sampan harbor, ends at the Spouting Horn where the sea pushes up through a shoreline lava tube with a moaning sound—the cry of a legendary lizard trapped in the tube. You pass Prince Kuhio Park and monument, at the birthplace of Hawaii's long-time Delegate to Congress; the hotel named for him; Tahiti Longhouse (restaurant-night spot) beside a small swimming beach; and an artists' studio and gallery.

Koloa to Hanapepe

You experience pastoral Lawai Valley on the meandering few miles of Koloa Road out of Koloa. At the approach to route 50, you'll find Hala-Kahiki of Hawaii, a place to buy or mail home fresh pineapple, fruit preserves, macadamia and coconut products. The hillside opposite is full of tiny stone shrines, each covering sacred soil from one of Japan's 88 Holy Places of Kobo Daishi, a Shingon Buddhist teacher many centuries ago. To visit, walk in from route 50 at the crest of the hill.

Poipu's beaches *are among Kauai's loveliest swimming spots, with both calm waters and good surfing waves.*

From Kalaheo, drive up to Kukuiolono Park, a once-private estate with golf course, Japanese garden, display of Hawaiian legendary boulders, and inspiring views out over Lawai to the sea. Beyond Kalaheo, a sign directs you inland to Olu Pua Gardens (daily, 8:30-5; adm. fee), where you can roam jungle paths and grassy expanses of another old estate, now a 12-acre botanic garden with native and exotic plants labeled. At the main house, which you may tour, you can buy dried plant material, and mail seeds and cuttings home.

From the lookout over Hanapepe Valley, you view taro patches and farm plots at the mouth of a lush canyon. At Eleele Shopping Center, ask the way to an interesting Japanese cemetery and "beach glass" beach below.

Turn into Hanapepe proper, an Old West town with box buildings, some balconied, and a narrow old bridge across its stream. Driving a dead-end road through valley farm plots back of town gives you the tone of old rural Hawaii. Stop at Shimonishi Orchids (all varieties), and at Green Garden or Mike's on the highway for homemade pie. Drive out to Salt Pond Park, a clean crescent of sand beside a reef-protected bay. Coarse *lu'au* salt is still made (in dry weather) by evaporating sea water in adjacent beds—early Hawaiians got salt this way to preserve meat and fish, and traders to cure furs.

Hanapepe to Polihale

In the cane country west of Hanapepe, turn off into tree-shaded Kaumakani, a model plantation village; and into old Makaweli camp to visit the plantation store. Well-preserved remains of Fort Elizabeth, built by Russians in 1817 (page 52), cover the bluff above Waimea River and Bay, Captain Cook's first Hawaiian landing place. Both fort and landing site are National Historic Landmarks. Of a European irregular-star shape, about 400 feet across, the fort flew the Russian flag briefly, mostly as a trading post; Hawaiian troops then occupied it until 1853. The state plans to repair the tree-shaded walls (laid Hawaiian style without mortar), reconstruct fort trappings, and add exhibits.

Waimea also boasts good vernacular architecture (note Badua Store) and Kauai's oldest mission, started in 1820. A handsome 1853 coral and sandstone church stands today with a mission graveyard on one side, an Oriental one on the other. Drive the narrow river road through town 1½ miles to Menehune Ditch, once a long watercourse allegedly built by the little people. You pass swinging bridges, taro and farm plots, *poi* factories, and an unusual Shingon temple. Like its Lawai relative, this temple has 88 outdoor shrines dedicated to Kobo Daishi, but they're bullet-shaped and also honor soldiers killed in World War II. Each has a deity which the priest—if he's in—will explain.

At Kekaha, note the boat harbor, view of Niihau, and the start of Kokee Road (route 55); ask for Kekaha Gardens, with orchids, anthuriums, tropical foliage, and packing-shipping service. Clear through the Pacific Missile Range gate to visit Barking Sands, where you can jump-slide down high dunes to make a "woof" sound, and explore tidepools in winter or swim in summer. From highway's end at Mana camp, follow signs along several miles of cane roads to 132-acre Polihale State Park at the south end of Na Pali. You can camp (rest rooms, showers; shelters to come), hike dunes or along the base of the bluffs, swim in summer—in the sea if it's calm, or in Queen's Pond, an often-exposed brackish water channel in the beach.

Waimea Canyon-Kokee

People visit Waimea Canyon State Park (1,866 acres) and Kokee State Park (4,640 acres) all year to take in magnificent views of Waimea Canyon and Kalalau Valley. In summer months, many stay to enjoy the outdoor life—to camp, fish streams, pick plums, hike luxuriant forests with native flora such as the *iliau* tree, *mokihana* berry, and lobelias found only on Kauai. You reach this wilderness on Kokee Road or Waimea Canyon Road from Waimea that travels the canyon rim and then joins route 55.

On Kokee Road you climb arid, scrub-covered hills above Waimea Canyon for 12 miles to the main lookout — 3,400 feet up and in greener country. From this point you can see most of this 2,857-foot-deep gorge which cuts into the Kokee Plateau. The canyon has a monumental quality as unexpected on a tropical island as the crisp, invigorating mountain air. It is like the Grand Canyon in character, if not in size, with the addition of the blues and mossy greens of lush vegetation to complement the reds and browns of exposed volcanic rock walls. Clouds usually hang over the rim, their moving shadows heightening the impression of vastness.

From Puu Hinahina Lookout, farther up, your eyes can follow the canyon out to the coast and pick up Niihau across the sea to the west. Just above, you pass a paved spur that goes 4½ miles down Makaha Ridge, through typical reforested country, to Na Pali Coast views; then Kokee Tracking Station for manned space flights (visit only by arrangement). Around Kokee Park Headquarters, you'll find Kokee Lodge, with restaurant, cabins, and dormitories; camp and picnic grounds; and Kokee Museum, with exhibits on flora and fauna, geology, petroglyphs.

The road climbs on to Kalalau Lookout, a 4,000-foot-high view point over broad, green-carpeted Kalalau Valley and the shimmering blue sea at its mouth. If a cloud obscures the view, as it often does, wait—it may lift.

Kokee Park has some 12 miles of dirt roads, normally in condition for passenger cars, and is the starting point for about 45 miles of trails. Here's a sampling:

Iliau Loop (*iliau* blooms there in spring), a 10-minute nature walk at the start of Kukui Trail, offers a good view of Waimea Canyon and distant Waialae Falls. For a long hike, but all downhill, you can walk the 3-mile Kukui Trail to the floor of Waimea Canyon, then follow it out to Waimea. Waimea Canyon Rim Trail, about 3½ miles, offers ever-changing vistas; start at Kumuwela Lookout or from above Kawaikinana Stream and arrange for a pick-up at the other end.

From Camp 10 Road, you can hike ⅓ mile to a scenic spot overlooking Poomau Valley; walk 1 mile into an area fragrant with *maile*; or explore part of the 9-mile Mohihi-Waialae Wilderness Trail—to picnic in a Japanese cedar grove or fish trout streams.

The Nualolo, Awaawapuhi, and Honopu trails, each several miles, start near Kokee headquarters and descend ridges that separate the Na Pali valleys. The 3½-mile Alakai Swamp Trail travels jungle and open bogs (expect to get soaked and muddy to your knees) to Kilohana Lookout atop Wainiha Pali. Or you can leave it after a mile and hike Pihea Trail 1½ miles to Kalalau's rim.

Fringed by palms *and pounded by a froth of white surf, Kaimu Black Sand Beach is a seascape for photographing.*

HAWAII . . . the Big Island

Hawaii, youngest and southernmost island in the Hawaiian group, is almost twice as large as the others combined; hence its most common nickname, the Big Island. In travel folders you also see it called "Volcano Island" and "Orchid Island." It is the one place in the United States where you are likely to see volcanic action. Of the five volcanoes that formed Hawaii, two—Mauna Loa and Kilauea—are still active and sometimes send enough lava to the sea to make the Big Island bigger. This island earned its third title by becoming the world's largest orchid grower.

With an area of 4,038 square miles, the Big Island is big only in Hawaiian terms. It is a small piece of land indeed to contain two single mountains that are probably the tallest and bulkiest on earth. Mauna Kea, which peaks at 13,796 feet above sea level, and 13,677-foot Mauna Loa, the world's largest active volcano, rise more than 30,000 feet from the ocean floor.

Glaciated areas on dormant Mauna Kea in the north are evidence of a glacier 250 feet thick that covered the summit during the Wisconsin glacial age. Today scientists consider Mauna Kea's top probably the finest spot in the world to study outer space. Its winter snow cap attracts skiers.

Astronauts tramped Hawaii's lava fields in preparation for a moon landing. The slopes of Mauna Loa are particularly noted for lunar-like features. This volcano has not erupted since 1950, but Kilauea on its southeast slope has spouted off more than a dozen times in the last decade. In the west is Hualalai (8,271 feet), dormant like Mauna Kea but active in historic time, last in 1801. Volcanism has ceased in the north corner, and the old Kohala Mountains (5,480 feet) have been eroded into cliffs and canyons where they face the northeast trades.

Hawaii's broad, rounded domes are shield volcanoes built up by very hot, fast-flowing lavas that burst out relatively gently. People flock to the fireworks which most often occur somewhere in Hawaii Volcanoes National Park. Eruptions are often predictable and although sometimes destructive, seldom disastrous.

The Big Island is only 76 by 93 miles and mostly lava wasteland, but it has an amazing variety of terrain,

At Parker Ranch, *horse races and cattle roping, held on Fourth of July weekend, draw a fascinated crowd.*

climate, scenery, and things to do. In 40 miles you can go from tropical beaches (some black sand) into fields of waving cane, up through rain forest or grassy pasture, and over lava slopes with snow banks and below-freezing temperatures.

Up high, old lava flows are barren or just sprinkled with lichen, but at lower levels pumice and ash have created fertile soils. This southernmost piece of the United States has the nation's only coffee industry. It is the state's biggest producer of sugar, papayas, avocados, macadamia nuts, anthuriums, vegetables, beef, and Christmas trees—but grows none of its pineapple. Six of the island's ten sugar plantations lie along the well-watered Hamakua Coast. On mountain slopes are truck farms and 240 cattle ranches ranging in size from 20 head to 45,000 on the vast Parker Ranch. The Kona District is famous for coffee, Puna for papayas, and Puna and Hilo for orchids and anthuriums. Other specialty crops, from established groves of macadamias to experimental plots of citrus, have sprung up here and there. The island also exports ginger, jams and jellies, hardwood flooring, and lava building stone.

More and more of the 70,000 Big Islanders are turning to the care and feeding of visitors. By 1975, the island will have tripled its present hotel capacity of 3,000 rooms. Resort complexes are developing from Kawaihae to Anaehoomalu Bay, from the new Kona Airport site at Keahole Point to Keauhou Bay, from Punaluu to South Point, and in Hilo. The National Park may expand along scenic drive corridors to the top of Hualalai and down to the City of Refuge and Kealakekua Bay.

This is the history island, the first one discovered by Polynesian settlers (by 750 A.D.), and the first to have Western ways implanted. It is the island that boasts Hawaii's most famous historic and legendary personalities. For 5 centuries, today's districts were "kingdoms." Kamehameha the Great, who was born in Kohala about 1753, unified them in 1792 and went on to establish a kingdom over all islands. He ruled his kingdom from Kailua, where he died in 1819. Later that year, also in Kailua, Hawaii's ancient *kapu* system—taboos related to the worship of pagan gods—was ended; it was begun in Puna in the 13th century. Captain James Cook, who put the Islands on the world map, was killed at Kealakekua Bay, in 1779. The first company of missionaries landed at Kailua, in 1820. And the state's most fascinating lady, the volcano goddess Pele, still lives in Halemaumau, Kilauea's firepit.

Festivals

At Big Island events (which include observances of statewide celebrations; see page 12), top billing usually goes to animals, fish, or flowers.

HILO. **Azalea Festival** (February). **Merry Monarch Festival** (April); horse races, flower show, costume and moustache-sideburns contests, parade, ball, and pageants dedicated to Kalakaua, the gay and stylish last king who revived Hawaiian culture. **4-H Steer Show** (June). **Orchid Show** (July); **International Festival of the Pacific** (July); dances of many ethnic groups, lantern parade, bonsai display. **Hawaii County Fair** (October); flower displays, horse races, horse show.

KONA. **Kona Stampede** (March); rodeo at Honaunau. **Captain Cook Festival** (July); solemn ceremonies at Kealakekua Bay; canoe races, fishing derby, pageantry, dancing, feasting in Kailua. **Hawaiian International Billfish Tournament** (July or August); Kailua. **Kona District Fair** (July or August in even-numbered years); Kealakekua.

WAIMEA. **"Old Hawaii on Horseback"** (May); pageant performed by riders. **Parker Ranch horse races and calf roping; quarter horse show** (July). **Bull and horse sale; turkey shoot** (November).

Rodeos occur at Honokaa on Memorial Day weekend and at Naalehu on Fourth of July. **A ski meet** is held in February at the summit of Mauna Kea.

How to Get There

You can fly to the Big Island directly from the Mainland, or see this island last and go home from Hilo's overseas airport. Hawaiian Airlines and Aloha Airlines jets make many daily round trips from Honolulu and Maui to the Hilo, Kona, and Waimea-Kohala (formerly Kamuela) airports. Royal Hawaiian Air Service flies scheduled trips daily from Honolulu to all three fields, shuttles between

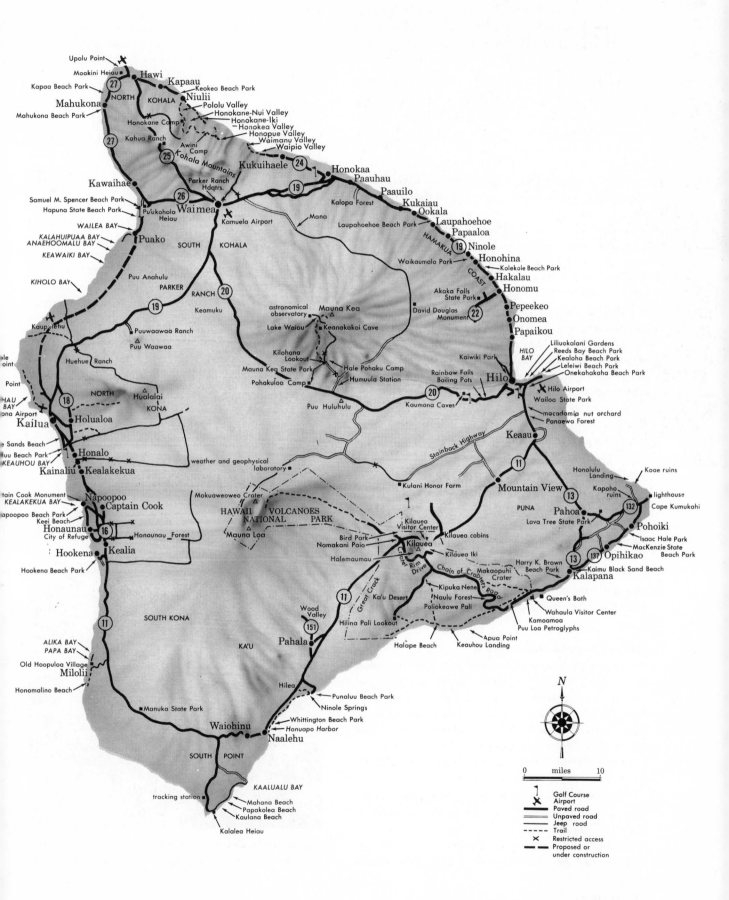

Upolu Point
Mookini Heiau
Hawi
Kapaa Beach Park
Kapaau
(27)
Keokea Beach Park
NORTH
Niulii
KOHALA
Pololu Valley
Honokane-Nui Valley
Honokane-Iki
Honokea Valley
Honopue Valley
Waimanu Valley
Waipio Valley
Mahukona
Mahukona Beach Park
(27)
Kahua Ranch
Awini Camp
(25) Kohala Mountains
Kukuihaele (24)
Honokaa
Paauhau
Kawaihae
(26)
Parker Ranch Hdqtrs.
(19)
Paauilo
Kukaiau
Ookala
Samuel M. Spencer Beach Park
Puukohola Heiau
Waimea
Kamuela Airport
Mana
Kalopa Forest
Laupahoehoe Beach Park
Laupahoehoe
Papaaloa
Hapuna State Beach Park
WAILEA BAY
SOUTH
KOHALA
HAMAKUA
(19) Ninole
Honohina
KALAHUIPUAA BAY
ANAEHOOMALU BAY
Puako
Waikaumalo Park
Kolekole Beach Park
Hakalau
KEAWAIKI BAY
Puu Anahulu
PARKER
RANCH (20)
astronomical observatory
Mauna Kea
Akaka Falls State Park
David Douglas Monument
COAST
Honomu
KIHOLO BAY
Keamuku
Lake Waiau
Keanakakoi Cave
(22)
Pepeekeo
Onomea
Papaikou
(19)
Puuwaawaa Ranch
Kilohana Lookout
Kaiwiki Park
Liliuokalani Gardens
Reeds Bay Beach Park
Kaupulehu
△ Puu Waawaa
Mauna Kea State Park
Hale Pohaku Camp
Kealoha Beach Park
Leleiwi Beach Park
HILO BAY
HAU
BAY
Huehue Ranch
Pohakuloa Camp
Humuula Station
Rainbow Falls
Boiling Pots
Onekahakaha Beach Park
Point
(18)
NORTH
KONA
△ Hualalai
Puu Huluhulu
Hilo
Point
Kailua
Holualoa
(20)
Hilo Airport
Wailoa State Park
Sands Beach
Kaumana Caves
macadamia nut orchard
uu Beach Park
Honalo
weather and geophysical laboratory
Stainback Highway
Panaewa Forest
KEAUHOU BAY
Kainaliu
Kealakekua
Keaau
Honolulu Landing
Koae ruins
tain Cook Monument
KEALAKEKUA BAY
Napoopoo
Kulani Honor Farm
(11)
Mountain View
(13)
Kapoho ruins
lighthouse
apoopoo Beach Park
Keei Beach
Captain Cook
Mokuaweoweo Crater
PUNA
Pahoa
(132)
Cape Kumukahi
Honaunau
City of Refuge
(16)
HAWAII VOLCANOES
NATIONAL PARK
△ Mauna Loa
Honaunau Forest
Bird Park
Namakani Paio
Kilauea
Visitor Center
Kilauea cabins
Lava Tree State Park
Pohoiki
Isaac Hale Park
MacKenzie State
Beach Park
Hookena
Kealia
Kilauea
△ Kilauea Iki
(13)
(137)
Opihikao
Hookena Beach Park
Halemaumau
Crater Rim Drive
Chain of Craters Road
Makaopuhi Crater
Harry K. Brown Beach Park
Kaimu Black Sand Beach
Kalapana
SOUTH KONA
(11)
Wood Valley
(11)
Great Crack
Ka'u Desert
Kipuka Nene
Naulu Forest
Poliokeawe Pali
Queen's Bath
Wahaula Visitor Center
Kamoamoa
Puu Loa Petroglyphs
ALIKA BAY
PAPA BAY
(151)
Hilina Pali Lookout
Apua Point
Keauhou Landing
Old Hoopuloa Village
Milolii
Pahala
KA'U
Halape Beach
Honomalino Beach
Manuka State Park
Hilea
Punaluu Beach Park
Ninole Springs
Waiohinu
Whittington Beach Park
Honuapo Harbor
Naalehu
SOUTH POINT
KAALUALU BAY
tracking station
Mahana Beach
Papakolea Beach
Kaulana Beach
Kalalea Heiau

N

0   miles   10

1   Golf Course
X   Airport
      Paved road
      Unpaved road
      Jeep road
- - - Trail
X   Restricted access
      Proposed or
      under construction

them, and uses Upolu Field and Kona Village Airstrip. Air Hawaii offers service from Kona to Kaanapali, Maui. Matson lines call at Hilo and Kailua on inter-island cruises.

Where to Stay

To explore this big island, stay in at least two widely separated spots. The big hotel bases are Hilo and Kailua, each with more than 1,000 rooms and a range from expensive oceanfront accommodations to modest apartment hotels. At Kailua, historic town turned resort village, are two landmarks: the large, sculptural Kona Hilton (lanais of the main building are stepped back to suggest the rise from sea to mountains), and the gracious Kona Inn (its original 1928 building is modernized inside); both have ocean-filled swimming pools. Most of Hilo's hotel rooms are near the airport, along the shore of Waiakea Peninsula, which is dominated by the Naniloa on the point.

Two alternate or additional bases are South Kohala (in Waimea or near Kawaihae), a 1 to 1½-hour drive from Kailua, and Hawaii Volcanoes National Park, 45 minutes from Hilo. The stunning 256-room Mauna Kea Beach Hotel is worth a sightseeing stop if you're not staying there—it is almost a Polynesian-Oriental art museum, and the buffet lunch is an experience. Up in cool Waimea are the new 40-room Waimea Village Inn (with some family apartments for outdoorsmen); and the Mauna Kea's tasteful small Ranch House. The National Park has the venerable Volcano House, with 37 rooms.

Kona Village Resort, with South Seas-like cottages on stark lava around a sandy bay, is a North Kona hideaway reached by private road, small plane, or boat. Other offbeat places are transient hotels in farm towns such as the Shirakawa in Waiohinu or Luke's Place in Hawi.

Inexpensive cabins are located in the National Park and just outside, and in Mauna Kea and Hapuna state parks (see Camping, page 67).

Getting Around on the Island

To sightsee all districts, plan at least four days. Most tours of all islands stop only one or two nights on Hawaii and take you over part of it fast on a bus or "stretchout" limousine. Rental cars available at all three airports range from foreign compacts to 4-wheel-drives. State Visitor Information Centers are located at Hilo and Kona airports and Hawaii Visitors Bureau offices at 180 Kinoole Street, Hilo, and outside Kona Inn, Kailua.

The around-the-island highway (Mamalahoa Highway, or the "Belt Road," for most of its 216 miles) is route 11 from Hilo to Kailua via Hawaii Volcanoes National Park and route 19 via the Hamakua Coast and Waimea. Each half can easily take a day to drive. You'll welcome a day, too, to explore Waipio Valley, and—when Chain of Craters Road is reconstructed (see page 73)—to loop from Hilo through Hawaii Volcanoes National Park to Kalapana and back through Puna, perhaps covering extra legs of the Puna triangle (routes 13, 137, 132); or, until then, to visit the park's two sections on separate trips to the point where the road is blocked. Figure a half day at least to travel about Kona from Kailua, and to loop North Kohala from Kawaihae or Waimea (using routes 26, 25, and 27). The Saddle Road (route 20) is the approach to the rugged roads that climb Mauna Loa and Mauna Kea.

For a fast look at all or part of the island, charter a Royal Hawaiian Air Service plane. You can leave from any field. For sightseeing or sport, take a ride in one of the Mauna Kea Soaring Club's sail planes, which fly from Kamuela Airport on weekends. You glide over the northern slopes of Mauna Kea and the Kohala Mountains—all the way to Waipio Valley on a good day. Make reservations with Hawaii Trails, Kamuela.

Country buses—mostly cars or station wagons—go from Hilo to some outlying towns, stopping at other towns en route. Fares are cheap and each journey an adventure, but at the distant places you have to wait overnight for the return trip. Check itineraries at Mooheau Terminal in Hilo. This is also the station for Hilo's distinctive sampan buses (page 70).

Recreation on Hawaii

Outdoor experiences on this island range from swimming to skiing. Hawaii is not as well endowed with beaches

Legendary boulders *are your chairs and table, pandanus trees your umbrella at Kalapana's Harry K. Brown Park.*

as the other islands—only a mile or so of its 305.5-mile shoreline is accessible, first-rate swimming beach, although 20 miles are at least sandy. But if you like to hike, hunt, ride, or camp, here is territory unsurpassed. A special sport is 4-wheel-drive exploring through rough and primitive country, much of it high and cool.

To tackle such activities on your own, note these sources of help: The State Department of Land and Natural Resources (with divisions of Fish and Game, Parks, and Forestry), 75 Aupuni Street, Hilo; "A Guide to Public Parks," a run-down on facilities and recreational resources at every park on our map, obtainable from the Hawaii County Department of Parks and Recreation, 25 Aupuni Street, or at the Hawaii Visitors Bureau, Hilo; Camping Headquarters Hawaii, 102 Kanoelehua Street, Hilo (or write Box 11), which rents equipment to adventurers (4-wheel-drives, tents, skis, fishing poles) and will field trip-planning questions.

Camping and Picnicking

Uncrowded shoreline and upland parks are spaced about the island. You can pitch a tent—and in most cases park a camper—in the following parks; these generally have one or more pavilions, rest rooms, picnic tables, water, and in many cases, firepits and electricity. Beach parks: Onekahakaha, James Kealoha, Isaac Hale, MacKenzie, Harry K. Brown, Punaluu, Whittington, Hookena, Napoopoo, Kahaluu, Hapuna, Samuel M. Spencer, Mahukona, Kapaa, Keokea, Laupahoehoe, and Kolekole. Inland parks: Hawaii Volcanoes, Manuka, Pohakuloa, Waikaumalo, and Kaiwiki. People picnic at all parks and camp and picnic also in Waipio and Pololu valleys (unimproved), at the beach or along streams.

Get camping permits, required for use of state and county campgrounds, at parks department offices (addresses above). Make reservations if you wish to use the state's low-cost cabins. Pohakuloa, at 6,500 feet in Mauna Kea State Park, has several furnished family cabins and a group camp—furnished sleeping cabins (capacity: 64) and cooking-dining hall (lounge and visitor center by mid-1970). Above at Hale Pohaku, 9,200 feet, are four furnished barracks (for 57 people). You can sometimes use three Mauna Kea hunters' cabins along restricted jeep trails. At Volcano, just outside the national park, are two furnished, family-size Kilauea cabins set in native forest. Another group camp (for 36 people) is located at Hapuna, 400 yards from the beach.

Hawaii Volcanoes National Park has three campgrounds and three picnic grounds. Get permits at Kilauea Visitor Center to camp or to use two cabins high on Mauna Loa. At Namakani Paio campground are 10 unfurnished cabins rented by Volcano House (equipment may also be rented).

Youngsters paddle *in Waiakolea Pond, at Harry K. Brown Park, bordered by a campground.*

You can rent a camper from Mauna Kea Motors in Waimea (Box 657, Kamuela) and from most of the firms listed on page 12.

Swimming, Surfing, Snorkeling

There is good ocean swimming and surfing on the Big Island, but you have to know where to go. The island is geologically so young that few coral reefs have built up to create surfable waves and be eroded into sand. But all sides have beaches, or sandy coves tucked between low-lying lava fingers—most of them in the beach parks.

Look first to the South Kohala-North Kona Coast. Hapuna State Beach Park has the outstanding accessible swimming, a generous swath of white sand, and some body surfing. The Mauna Kea Beach Hotel's beach (Kaunaoa) and its cove at Hapuna (another hotel site) are superb, too. Try skin diving at Spencer Park and shallow, sandy coves up the coast from Kawaihae and south, off Wailea and Puako. Corals are colorful and there are shells. The connecting road being built from Puako to Kailua will make accessible a dozen or so sand-fringed bays. You can reach a few by road (mostly private) now, or all by boat. Kaupulehu already has a hotel (Kona Village); Anaehoomalu has one in the works. There are fishponds at Kalahuipuaa, Anaehoomalu, Kaloko, and Honokohau. Keawaiki has black sand; Makalawena, a native waterfowl pond. Kiholo may become a major park.

The rocky Kona Coast has interruptions. You can swim in shallow Kahaluu Bay, body surf at famed "disappearing" White Sands (Holualoa), and do both at

A successful day *off the Kona Coast. Marlin grounds here yield record game fish (this one weighs 480 pounds).*

Hookena. Kailua, Keei, Honaunau, and Milolii have sandy coves good for children, and Keauhou and Kealakekua (off Napoopoo Park) bays, protected deep water. Banyans (year-round) and Lyman's (in winter) are popular surfing spots a couple of miles south of Kailua. Honokohau, two miles north, has surf to rival Waikiki's, but still takes a boat, jeep, or board-hauling walk to reach.

Kau's Whittington Park has mud-bottom tidal pools, and Punaluu, black sand and some body surfing. Kaulana Bay is sheltered, and to the jeep explorer, this east coast of South Point (page 79) offers beachcombing, including strips and patches of green sand (olivines). In Puna, swim off Isaac Hale and Harry K. Brown parks when the sea is calm, and any time in the latter's brackish and fresh-water ponds, or at nearby Queen's Bath, a volcanic crack with cold ground water.

At Hilo, Reeds Bay has sand and fresh-water inlets to keep it free of the sharks that like the rest of the harbor. (They don't discourage surfers when exciting waves come up at Bayfront, right off downtown.) Just two miles north is Honolii, blessed with swells from the north or south and the island's best all-year surfing. The

parks east of town have coves and tidepools, and you can follow residents to others in the neighborhood.

Don't tempt fate along the wave-lashed north coast. Streams in Waikaumalo and Kolekole parks and in Waipio Valley have dipping places. Keokea and Kapaa parks front a sea generally free of storm swells in summer and promising for skin divers, and Mahukona Bay is crystal clear and sheltered—youngsters dive off the old landing.

Fishing, Boating

Sport fishing center is Kailua. Only minutes away from Kailua Wharf, and with scenic coast in view, you can troll smooth seas that have yielded the world's record 1,100-pound Pacific blue marlin. A lot of fighting *mahimahi, ono, 'ahi,* and *aku* have succumbed to Kona Coast fishermen, too. Some two dozen boats are available for full or half-day trips on a per-person or exclusive charter basis. Make reservations with Kona Big Game Fishing Association, Kona Charter Skippers Association, or Kona Activities Center, all in Kailua (Kailua-Kona Post Office), or Pacific Game Fishing Unlimited, 1777 Ala Moana, Honolulu. Make reservations with Mauna Kea Beach Hotel for charters out of Kawaihae; there's a good *mahimahi* run offshore.

You might talk a resident of Kawaihae, Mahukona, Puako, or Milolii into renting you a skiff or motor-powered outrigger canoe to go bottom-fishing for snappers and mackerel. All along the west coast, anglers surf cast for *'o'io,* pole fish from rocks or piers for *papio,* and spear-fish. You need an aqua lung for the deep water off most of Kona but can skin dive off Puako and Hapuna, Mahukona, and Kapaa beach parks. On the Hamakua Coast the poling is for *ulua, kawakawa, moi,* and *'u'u.* Hilo and Puna parks are good bases for casting or poling, and fishermen sometimes go out at night from Isaac Hale Beach Park to troll for *'u'u* and *'o'io.* They catch *'u'u* from South Point's bluff, cast for *ulua* and *papio* from its beaches.

Mullet and *aholehole* are plentiful in 26-acre Waiakea Fishpond, part of Hilo's Wailoa State Park. Five Kohala reservoirs south of Hawi, totaling 55 acres, are stocked with channel catfish, bluegills, large-mouth and peacock bass. A license and permit (State Fish and Game office) are required for pond fishing.

At Kona Activities Center in Kailua (Box 1035, Kailua-Kona), you can sign up for glass-bottom boat trips, skin-diving charters, an outrigger picnic cruise, and excursions to the Captain Cook Monument at Kealakekua Bay where you transfer to a glass-bottom boat for a look at colorful fish and coral. All trips start at Kailua Wharf; you can also book with skippers. At Kawaihae, Gary Nagasawa runs glass-bottom boat trips. Catamaran cruises depart from Mauna Kea Beach Hotel.

Golf

Golfers have a choice of six courses: the championship Mauna Kea and Keauhou-Kona courses; 18 and 9-hole courses at Hilo; the 18-hole Volcano course; and a 9-hole course at Honokaa.

Bicycling

You can rent bicycles at the Naniloa in Hilo and at Pedal 'n Paddle, Kailua.

Driving Rough Country

If you want to roam the wilderness, you should know that some of it is off-limits unless you're on a guided trip. And if you're unacquainted or unused to driving rough terrain, it's wise to cover on tour even some out-of-the-way areas you can arrange to travel yourself.

All-expense outings by 4-wheel-drive are simply organized adventures. Hawaii Island Safaris (Box 11, Hilo) and Hawaii Trails (Waimea Village Inn, Kamuela) are the adventure specialists. Trips can take from half a day to two or more. They can be catered to special interests—native birds and plants, volcanoes, archaeology.

On one tour, you travel through private ranch and wild lands to the cinder-pocked summit of Hualalai, and explore the Mauna Loa-Hualalai saddle. Here you see sandalwood and odd, stunted plants; remnants of the Judd Trail, a perfectly straight horse path with curbstones started from Kona to Hilo but halted by the 1859 lava flow; and remains of Ahua-a-Umi, a curious 16th-century temple with individual rock piles said to have represented a census of each district's warriors.

You might explore Waipo Valley (page 89) or South Point (page 79); ascend the summit bog of the Kohala Mountains for a look down into Waipio Valley (page 89); climb to the summits of Mauna Loa and Mauna Kea (pages 91 and 92).

Skiing

Ski buffs (mostly those who live in the Islands) try runs 1,000 yards to 5 miles long over the fast, wind-packed corn snow that usually covers Mauna Kea's summit cones in winter. Access to the slopes is via the restricted 4-wheel-drive summit road controlled by the State Parks office in Hilo. Camping Headquarters Hawaii (102 Kanoelehua Street, Hilo, or write Box 11) has some rental equipment, and it is possible to arrange a trip with Hawaii Island Safaris or Hawaii Trails, or even to join the excursions they handle for the Ski Association of Hawaii (Box 8327, Honolulu). The Association has a portable rope tow.

Hiking

Hikers can consider some ultimate challenges—to lungs as well as legs: scaling lava-encrusted Mauna Loa on the national park trail (pages 73-74), or climbing up through cinders from Kilohana Lookout in Mauna Kea State Park to the very top of the island (page 91). The national park has about 30 miles of trails of varying length and difficulty (see section on park, pages 72-75). Check in at Kilauea Visitor Center before venturing out on the tough ones.

In about 6 hours, you can hike a switchback trail up Waipio Valley's west bluff, cross 13 smaller gulches, descend into even-more-isolated Waimanu Valley, and camp on the beach. There's a trail-side cabin about half way.

You can hike into Pololu Valley and on through gorges as far as Honopue on the Kohala Ditch Trails (page 88). To hike for a day, or to cover the 2-to-3-day loop, using free cabins, make arrangements with Kohala Sugar Company, Hawi.

Look for short trails or streams to follow in many of the parks. Along many shores are sections of old Hawaiian foot or horse trails. You'll find these at City of Refuge and MacKenzie State Park; longer sections are shown on our map.

Four-wheel-drive *vehicles can explore parts of Hawaii not accessible by ordinary car. This is Waipio Valley.*

Riding party *heads into drifting clouds on high grasslands of Parker Ranch on slopes of lofty Mauna Kea.*

Hunting

Hunters go after game birds, goats, sheep, and wild boar in the 100,000-acre Mauna Kea and Pohakuloa public hunting grounds and many more acres of private territory. The season for pheasants, chukar partridge, doves, gray and black Francolins, California and Japanese quail is generally weekends and holidays from November through mid-January. The usually-longer animal seasons are set periodically and apply only to the public grounds and several forest reserves. In special areas you can hunt sheep and pigs all year with a bow and arrow. The Fish and Game office in Hilo issues the permits required to hunt public areas and can tell you of available guides.

For all-expense safaris, mostly on private lands, write Hawaii Trails, Kamuela, or Slim Holt-Hawaii (Box 1938, Hilo). Hawaii Trails represents Winchester World-Wide Safaris, has hunting rights over 300,000 acres in North Kona. Mauna Kea Beach Hotel guests can hunt the vast Parker Ranch.

Horseback Riding

From Parker Ranch Livery Stables in Waimea, you can ride nearby range or head for distant Kohala and Mauna Kea flanks with a guide for a few dollars per person an hour. Pack trips are possible, too. You can also hire horses, and a guide, at John Silva Riding Academy, Hoolulu Park stables, Hilo (to ride around the town).

Hilo

Hilo, the Neighbor Islands' largest "city," is really a cane field town now grown to 30,000. It sprawls along crescent-shaped Hilo Bay and stretches upward 1,500 feet. Both Mauna Loa and Mauna Kea are backdrops on clear days, but it is Mauna Kea that rises back of the harbor.

Two important rivers empty into the bay. The Wailuku, the state's second longest, flows 32 miles from its source high on Mauna Kea. The Wailoa is the state's shortest, less than half a mile.

Other kinds of water have shaped the town's character. You can expect rain (almost 150 inches a year). That's what makes the green growth heavy and the tropical flowers abundant. Hilo is particularly vulnerable to seismic waves (tsunamis). Its bayfront was washed out in 1960 in a disaster that saw 61 killed, 282 injured, and 220 homes and 308 businesses destroyed—some of them buildings rebuilt after an even more destructive wave in 1946. The spunky town is capitalizing on being handed a waterfront greenbelt, gradually sculpturing and planting to make it a handsome, usable park with separate fishing and pleasure boat harbors, boating canal, golf course, promenades, equestrian and bicycle paths, shelters, and flower displays. Shopping and hotel complexes are going in around it—out of any wave's reach. In part of the redevelopment area known as Kaiko'o, a new government center (with large state and county buildings) is functioning. Just below is Wailoa Visitor Center with an information counter and interpretive exhibits on the Big Island's history, natural history, and archaeology.

Jets landing from the Mainland made Hilo a tourist playground almost overnight. There's some night life now and high-rise building. But still the town is unpretentious, busy with its flowers, with shipping sugar, and as seat of government for Hawaii County. Most buildings are wood, with metal roofs (note the pastel façades along Kamehameha Avenue). Theaters screen Japanese and Filipino movies as often as American, and Japanese martial arts (*judo, karate, aikido, kendo*) are popular recreation.

Hilo's branch of the University of Hawaii (enter campus off Lanikaula Street) has new classrooms and dormitories, more than 800 students, and a unique Cloud Physics Observatory.

The town has an unusual Yacht Club, on Kahoai Street. The club has no boats, although it did when it began in 1925 on the site of the Naniloa Hotel. Its oceanfront dining room and pool are open to members of Mainland clubs with which it has reciprocity agreements.

Sampan buses are a Hilo landmark—like San Francisco's cable cars or Tahiti's *le truck*. Actually the sampan is not a bus at all but a low-profile jitney built by metal smiths and carpenters on an automobile chassis, painted and appointed to suit its owner's whims. It's a workhorse like the Island-made fishing boat called a sampan.

Riders step up to board, then walk stooped over to their places. Twelve can squeeze into side and back seats, but even with a full load a sampan is airy—it has no windows except for the windshield. When it rains, curtains are unrolled and buttoned down.

Sampans leave Mooheau Terminal for the outermost points of town every 10 to 30 minutes between daybreak and 5 P.M. The drivers (some are women) alternate routes and run on a schedule of sorts past tidy homes and gardens in sections most tourists don't see. The only marked bus stops are downtown. Elsewhere drivers stop or pick up at any points along the routes, and may detour to show sights to visitors—without extra charge. Most any time you can hire a sampan for touring.

The sampan fleet that numbered 75 vehicles right after World War II has dwindled to about a dozen now that most Hilo residents go about in their own automobiles and children ride orthodox school buses. But the community is so fond of its aging curiosities it will probably help a few to survive.

Sampan buses are *fun to ride. Here the driver has detoured to show tourist passengers Hilo's Haili Church.*

Shops and Factories of Special Interest

In and around Hilo, visitors are welcome at many shops and factories that turn out Hawaiian specialties. Unless otherwise noted, places listed are open during business hours. Locate them on a city map.

Commercial flower plants. At more than a dozen places you can see how orchids and anthuriums are grown and packed for shipping; buy flowers, dried arrangements, and curios. Biggest operations are **Hirose Nurseries, Inc.**, 2212 Kanoelehua Ave. (also good artifact collection); **Kong's Floraleigh Gardens**, 1477 Kalanianaole Ave. (most photogenic gardens); **Mauna Loa Orchids, Ltd.** (also called Hawaiian Exotic Flowers), 784 Kinoole St.; and **Orchids of Hawaii**, 575 Hinano St. The **airport flower stalls** sell or ship *leis* (some unusual) and cut flowers. Inquire about other nurseries and their specialties and which spots welcome Sunday visitors. For a continuous display of prize flowers, visit the **Orchidarium**, 524 Manono St. (daily 9-5; small charge); judging takes place every second Wednesday at 7:30 P.M.

Fish auction, in shed at Sampan Harbor (daily, 7:30 A.M.). Spirited bidding goes on in several languages plus "pidgin." Sampans come in with catch around 5:30 A.M. and 4 P.M. Also at the shed: **Suisan Company's wholesale fish market** (85 Lihiwai St.).

Sumida Fish Cake Factory, 399E Kawili St., makes the popular Japanese *kamaboko*—it's rubbery and sweet.

Hilo Meat Cooperative, Ltd., 230 Kekuanaoa St., makes Miko Portuguese sausage, Scottish bangers.

Okura Pickle Factory, 261A Kekuanaoa St., puts out two kinds of Japanese pickled radishes—*takuwan, sambaizuki*.

Mr. Papaya Cooperative, 866 Mililani St., packs papayas and also sells gift boxes at factory prices.

Hawaiian Luau Foods, 76 Kilauea Ave., offers such exotics as dried fish, canned fern shoots, fresh or frozen *opihi*.

Poi factories. Action starts at dawn, is over by noon at **Ah Hee Poi Shop**, 140 Kilauea Ave.; **Hilo Poi Factory**, 265A Kekuanaoa St.; **Puueo Poi Shop**, 265D Kekuanaoa St.

Hulaberry Farms, Inc., 31 Makaala St. (call ahead), and **Niolopa Jams & Jellies**, 1965 Kamehameha Ave., turn out jams and jellies of guava, *poha*, passion fruit, papaya, pineapple.

Candy Box, 319 Manono St., makes an assortment of candies with macadamia nuts.

Royal Hawaiian Macadamia Nut Company, near Keeau, 5 miles from airport on route 11, then 3 miles on farm road. You watch processing and packing of nuts from observation gallery, taste samples, take self-guided walk through orchard of 80,000 macadamia nut trees (planting holes were drilled in lava).

Woodcraft plants. Blair, 300 Manono St., makes Hawaiian hardwood flooring and furniture as well as tableware. **Aloha Hawaii Woodcraft Shop**, 262 Kekuanaoa St., makes tableware and carves images from tree fern trunks. **Hawaiian Tiki Products**, 271B Kekuanaoa St., makes images.

Hilo Art Gallery, 175 Keawe St., features painting on the spot by local artists.

Hale O Lima Hana, 330 Kamehameha Ave., is a headquarters for ceramists, weaving and feather-work artisans; it also sells paintings.

Hale Manu Craft, on route 11, 3 miles from airport, is one of few places to see hats, purses, mats, and baskets hand-woven from *lauhala*, the leaf of the pandanus tree. Weaving is in the morning; sales, all day.

Kulani Honor Farm, 19 miles up Stainback Highway from turnoff on route 11, 4 miles from airport (daily 9-3). No prison setting is this clearing in the wilderness at 5,000 feet. Men raise livestock, do fine woodcarving and sell it. You drive up on good gravel through superb native forest.

Mauna Kea Sugar Company Mill, at Wainaku, atop the town's north bluff, has tours (Mon.-Fri., 10 A.M. and 2 P.M.).

Bulk sugar plant, Pier 1—Kuhio Wharf (call Hilo Transportation & Terminal Co., Ltd., to arrange tour, weekdays). Equipment takes in 300 tons of sugar an hour from trucks, loads 800 tons an hour into freighters.

Hilo's Parks

In Hilo's array of parks (besides beach parks), attractions range from caves to waterfalls.

Wailoa State Park embraces Wailoa River, Waiakea Fishpond, and Waiolama Canal; has picnic tables, outdoor stoves, pavilions, tropical garden displays, visitor center. You reach picnic area at end of Piilani St., or cross footbridge from State Office Building.

Banyan Drive. On the tree-shaded parkway that rounds Waiakea Peninsula, past the hotels, each banyan has a plaque telling you what celebrity planted it.

Liliuokalani Gardens. Almost 30 acres of Waiakea Peninsula is an Edo-type Japanese garden with ponds, lanterns, bridges, and picnic grounds.

Coconut Island, the palm-fringed islet in Hilo Bay, was once a Hawaiian sanctuary with birth and healing stones, now is a pleasant picnic place reached by bridge from Waiakea Peninsula.

Hawaii County Zoo, at Onekahakaha Beach Park, 3 miles out on Kalanianaole Ave. (Tues.-Sun., 10-4:30). Small collection of exotic birds, Big Island game animals.

Tree Nursery, 1643 Kilauea Ave. (Mon.-Fri., 7:45-4:30). An arboretum of 17 acres with more than 600 different tropical trees.

Kalakaua Park, Waianuenue Ave. at Kinoole St., is a tree-shaded green with World War II memorial fountain.

Wailuku River Park has two sections. Its **Rainbow Falls** (take Rainbow Drive off Waianuenue Ave.) is a torrential waterfall noted for the rainbow visible in its spray and mist many mornings. A short trail to a secluded picnic spot starts near the lookout. An old hospital just below the falls has become a Peace Corps Training Center for volunteers headed for Southeast Asia. **Boiling Pots and Peepee Falls,** a mile farther inland, are at the end of a foot trail from the corner of Wailuku and Peepee Falls drives. The river has cut a chain of deep, round pools in the lava stream bed and linked them with falls and rapids. Turbulent water also flows beneath the surface and bubbles up as if it were boiling. The "pots" are 20 to 50 feet across, just right to splash about in.

Kaumana Caves, on Kaumana Drive (route 20), about 5 miles from downtown. From a picnic ground, a stairway goes down to a fern grotto between two large facing tunnels. These lava tubes and many branching caverns were formed during Mauna Loa's 1881 flow, which lasted nine months and came closer to Hilo than any other on record. The tunnel leading toward Hilo is 2½ to 15 feet high and 10 to 60 feet wide and has been followed for more than half a mile (take flashlight). The other is dangerous to enter.

Churches, Temples, and Museums

Hilo's heritage shows in these buildings and their furnishings.

Haili Church, 404 Haili St. This yellow frame, New England-style church was built in 1859 by Protestant missionaries. Services are in Hawaiian and English. Half of outstanding choir is from one family.

St. Joseph's Catholic Church, corner of Haili and Kapiolani streets. Hilo's largest church, a stucco building dating from 1919, resembles an early Spanish mission, has an interesting cracked bell.

Lyman House Memorial Museum, 276 Haili St. (Mon.-Sat., 10-4; Sun., 1-4; small charge). Missionaries, the David Belden Lymans, built this New England-style house in 1839 out of hand-hewn timbers and planks from local forests and stones mortared with coral. Inside are missionary furnishings and costumes, whaling relics, rare Hawaiian bows, featherwork tools, fine tapa. In 1970 some of the collection will go into a new building next door.

Naha and Pinao stones, museum pieces in front of Hawaii County Library on Waianuenue Ave. In ancient days the huge rectangular Naha Stone stood before the temple of Pinao, near the present library site. Hawaiians used it to determine the legitimacy of claimants of Naha line royal blood. One who could move the stone (presumably a Naha chief) would become king of the island, and one who overturned it would conquer all the islands. It is said the prophecy was proved because the stone was overturned by Kamehameha the Great (who was not even a Naha). The Pinao Stone was the temple's entrance pillar.

First United Protestant Church, corner of Haili and Kinoole streets. Hiloans have gone by the four-face steeple clock on this imposing red frame Victorian since the turn of the century. The church was established as the First Foreign Church of Hilo in 1868 when services at Haili Church were only in Hawaiian. This sanctuary is destined to make way for a shopping center, and the new one will go up on a new site.

Central Christian Church, corner of Haili and Kilauea streets, is a quaint wooden Victorian built in 1892 as the Portuguese Church by descendants of missionaries who fled Catholic control of their native Madeira Islands. Today's congregation is an ethnic mixture.

Hilo Hongwanji Temple, 398 Kilauea Ave. The characteristic three-domed building was built in 1925 for the oldest Japanese Buddhist mission in the state, founded in 1889. Its first building was across the street.

United Community Church, corner of Kinoole and Mohouli streets, looks like a temple. It was built in 1937 as the Hilo Chinese Christian Church and has a striking Oriental roof and tower. Now it has a "melting pot" membership and services are in English.

Ke Kilohana O Ka Malamalama Church, 558 Manono St. A simple box of a building with charming Victorian details serves 200 members of a small Protestant sect, Hoomana Naauao O Hawaii. The church has Hawaiian-English services, two choirs, Hawaiian language classes. The 1922 structure was modeled after the original building of the mother church in Honolulu (page 38).

Hawaii Volcanoes National Park

Kilauea Volcano may erupt anytime. And its bizarre landscape, even without liquid lava, abounds in fantastic volcanic features. It was to protect this live volcano land, its rain forests and rare plants and birds that a national park was established back in 1916. Mauna Loa's summit caldera and upper northeast flank were included. Now the park covers 344 square miles and takes in a stretch of coast with ancient Hawaiian ruins.

Steep, symmetrical cones like Vesuvius are the explosive type. When gently-rising Mauna Loa or Kilauea crack open, people are usually allowed close to the scene—if it's accessible—and can view flaming fountains and rivers from sightseeing flights at night.

Mauna Loa's flows have covered half the island. Many

times erupting lavas have stayed within its summit caldera, Mokuaweoweo; other times (including the last eruption in 1950), lava bursts started in the caldera, then split open the mountainside far below.

Kilauea, 9,500 feet below, is called the "drive-in volcano" because of its frequent, easy-to-reach action. Its summit caldera, Kilauea Crater, is 2½ miles long, 2 miles wide, 400 feet deep, and contains Halemaumau, the fire-pit which Pele, the volcano goddess, now calls home. This main lava vent is ½ mile in diameter; its depth changes with each refilling or collapse of its bottom. For more than a century, Halemaumau was a bubbling—and sometimes overflowing—lava lake, but the almost-continuous activity ended with steam explosions in 1924—one of the rare times Kilauea has become violent. There was lava lake activity in Halemaumau again for eight months in 1967 and 1968; it raised the level of the firepit 375 feet, to just 175 feet from its rim. Kilauea's outbreaks in the last few decades—so many it's hard to keep count—have also included flank flows in Puna and fireworks in its satellite craters.

Planning Your Visit

Enough roads, trails, and interpretive plaques are laid out in the park to keep you busy for several days. But you can get a fair sampling in a few hours on a 90-mile loop trip from Hilo or even traveling between Hilo and the Kona Coast (this makes a long day). On the loop trip, if you visit the summit section first, you can have a lesson in volcanology before you sightsee; then drive downhill to the coast and take in the sweeping marine view. Going from Hilo to Kona, you can visit the coastal region first by entering the park at Kalapana.

Note: The standard loop trip is out until reconstruction of a 3-mile stretch of the Chain of Craters Road between Aloi and Makaopuhi craters overrun by lava in several 1969 eruptions. You can drive from each entrance almost to the lava barriers, and will find fascinating new landmarks near the Aloi turn-around (see page 74).

Visitor centers at both entrances are stocked with map-guides (free) and booklets on the volcanoes, plants, and wildlife. At Kilauea Visitor Center (open daily but hours vary), museum exhibits and programs several times a day (with movies of eruptions) explain volcano action. Displays at Kalapana's Wahaula Center (days and hours vary seasonally) depict early Hawaiian life.

Close by Kilauea Visitor Center and on the crater rim is Volcano House, a hotel Islanders visit for a climate change—the air is crisp at 4,000 feet—and where hundreds eat every noon. Military families can stay at Kilauea Military Camp, a recreation center a mile away. To avoid luncheon crowds, try the park's picnic grounds or Volcano Lodge, just outside the park on the Hilo side.

Rain forest *in Hawaii Volcanoes National Park has 'ohi'a trees with understory of tree ferns 20 feet high.*

Crater Rim Drive

The 11.1-mile Crater Rim Drive takes you from Kilauea Center around and into the summit caldera, across both rift zones, through native jungle and over bleak desert. A nearly parallel foot trail takes a day to walk but crosses the road at several good pick-up points.

If you head west, you come first to the Sulphur Banks, where volcanic fumaroles emit gases and vapors which cool when they reach the surface, leaving colorful mineral deposits. Along Steaming Bluff, you can be engulfed by steam from hot ground water released through deep cracks in the ground.

Mauna Loa Strip Road takes off up the mountain to a shelter and overlook at 6,662 feet, the start of an 18-mile trail to Mokuaweoweo firepit. Along its lower reaches are Tree Molds as large as 5 feet across, formed when liquid lava cooled around trunks, crusting on the outside but burning the inside out; and Kipuka Puaulu (Bird Park), an oasis (*kipuka*) created when a Mauna Loa flow split, leaving intact 100 vegetated acres with unusual native plants (some varieties are found nowhere else) and some

Oddly beautiful *skeletons of 'ohi'a trees rise from a deep carpet of cinders along the ½-mile Devastation Trail.*

edible berries. You'll find picnic grounds, an exhibit describing the plants and native birds, and a pamphlet to guide you on an easy, mile-long trail.

The drive up from Bird Park, over 10 paved but narrow miles, rewards you with a wide view—on clear days. To hike on to the top takes three days or more round trip. You trudge over seemingly endless lava crust—even snow or ice—and stay in cabins at 10,035 feet and at the summit (arrange hike, cabin use at Kilauea Center). For another way to the top, see page 92.

Continuing counter-clockwise on the rim drive you come to Kilauea Overlook (a picnic spot on the edge of the vast lava-streaked depression), and the only permanent volcano observatory in the nation, on the high point of the caldera's west wall, where you look through a window at seismographs that record hundreds of slight earthquakes every month. Parallel cracks that run from the summit into the Ka'u Desert, the volcano's leeward flank, mark the southwest rift zone.

At the halfway point on the drive, stop to peer into Halemaumau from a couple of safe terraces on its cracked and crumbly brink. Depth and coloring depend upon what Pele has been up to. The temperamental lady may just send up smoke to irritate your eyes and throat.

Park again at Devastation Trail, a half-mile of boardwalk atop cinders that takes you through a skeleton forest wrought by the violence in Kilauea Iki (Little Kilauea)

Crater in 1959. The walk ends at Kilauea Iki Overlook (also reached on the rim drive) and Puu Puai, the 400-foot cone of pumice and ash formed during the eruption when dazzling fountains of lava shot as high as 1,900 feet. The cone straddles the crater rim and rears up 150 feet from the old, now-buried roadbed. From the Overlook, the drop is 350 feet. You can cross the floor of the chasm and check the lava thermometer in a hole drilled through the floating crust to magma 100 feet below. The mile-long trail connects two rim drive stops—Thurston Lava Tube and Byron Ledge (the divide between Kilauea Iki and Kilauea craters).

Thurston Lava Tube, easternmost point on the drive, is in the famous Fern Jungle, a moist tangle of giant tree ferns and several varieties of smaller ferns growing in the shade of weathered 'ohi'a trees. You can walk here, too, on a ¼-mile loop through forest and the 450-foot tunnel, 20 or more feet high, formed in prehistoric time when the outer crust of a flow hardened while the molten river within traveled on.

Halemaumau Trail

The "World's Weirdest Walk" is an apt subtitle for the 3.2-mile, self-guiding Halemaumau Trail, the park's most popular hike. It starts near Volcano House, crosses the scorched and scarred floor of Kilauea caldera to the rim of Halemaumau. Warped grayish trees and plants, ash beds and rock, some sporting lichens and other growth, are described in a park pamphlet. Start early, before sun bakes the crater floor. Arrange a ride back from Halemaumau Overlook, or walk out and back on Byron Ledge Trail, 3½ miles.

Chain of Craters Road

The Chain of Craters Road branches south off the rim drive and travels the volcano's east rift zone for 7 miles, past old craters that have been firepits in recent months. For another 19 miles, it drops to the sea and follows the coast to Kalapana.

You can look into most of the nine chasms. Some have hardened lava lakes that will stay hot beneath the paving for centuries; others have islands of vegetation; a few have double pits. The chasms were formed long ago by ground collapse when lava underneath drained away, but they keep changing. More than half (Heake, Aloi, Alae, Makaopuhi, Napau) are newly famous for spectacular outbursts within or close by. Magma geysers have spurted up inside; hot lava rivers have tumbled over their high walls. In the 1969 flare-ups that buried roadway under molten rock and pumice, high fountains sent a river of flame down the mountain all the way to the sea, plunging over two *pali* along its way, and left "draperies" on Aloi's walls, along with 30-foot cinder cones, deep ground cracks, and weird lava trees that are easy to see.

Hilina Pali Road veers off the main drive and ends after 8½ miles at a lookout 2,250 feet above the coast on a cliff formed by prehistoric slumping of the volcano's slopes. Trails from Kipuka Nene campground (part way along) and the lookout go down to Halape Beach (blanketed with morning glory).

Road to Kalapana

The broad road on to Kalapana from Makaopuhi leaves the rift zone and rain forest for the 1,500-foot crest of Poliokeawe Pali, a fault scarp similar to Hilina Pali. From turnouts you look over Mauna Loa's southwest shoulder all the way to South Point. At Naulu Forest picnic area, 20 species of native trees grow on an old *aa* flow. On the descent to shore, park at Puu Loa and walk the old Puna-Ka'u Trail ¾ mile east over *pahoehoe* fields to mounds etched with hundreds of petroglyphs (most are dots-in-a-circle tally marks).

On the stretch of coastal road atop 60-foot cliffs, look inland over the undulating *pahoehoe* to *kukui* groves up on Holei Pali; one once shaded a large settlement. The Kamoamoa campground and picnic area overlook an arch created by wave erosion of a 100-foot lava tube. On its Ka'u side, back of a boat landing, are long, narrow enclosures that were canoe sheds. Rock walls all around formerly outlined village compounds. One long wall, from sea to *pali*, is of turn-of-the-century construction and now separates the campground from partially-repaired ruins of Moa Heiau. Make a roadside stop at Oloua, a fishermen's cave whose excavation yielded Stone Age tackle— you push a button for a description.

Next to Wahaula Visitor Center are the ruins of Wahaula Heiau, probably the Islands' oldest, built about 1250 A.D. by the Tahitian priest Paao, who introduced the severe system of taboos and sacrifices practiced until 1819. The temple was rebuilt twice (last about 1770), and during two reigns (including that of Kamehameha the Great), was one of six *luakini*, or state, *heiaus* where ruling chiefs prayed and humans were slain and offered to the gods. The last human sacrifices took place here. It is a scale model of this temple that is in Honolulu's Bishop Museum.

Puna District

Puna has few people but lots of subdivisions awaiting houses. It also has papayas, and contrasts of bucolic tranquility and upheaval—the freakish evidences of Kilauea's fiery behavior in 1955 and 1960 when roads, farms, buildings, even villages were buried under ponderous lava flows.

You see Puna on a 35-mile triangle of roads out of Pahoa. One leg is the direct route between Hilo and the Kalapana end of the national park.

Visitors explore *Kekaloa Heiau, supposedly built by a wizard, on bank of Waiakolea Pond in Kalapana park.*

Queen's Bath, *on coast near Kalapana, is a natural pool in a volcanic crack—a refreshing place for a dip.*

Pahoa to Kalapana

Pahoa has false-front buildings, some wooden sidewalks, and three large anthurium nurseries to visit (Taira's Big Isle Anthuriums, Hawaiian Green House, and Puna Flowers & Foliage, Inc.). Townsfolk grow the flowers in their lava-crust yards under orange and tangerine trees. Pahoa School has several times been converted to eruption headquarters—for volcanologists, evacuees, reporters, and spectators.

Kalapana-bound on route 13, park at the marked turnout about 4 miles out of Pahoa and have a look below at still-impressive remains of the 1955 eruption. But watch out for obscured holes, cracks, even hot mud. You can climb a 20-foot cone and peer into its still-steamy interior. In the old (now partly brush-covered) roadway it cut off, note the deep cracks. Here is where scientists for the first time watched an eruption start. A fissure opened, the road split, and small explosive fountains shot up through a bulge of lava. Hunt in the tall grass below for Kamaili Crater (popularly known as "the hole in Nii's cucumber patch"), a 135-foot-deep pit formed when the ground collapsed with sharp explosions. It steams after rains; other times you can see the underground hardened lava it exposed. In "Pele's Kitchen" are old tree molds, yellowish from sulphur and other gases that steamed out of them after this eruption.

The highway crosses two 1955 flows that reached the sea. Outlined against the sky, you can see the cones from which they came. The lava—as happens quickly in rainy regions—is already acquiring a silvery cloak of lichen.

Downhill the road cuts through more tropical forest and an old lava flow. It passes scattered, unpainted wooden houses with rusty iron roofs that are mossy around gutters that feed rainwater through a trough to a wooden tank.

Cave of Refuge *at Kalapana comes out on ledge above sea. Take a flashlight; you'll be in total darkness in tunnel.*

The road reaches the sea at the striking black sand beach of Kaimu, washed with foam that laps the trunks of its overhanging coconut palms. The black sand was formed when lava exploded into bits as it hit the ocean and then was ground finer by wave action and friction. Picnic, walk the long crescent barefoot, but don't swim— there are hazardous currents.

Kalapana, a few road curves to the west, has a beach park (Harry K. Brown) with legendary boulders, some arranged as picnic furniture under umbrellas of palms and pandanus, and the remains of Kekaloa Heiau. The story goes that a wizard built this *heiau*. He proved his powers by eating the pulp of bananas; skins left hanging would develop new pulp. You can splash about in Waiakolea Pond, swim in a brackish pool built in gray sand dunes and usually in the sea below.

Nearby Star of the Sea Church is a tiny treasure-house of painting. The work (finished in 1929) is by Belgian Father Evarist Gielen, who studied briefly in Europe with Father John, artist of the Kona churches (pages 83-84). Two barrel-vaulted ceilings, one over the altar recess, appear supported by columns which are just painted on; six pictures, with large designs and soft colors, float between painted ceiling ribs; and windows have painted canopies. A large Nativity scene over the door is Florentine in tone. Angels over the altar resemble early ship figureheads. In 1963-64, a visiting artist, George Heidler, filled the empty spaces below Evarist's work, painted the outside entrance, and added a roadside mosaic.

On the shore behind the church is a Stone Age canoe ramp. Villagers still use the huge rock slabs to launch their outriggers swiftly, between wave breaks. A plaque explains how the ancients did it. At Kalapana's 'Awa Factory and Lauhala Hut, pandanus leaves (*lauhala*) are processed for weavers, and roots of 'awa (which Hawaiians mashed for a drink that relaxes muscles) are dried for shipping to drug manufacturers. Chew on a stalk (it's like mouthwash), but not too long or it will numb your tongue and throat.

The bluff above the village has a long lava tunnel, the Cave of Refuge, that comes out on a ledge above the sea. From the overgrown entrance in the ground—on a line between two red and white survey marker flags—you soon get into total darkness; so take a flashlight. You can climb the hill on a trail from back of a white house with red roof and gate (ask permission and directions). Queen's Bath, a marked swimming hole along the 4-mile stretch to the national park, is about 10 by 100 feet; youngsters dive from its rocky banks.

Kalapana to Kapoho

On the jungle drive along shore toward Cape Kumukahi (route 137) are stunning break-throughs to the ocean, three of them to black sand beaches (1955 lava). A trail goes over sun-baked rocks to the largest.

Houses closer together than others in the region identify two old villages—Opihikao and Pohoiki. Approaching Opihikao, watch for concrete tombs atop old lava, and a marked remnant of an ancient paved trail. The settlement's wooden church is more than 100 years old. You'll spot MacKenzie State Beach Park by its campground in a shady grove of ironwoods just past Opihikao. Isaac Hale Beach Park is on Pohoiki Bay, once Puna's shipping port (note abandoned buildings), now a launching place for small boats. Country lanes that go inland from the two villages pass small farms, subdivision plots, sources of 1955 lava, and emerge onto the main roads below Pahoa. On the Opihikao road, near the route 13 intersection, watch for the sign Puu Lapu. Follow directions on the marker to get the illusion your car is rolling.

Up the coast from Pohoiki lie some startling contrasts: a vast wasteland of recent origin, fields of orchids and papayas thriving in crushed old lava which heavy rain has helped make into fertile soil, and Kapoho Cone—a green-cloaked prominence from an old eruption. Drive up a grassy road to the cone's low rim, then walk down inside to an almost jungle-covered "green lake" of perhaps 10 acres, its color the result of abundant algae.

Pele went on a month-long rampage in this region in 1960, destroying two villages, 1,500 acres of cane and other farm land, a photogenic natural pool with springs, inshore waters rich in mullet, and beach lots so desirable they're in use again (turn seaward on one of several spur roads). Lava fingers buried a dozen of the homes, but new ones have gone up to take advantage of a wake of small black sand beaches.

From their junction, routes 137 and 132 continue to a few things miraculously spared. A spur off route 132 leads to 16 gravestones (usually flower-decked) that were left on the side of an old cinder cone when a molten river temporarily forked and went around them. Route 132 ends at the lucky lighthouse on Cape Kumukahi. The river stayed away from its door, but just barely, and it crushed the station's cottages before dividing. The tower, now automated, stands on the state's easternmost point, which was extended about 500 feet closer to California. About 100 yards north of the road, atop the mile-wide flow, is an ancient Hawaiian graveyard.

Route 137 goes north through a blanket of cinders, alive with new orchid fields, to Koae, virtually abandoned when its houses buckled under a heavy cinder shower. A cream-colored church punctuates the blackness. Fishermen's trails lead to more black sand beaches. Beyond Koae go into a grove of ironwoods to see, on the shore, 1840 cinder cones hard enough to drive on. In a passenger car, turn around at Honolulu, an old landing, or take a subdivision road to route 13.

Sightseers *watch the sea thunder into famous black sand beach at Kaimu. Coconut grove is a fine picnic spot.*

Kapoho to Pahoa and Route 11

When you drive route 132 inland, you pass right over buried Kapoho village. To the north is the 420-foot black cone built up on the eruption site. Most of Kapoho's 250 people moved to Pahoa and grow anthuriums there, but their new orchid fields lie in a graben above the old town site that has ideal growing conditions. The Kapoho region's newest crop is Norfolk pines for Christmas trees (many are shipped to the West Coast). Groves of the spare, symmetrical evergreens are easy to spot.

The road into Pahoa cuts through a cone formed by the 1955 eruption's largest vent and producer of 800-foot fountains. Lesser cones, turned yellow, red, and burnt orange by gases, are visible. That year lava activity jumped about in Puna for three months.

At Lava Tree State Park, you visit the "petrified Hawaiians," weird lava-encrusted tree trunks left standing after an old flow had drained away.

Rolling cane fields and more embryo real estate developments lie between Pahoa and Keaau, where route 13 meets route 11, 21 miles from the national park via Mountain View and 7 miles from Hilo through the lower

Panaewa Forest. At Mountain View is St. Theresa's, the other church Father Evarist built and decorated (in 1936). Here he did a profusion of paintings because parishioners subscribed to them in a money-raising venture. They're not carefully related to each other or the building (wall scenes were done on plyboard, then affixed, and their colors have not mellowed), but they include fine baroque details. Keaau has a striking Hongwanji Buddhist Temple and popular Olaa Steak House.

Ka'u District

Ka'u is farm country soon to sprout resort villages down on its seashore. You sample it driving the 50-mile stretch of route 11 between Hawaii Volcanoes National Park and Kona, but there's exploring to do.

From Kilauea's summit the highway swoops down the volcano's southwest slope—the Ka'u Desert, barren and bleak except when winter and spring rains make it bloom with native yellow *mamani* and white *alahe'e* (a coffee relative with carnation scent). Just inside the park boundary, walk .8 mile on the Mauna Iki (Footprints) Trail to the spot where warriors battling Kamehameha the Great for control of this island were asphyxiated by fumes and dust while fleeing the boulders and mud balls Halemaumau belched out in 1790. (Hawaiians believed Pele interceded to help Kamehameha.) Most of their footprints left in the hardening ash have eroded, but you'll find a set protected under glass. The trail continues a mile to a dome that fired in 1920 at the head of the Great Crack, a huge fissure that extends to the sea.

From the park to Waiohinu, the road travels mixed grasslands ribboned with windbreak trees that run up onto Mauna Loa's steeper flanks through the highest cane fields in the country. Plantings go up to 3,300 feet and take more than three, rather than the normal two, years to mature.

For an adventure, turn off into pretty Pahala village. If it's the dry season, ask permission at the plantation office opposite the mill to drive the cane haul road uphill several miles to luxuriant Wood Valley. In 1868, in the mightiest cataclysm in Hawaii's history, a village here was smothered by an avalanche of mud set loose by an earthquake. The quake also triggered simultaneous eruptions of Mauna Loa and Kilauea and lethal seismic waves that swamped Puna and Ka'u villages and depressed the south coastline about 7 feet.

You can wind southward out of Pahala back to the highway on a parallel strip of the old Belt Road, past weathered houses, eucalyptus and African tulip trees entwined with bougainvillea, and part of a large, growing orchard of macadamia nut trees. Commercial or experimental navel oranges, grapefruit, mangoes, guavas, and avocados are also sprouting in Ka'u pastures that still harbor remnants of old sisal.

Drive downhill a mile to Punaluu Beach Park and settlement, guarded by a tiny church on the hill above. In its graveyard is a shrine to Henry Opukahaia, a Punaluu boy who sailed to New York in 1809, became a Christian, and died in New England—but not before he had influenced missionaries to come to Hawaii and teach his people. On the black sand shore, you are likely to find ladies selling Hawaiian jewelry from rickety stalls, outrigger canoes under palm roofs, and a throng of jolly children.

A fishermen's road continues southward .7 mile to Ninole Springs, a cove where fresh water bubbles up through lava at the ocean's edge. There's a pebbly beach with "stones that give birth"; they have holes with baby stones that multiply—so they say. Ruins of two ancient temples are accessible to walkers. One, Kaieie (and some pebble-paved grass house platforms), is up a ¼-mile path to the top of a broad lava flow. Well preserved Keeku Heiau is south of the flow, above the sea, along the old Hawaiian shoreline trail to Honuapo.

Honuapo is where the main highway meets the shore. A spur road opposite Hutchinson Sugar Company mill goes into Whittington Beach Park (with tidal ponds) and to a decaying old sugar-shipping wharf.

Signs proclaim Naalehu, 3 miles on, as the nation's southernmost town. It has a store named Green Sands; a coffee shop with craftwork and paintings for sale, antique bottles on display, and a bonsai garden; and a broad, shaded main street. Here and just west at Waiohinu are the last places to buy gasoline for South Point exploring or, if Kona bound, for 50 miles. Jungled Waiohinu village is distinguished by the Mark Twain tree (a new monkeypod growing from roots of one Twain planted in 1866 which was felled by a storm in 1957); the island's most elegantly trimmed frame church, Kauahaao, about 90 years old and set beside a tidy graveyard even older; the Shirakawa Hotel with a Japanese *furo* (and conventional baths), largely an oversize house set in a garden of hibiscus and orchids with a coffee-drying shed; and evidences of a golf course subdivision to come.

The highway next crosses miles of old Mauna Loa lavas. Because of rainfall differences, some with forest cover are more recent than others that are carpets of tumbled black rock. You'll wonder about the roadside water pipe that spans a particularly bleak section: It serves cattle. But the harsh land has its oasis—Manuka State Park, a wayside picnic ground and arboretum of native and imported plants.

Kauahaao Church *in Waiohinu is colonial in style but with decorative trim. It is set beside a tidy old graveyard.*

The Nation's Southernmost Tip

Ka Lae, or South Point, the most southerly piece of ground in the United States, is a ruggedly beautiful, windswept cape with remnants of the oldest known Hawaiian settlement (750 A.D.) and green sand (olivines) on its beaches.

You drive downhill for 9 miles from a turn off route 11, 3½ miles west of Waiohinu, through pasture that is sometimes parched, sometimes verdant and abloom with lantana and native wild flowers. Any people about will likely be fishermen or the caretaker of an inactive spacecraft tracking station 1½ miles from the end. The currents that meet off the treeless point make fishing outstanding.

On the grounds of an automated light tower, where pavement stops, are salt pans (lava boulders with depressions in which sea water was allowed to evaporate), and the remains of Kalalea Heiau, part of the complex of ruins designated a National Historic Landmark. Modern fishermen consider the prehistoric fishing shrine still so potent with *mana*, or spirits, that they bring offerings of food and drink and advise you not to go inside.

On the point where the lava slope dribbles away, look for the rings (more than 80) chipped in leeward edges; the earliest Hawaiians secured their canoes by running the bowlines through these rings. The moorage of today's fishermen is just up the west side beneath a 50-foot cliff with hoists and ladders welded to its face. Just inland you'll see a turbulent rock-bound pool, a lava tube formed when a hot spot in a cooling flow collapsed into the ocean. A bit farther north, a spur road goes out to the edge where there is a fine view along the rising bluff of black rock to Mauna Loa.

On the windward side of the cape, breakers pound dunes of yellowish ash and patches of green sand. Bishop Museum archaeologists, excavating a habitation site dating from 1,000 A.D., ½ mile east of the canoe mooring holes, turned up a fish hook "factory." Just inland is Palahemo, the early settlers' well—a tidal waterhole on which fresh water floats. It has petroglyphs on its rim and was marked centuries later for World War II pilots bound for an emergency landing strip by the row of cairns you see nearby.

Search for Makalei Cave, where the ancients slept on stone platforms, about 100 yards downhill from a row of old army barracks foundations (along a spur road of sorts that connects Kaulana Bay with the main road south of the tracking station).

Following tire tracks up the windward coast, the going gets rough even for 4-wheel-drive vehicles beyond Kaulana (protected swimming cove with boat ramp). You will find, about a mile apart, Papakolea, a coral-and-lava beach strip with some olivines; and Mahana Bay, backed by a steep cone of fine green sand that drops into the sea. You can continue 3 miles to Kaalualu Bay (with abandoned cattle-shipping pier) where a dirt road runs inland to join the main drive.

Kona District

Tourist Kona is the village of Kailua and thereabouts, but on 60 miles of Mauna Loa's and Hualalai's western slopes are several other Kona worlds. The highway travels the district north-south at 1,000 to 1,500 feet and swoops down to the sea only at Kailua. Fingers branch off to other settlements on the shore. Two short coast roads connect Kailua with Keauhou Bay, Napoopoo with the City of Refuge. Many visitors catch the district's outer reaches on drives between Kailua and Ka'u, the national park, and Hilo; or between Kailua and Waimea and Kawaihae.

Kailua to Keauhou

In Kailua you shop, try the eating and night spots, cool off in a hotel pool, mix with other visitors. You'll stroll Alii Drive, past a tumble of hotels, cafes, snack bars, small shopping centers, Hawaiian boutiques, tourist agencies, and historic treasures. At the north end, you can sit on the seawall and people-watch or view the bay. Walk out on the wharf in late afternoon to welcome the fishing boats. On the pier's north side is tiny Kamakahonu swimming beach and lagoon, its other boundary a once-royal lava point. Hotel King Kamehameha stages pageantry

Remote, friendly, picturesque—*the tiny fishing village of Milolii is a cluster of cottages alongside the sea.*

in thatched buildings constructed on the site of Ahuena Heiau, part of the Kamakahonu ground (a National Historic Landmark), where he died in 1819, and where his son Liholiho was installed as Kamehameha II later that year and soon broke the ancient *kapu* system of taboos by eating with women at a feast—he later ordered temples and images destroyed.

Two-storied Hulihee Palace stands gracious and secluded, its verandas with carved balustrades overlooking the bay. Built in 1837-38 by Kuakini (brother of Kamehameha's favorite wife), who became governor of the island in 1820, it is now a museum (Mon.-Sat., 8:30-4:30; adm. fee) furnished mostly from the elegant 1880's when it served as King Kalakaua's summer palace. One room has early Hawaiian artifacts and on the lawn is a *pili* grass house.

Just across the street is Mokuaikaua, the Islands' oldest church, product of the first missionaries who landed close by (in 1820). With Kuakini's aid, they put a thatch church up first, then another, and finally this building completed in 1837 and as solid as their faith. Its rock walls are mortared with coral; hand-hewn *'ohi'a* beams more than 50 feet long are joined with *'ohi'a* pins. You enter the grounds through a 1910 missionary memorial arch. After Sunday night services, Mokuaikaua's choir sings hymns, some in Hawaiian, at one of the hotels.

On the road to Pacific Empress Hotel you can see fragments of the 4-mile-long Great Wall of Kuakini,

which the governor built to keep animals within the village area. Another piece stands behind the ruins of pioneer missionary Asa Thurston's home.

At the south end of town is St. Michael's, a lava stone church finished in 1848 at the first Catholic mission established on the Neighbor Islands. It is painted pink, framed by two spreading monkeypods, and has a quaint coral grotto shrine. Hale Halawai, the open-sided community hall, is opposite, in a coconut grove.

Alii Drive south to Keauhou Bay is filling in with hotels and houses, some in a huge planned community developing around Keauhou-Kona Golf Course—built on top of a lava flow with some rock left for hazards. Eventually it will have seven hotels with 3,400 rooms, hundreds of homes and apartments, shopping and cultural centers, and more golf. Still you pass tangles of gnarled *kiawe*, openings to the restless ocean spurting foam as it pounds black, jagged points, and accents of bougainvillea.

Holualoa Beach has popular names more descriptive: White Sands, Disappearing Sands, or Come and Go Beach. Occasionally the waves and currents that challenge expert body surfers take out the sand and expose its lava base. Take a peek at St. Peter's Catholic Church at Kahaluu Bay; it's scarcely larger than a playhouse and was put on a *heiau* site to surmount superstition. On the Kailua side are a royal spring and "bathtub" of rock construction and the well-preserved temple, Kuemanu. From the well-furnished beach park spread over Kahaluu's south shore, you can swim in the bay or examine remnants of three *heiaus* on adjacent hotel grounds. Keauhou Bay, long an anchorage and canoe landing for Kona's resident fishermen, is gaining hotels. A monument just south of the pier marks the birthplace of Kamehameha III, and high on the hill above lies part of the ancient royal *holua* (slide), a National Historic Landmark. A marker on the coast road points to it, but you can barely make it out, and there's no trail to climb. The hand-laid rock course was about a mile long and as much as 30 feet wide. Kings and chiefs covered it with *pili* grass and rode it on wooden sleds. A ruin of the 1850's you can get to is a stone church, Keauhou-Kai, on the Kailua side of the bay, inland a bit, off a winding side road.

The Coffee Country

Between 800 and 2,000 feet, Kona is coffee country, cooler and greener. A dependable afternoon cloud cover does away with the need for space-taking trees to shade the plants, and this, coupled with rich volcanic soil and proper moisture, gives Kona the world's highest coffee yield per acre.

The coffee belt extends some 40 miles, from Hookena to Honokohau, and is bisected by route 11 and route 18 (a strip of old Belt Road). All the way along your out-look is down, over the long slope to a sweep of coastline, and it's easy to observe the weather pattern. Generally the great mountains block the trade winds, and Kona is ruled by alternating land and sea breezes. Mornings, all the land is sunny. The warmed hillside draws winds off the sea which form clouds above the coffee land and tend to hold them there. In late afternoon the mountainside cools, winds reverse for the night, clouds drift down and dissipate over the parched coast and may freshen it with showers.

The bushy, glossy-leafed coffee trees are set out in family plots of 5 to 10 acres. About March, fields turn to "snow" when fragrant white flowers suddenly appear—usually after a storm. Harvest time is fall when the berries—known as cherries—are red.

Time is up for family-enterprise farms healthy enough to survive the vicissitudes of the world coffee market. The first growers were Japanese contract laborers who fled East Hawaii cane fields, sent home for "picture" brides, transplanted their strong-family culture. They formed combines and built many small mills, got Kona's school vacations set in the fall so children could help pick the crop. But the traditional system has broken down in the last decade. Now most schools operate on a normal sched-ule and most students take summers off; young people are leaving the farms to staff hotels or take up other work. Most farmers have joined large processing and marketing cooperatives. They have made Kona coffee a gourmet variety as well as an ingredient of blends, are pioneering with mechanical harvesters, and are growing macadamia nuts to diversify. But enough born farmers (also Filipinos from a later cane field exodus) are around to keep coffee

At City of Refuge *National Historical Park, reproduc-tions of ancient images stand in courtyard of temple.*

percolating and ultimately farms may merge and thor-oughly mechanize.

Tour parties stop in Kealakekua near Kona Hospital to look down on the layout of one of a few old-timers who still remove pulp from berries and sun-dry them at home on flat platforms under roll-away roofs.

At Sunset Coffee Cooperative Mill on the road down to Napoopoo you can watch the whole process from red cherry to roasted bean and there, or in a store on the highway opposite Honaunau Post Office, taste and buy the cooperative's Kona coffee. The mill store also sells macadamia nuts that come from Sunset's factory across the way. Another macadamia plant, Kona Groves, is just uphill. Both welcome visitors.

The narrow coffee highway also plows through a string of towns cluttered with tin-roofed wooden build-ings and autos, jeeps, and pickup trucks where you note general stores (some have astonishing inventories) and box houses (some precariously perched on the slope) that claim big TV aerials and luxury cars. It winds under spreading trees and past colorful blooms: white and yellow ginger in summer; gold Timor showers and wild sunflowers in November; red and white poinsettias and bougainvillea in winter; jacaranda, coral shower, and silver oak trees in spring.

The route 18 section is the most like *mauka* Kona of a few decades ago—except for its lively Kona Arts Center, in an abandoned Holualoa coffee mill, which has classes

Palms, birds, and stars *are hand-painted decorations on the Painted Church; religious phrases encircle pillars.*

Ceremony in July *at Captain Cook monument on Kealakekua Bay honors Islands' discoverer killed near here.*

Kealakekua Bay is where Captain James Cook, the Islands' discoverer, was killed in 1779 while trying to end a melee between his men and the natives. Only a month before, on his first landing, Hawaiians had taken Cook for their god Lono and led him into Hikiau Heiau for rites. In this same *heiau* at Napoopoo, Cook read the Islands' first Christian burial service over one of his men. You'll see plaques commemorating this ceremony and Henry Opukahaia, the native son who was instrumental in bringing out the first missionaries (see Punaluu, page 78), at the foot of the stone path up to the sun-scorched temple platform.

From the *heiau* or Napoopoo's shore, you look across the vast bay to a 27-foot white obelisk erected in 1874 on the lava benches of Kaawaloa near the spot where Cook died (denoted by a tablet at water's edge). The monument is isolated by soaring bluffs riddled with ancient burial caves, at the head of the bay. You might hire a villager to take you across in a motor-powered outrigger, or take a rough jeep road downhill from Captain Cook town; it passes remains of Puhino o Lono Heiau where Cook's body was taken (bones were returned to his sailors). Most people settle for seeing the monument up close on a cruise (see Boating, page 68).

Typical Napoopoo houses are engulfed in foilage and set behind low stone walls. Townsfolk market *leis* and bracelets of seeds and shells at the road turn-around by the bay. The beach at Napoopoo Park is pebbly, but you swim in remarkably clear ocean water laced with cool springs in a bend of a bay so rich in sea life (striking corals, urchins, fish, spinner porpoises) that it has been made a marine preserve.

There's exploring to do on Kealakekua's south shore. Just out of Napoopoo, turn off to Keei settlement on a narrow lane off the 3-mile coast road to Honaunau (better ask the way). You'll find a black sand canoe cove, white sand beach and shallow channel out to acres of colorful coral, a *pahoehoe* shore chipped with holes in which Hawaiians once ground sea urchins, and an ocean grotto. From the last houses, you can walk or 4-wheel-drive the dirt tracks that loop the bay's south point, Palemano. Look for the remainder of Kamaiko, a human sacrifice temple; fragments of other ancient stone-craft; an abandoned camp; a man-made ocean-filled swimming pool in the lava.

From the Honaunau road, you notice a picturesque church on the hill, above Keei. It's old Kahikolu, built of stone in 1838-41, once partly rebuilt, but now a derelict. You'll find a road through the brush to it about 1/2 mile up the road that goes from Napoopoo to the coffee mill. Some stenciling remains on peeling interior plaster and the graveyard is impressive.

and displays and sells local paintings and crafts (open only a few times a week; check schedule at your hotel).

At Honalo, where routes 18 and 11 meet, you'll find Teshima Restaurant (seafood, Japanese and Hawaiian dishes), almost a local institution; Daifukuji Buddhist Temple (a tour stop); and St. Paul's Catholic Church, its steeple a hillside landmark. Kealakekua has a Hongwanji Buddhist Temple and three fine mission churches: Central Kona Union Church, built in 1859 of rocks mortared with coral plaster; diminutive Lanakila, a wooden chapel that has stood since 1866; and frame, spired Christ Church, the island's oldest Episcopal sanctuary (1867-74). At Captain Cook are the district's Civic Center buildings and colorful Machado Garden, a steep bank with about everything that grows in the area. Upper Honaunau's old wooden Japanese church on a knoll beside the highway has turned Filipino. It's Guadelupe Church now and all spruced up. Note the unusual Sausage Tree (named for its fruits) at the route 16 junction.

Kealakekua Bay to City of Refuge

Hawaii's most historic places lie on the seacoast, at the end of roads to Honaunau and Napoopoo: the sacred refuge, now a National Historical Park, where the old culture comes alive; and Kealakekua Bay, scene of Hawaii's first sustained contact with the western world. The entire region is under the protection of a federal-state-county historic and scenic conservation plan.

The coast road passes the Keei lava field, Mokuohai, where Kamehameha the Great won his first battle, and ends at the City of Refuge.

The remaining Great Wall and reconstructed temple of Old Hawaii's most important *pu'uhonua*, or place of refuge—that of the Kamehameha dynasty—are the prominent features of the 180-acre City of Refuge National Historical Park on the south shore of Honaunau Bay. The site is being restored to look the way it did when Kamehameha the Great conducted ceremonies here in 1782.

A refuge was an inviolable haven for defeated warriors and noncombatants and breakers of a *kapu* (taboo) —for example, women who ate bananas (reserved for men), or a commoner who interfered with a king's godly power, perhaps by letting his shadow fall upon royal ground. For perhaps 400 years, until the old religion was abandoned, people scurried by trail from the south or swam Honaunau Bay from the north to reach this then-sacred lava shelf of 20 acres ahead of their pursuers and escape death. They were purified by a priest and released, protected by the king, priest, and refuge gods (spirits of dead chiefs). A benevolent king used the system to bestow mercy on subjects with whom he could have no direct communication.

The park is always open and you can guide yourself about with a map-folder, picnic at a palm-shaded ground beside the sea. A visitor center (open 8 to 5) has an ancient Hawaii story wall (tile murals, sculptures, recorded narration). Rangers give talks in the amphitheater and conduct tours several times a day.

Inspect the extraordinary wall that barricades the landward side of the refuge. It's more than 1,000 feet long, about 12 feet high and 17 feet thick, and was hand-laid without mortar. In about 1650, one end was torn down to make way for Hale-o-Keawe, the tomb-temple of a king made the major refuge god (ruins of earlier temples are inside the wall). Between then and 1818, the deified bones of 22 other ruling Kona chiefs were interred. This temple was not destroyed the next year along with others; it stood into the 1840's. But in 1829, Queen Regent Kaahumanu, a Christian convert, had the images taken and bones removed and hidden— the locations are still unknown. The house of *ti* leaf thatch that stands on the ancient foundation was rebuilt from sketches and descriptions of early European visitors. Reproductions of images, which represented gods and guards, within and outside the palisade were carved from giant *'ohi'a* logs.

Outside the wall are the royal canoe landing, grounds of chiefs' houses, and king's turtle pond, and elsewhere in the park, remnants of a horse ramp, toboggan slides, and an ancient village.

Visitors are welcome *at Sunset Coffee Cooperative mill where beans are sun-dried, sorted, readied for shipment.*

A side road off route 16 up to the main highway leads to St. Benedict's, the "Painted Church" of Father John Berchmans Velghe, a Belgian priest who wanted to bring to his parishioners the splendor of medieval Europe. He turned his 1902 gable-roofed box into a miniature cathedral by painting its walls, ceiling, and pillars with copies of religious works and Hawaiian motifs—a folk art masterpiece. On the wall behind the altar, perspective painting of the light-dome, apse, and transepts of Burgos Cathedral in Spain gives you the illusion the vaulted nave continues. Outside, the church has charming carpenter's Gothic—a frontal lattice and a belfry that resembles a storybook castle. Some of the adjacent fenced gravestones have iron pipe crosses and markers with photographs.

The South End of Kona

In south Kona are Mauna Loa's last lava, new forests and orchards, few—but interesting—settlements.

Route 11 passes below the 100,000-acre Honaunau Forest where more than 800,000 Australian red cedar and tropical ash trees have been planted for harvest starting at the end of the century. It crosses all three 1950 Mauna Loa flows, which buried several buildings in their path to the sea. It spans Honomalimo farmlands occupied by a huge macadamia nut orchard, which supplies the Honokaa factory, and healthy plantings of bananas, avocados, citrus, and vegetables. It passes by housing tracts in rough lava; some have wide streets with fancy names and flower gardens.

Hookena, a semi-ghost town with swimming beach, lies a couple of miles down a narrow, twisting—but paved—spur road. It has a handful of cottages and a park pavilion (no drinking water or lights). A few families are still in residence, and others come weekends to camp and fish. You'll note pilings of the wharf where inter-island steamers once loaded coffee, oranges, cattle, lumber, and passengers; it was abandoned in the early 1930's when the road from Hilo finally reached Kona. To the north lie remnants of a "Main Street"—a stone wall with gates, shade trees, posts that supported gas lamps, ruins of houses and a pre-1900 Congregational Church, its Hawaiian altar inscription still visible. The cliff above the beach is honeycombed with burial caves, some respectfully untouched.

To explore further, walk the shore ⅜ mile north of the village and look for the walls and upended steeple of Maria Lanakila Church, in jungle about 100 yards from shore—near a pond mynah birds frequent. Here Father John (of "Painted Church" fame) had turned a tiny 1866 plastered lava structure into a jewel with religious murals in perfect scale. A 1950 earthquake wrecked it, but in early 1969, fragments of weathered craftwork and painting were taken to Bishop Museum, where the church's altar end will eventually be reconstructed and displayed.

Milolii is a thriving village for all its vestigial ways. The Hawaiian-Filipino fishing community of about 80 residents lies 2,000 feet below the highway, down a 5-mile traverse of the 1926 lava flow that wiped out (no casualties) its forerunner, Hoopuloa, a mile away. A couple of rebuilt homes at Hoopuloa and new house lots on bleak lava just north at Papa Bay will astonish you.

Milolii is also strung out on lava rubble that supports only *kiawe* and palms (villagers grow anthuriums and ferns on hauled-in soil). It has a bay where outriggers beach and nets dry on a black sand-and-pebble shore. Children frolic here in a shallow channel, or in a lagoon with a fringe of white sand at the south end of the settlement. Men fish with handlines for *'ahi, aku, mahimahi, ono,* even marlin, and use nets for *'opelu.* They steam in around noon and late afternoon in motorized canoes and skiffs with the catch they will truck to Hilo's fish auction. Sometimes they go out overnight for *'u'u, ulua, 'aweoweo,* and *akule.*

Houses are of old lumber and corrugated iron. Most families have kerosene or gas stoves and refrigerators and a few, generator-powered lights, television, and telephone (others get by with gas lanterns). They have goats, tied up, and pigs that nose about for food.

The store has canned and packaged goods and cold drinks—honk your horn out front to have it opened. Owner Eugene Kaupiko is unofficial mayor and conducts services at century-old Hauoli Kamanao Church (there's a Catholic church, too). You're welcome to camp in the old school yard. Children now go *mauka* to school, the older ones to board during the week.

North Kona

You cruise North Kona on a high road going from Kailua to Waimea (40 miles) and Kawaihae (12 more), but before long you'll be able to drive a new straight course (about 35 miles) just above the sea all the way to the South Kohala port and resort center.

Already you can drive enough of this sunny shore to envision its future. It's wasteland, but there are beaches and archaeological treasures, and plants will grow. Bougainvillea crawls over the lava banks of the mile of road from Kailua to Kona Airport, through an area marked for resort use when the new airport opens at Keahole by fall of 1970. You can get to Keahole now on foot or by 4-wheel-drive on the old shoreline trail from the airstrip (petroglyphs lie near the start), or by driving the 7-mile beginning of the new arterial, which turns off Palani Highway (route 19) just above town and goes past Honokohau Harbor, blasted out of lava and dredged.

What's left of ancient Honokohau comprises a Na-

White Sands *is Kona's body surfing beach—for experts. The beach is lovely, but it disappears when surf is high.*

tional Historic Landmark. To see remnants, whose secrets are being unraveled, take the paved spur that turns sharply toward the coast just short of the 2-mile point. At the harbor, a dirt road goes off to the right to a sandy beach—less than a mile—past ruins of a century-old salt-making system (rocks hollowed to evaporate sea water); walls of what may have been the Islands' oldest church; a petroglyph field; a *heiau* that bridged a watercourse to the sea; a fishpond wall. To the north, now inside sand dunes, are two still-used fishponds; lava on the south shore of the first has bait-pounding "cups." At Keahole, strange circular house platforms and shelter and burial caves have been discovered.

Farther north, on the encrusted last sputterings (1800-1801) from dormant Hualalai, is a cave with intact skeletons that can be visited by guests at Kona Village Resort. The secluded hotel harbors other mysterious ruins and a restored waterfowl pond, opens the gate to its road down the mountain from route 19 to people with luncheon or dinner reservations.

The present highway (route 19) climbs gradually, past some of the new homes that are taking over the hillside above Kailua, through coffee farms, wilderness, and ranches, and finally emerges onto the Waimea plateau where on clear days your eye sweeps all of this island's volcanoes but Kilauea, and you can see Haleakala on Maui. At Kalaoa settlement, in forest north of where routes 19 and 18 meet, notice two wooden churches: aging Mauna Ziona, and Holy Rosary, a bold blue-and-white gingerbread type. Swaths of black cut the grasslands: the Hualalai lavas, and north, *pahoehoe* from Mauna Loa's most voluminous eruption in historic time (1859). In between is Puuwaawaa Ranch with undulating meadows and the islands' largest cinder cone, Puu Waa-waa, that looks like a cupcake, has a unique chemical makeup, and furnishes pumice for manufacture of a lightweight aggregate. In late spring, stands of silver oak turn gold, the red *lehua* blossoms (the island flower) of the 'ohi'a are used to make honey, and on the southern reaches of the Parker Ranch, roadside 'a'ali'i shrubs bear clusters of red and chartreuse fruit. Here the landscape seems endless—a carpet of green and tan that stretches from sea to the silhouetted domes of the great volcanoes often lost in clouds.

Kohala District

The wonder of this vast region is its contrasts, within very few miles. Kohala, the Big Island's northwest corner, includes Mauna Kea's lower western slope—the high (2,500 feet), windswept Waimea plateau with ranch and truck farms; the sun-baked Kawaihae coast, a budding

Snow-capped *Mauna Kea looms above seaside golf course (open to the public) at Mauna Kea Beach Hotel.*

resort center; and the old Kohala Mountains whose verdant grasslands roll up to 5,000 feet, flatten out into cane land on the north, and break apart on the northeast into spectacular green canyons wrought by wind and water.

Embracing the varied landscapes is the Parker Ranch of more than 200,000 acres. Its largest part is a swath running from Kawaihae up 7,000 feet on Mauna Kea and into the Kohala foothills; another covers about half the northwest side of the Kohala Mountains; a third, Humuula (in the Hamakua District), is a belt around Mauna Kea's southeast flank between 7,000 and 9,000 feet.

Route 19 spans the plateau and passes through Waimea (Kamuela Post Office, 40 miles from Kailua and some 55 from Hilo; and Waimea lies along a loop of some 50 miles through the district.

Waimea

Waimea, cool (50's and 60's), backed by turf-carpeted Kohala hills, and facing out over the tableland to Mauna Kea, is the bustling Parker Ranch town. You also hear it called Kamuela, the name given to its post office to avoid confusing it with Kauai's Waimea.

The name Kamuela is Hawaiian for Samuel, grandson of the seaman John Palmer Parker, who started the ranch. Back in about 1815, John Parker left his ship and went to hunt cattle for Kamehameha the Great. (The king had placed a protective *kapu* on the Islands' first cattle, a few animals given to him in 1793 by Captain George Vancouver, and they had multiplied and gone wild.) Parker developed a domestic herd from the captured stock, married a Hawaiian chiefess, and acquired land. Subsequent generations of Parkers increased the spread. Still family-owned, it is one of the nation's largest ranches, with 45,000 head of Hereford cattle and some 1,200 horses. A few of the cowboys are descendants of the first ranch hands. (A Hawaiian cowboy is called a *paniolo,* the name Hawaiians gave to Latin Americans brought in before 1830 to teach riding and roping.)

Waimea has gingerbread houses with yards, flower gardens, and picket fences, and carpenter's Gothic on some buildings—notably the Kahilu Theatre, the bandstand, Lanakila Park pavilion, Parker Ranch Headquarters, and even a bank and filling station. The New England-like village has new shops, markets, and places to eat, and more hotels, motels, and apartments on the way. But still you can dine out on Hawaiian favorites (tripe stew, chili pepper water, *poi*) as well as enormous ranch steaks, or shop for ropes, saddles, *palaka* shirts, and pansy *leis,* in addition to gourmet foods and the latest fashions. Kamuela Roadside Vegetable Stand has that rare treat for Islanders—temperate zone produce fresh from the outskirts of town.

In the 10-acre Centralized Tree Nursery (weekdays, 7-3:30), opposite Waimea-Kohala Airport and landscaped with temperate zone flowers, state foresters for the first time are growing hardwoods from seed for direct transplanting for watersheds, windbreaks, or timber. On the Honokaa side of town, you'll find several churches and temples around an open green beneath rolling, forest-capped hills of emerald or tan (depending on the season). Visit well-preserved Imiola, built in 1857 by Waimea's missionary Lorenzo Lyons, who composed Hawaiian hymns that are still sung. Its walls are paneled in *koa* and chandeliers are *koa* bowls.

Along route 25 you pass the Mauna Kea Beach Hotel's Ranch House, once the home of the Parker Ranch manager, with handsome furnishings, a formal side garden, and an exquisite waterfall in the stream behind. Farther on is the attractive hillside campus of Hawaii Preparatory Academy, a high-caliber boarding school for boys. Kamuela Museum (daily, 9-5; adm. fee), at the junction of routes 25 and 26, has a private collection of Kohala artifacts.

Kawaihae Coast

On the 15-minute drive from Waimea down to the *kiawe*-cloaked shore, the temperature rises one degree per minute. An immense complex of hotels, apartments, houses, shops, and parks is planned for this long slope. To see the start of it, fork to the south, toward Hapuna, and

Youngsters walk *the dry-laid wall around platform of last sacrificial temple, Kamehameha's Pu'ukohola.*

turn into Mauna Kea Beach Hotel and Golf Course, a 300-acre tropical oasis fronting sparkling, sand-fringed Kaunaoa Bay. It was the work of quality-resort-builder Laurance S. Rockefeller and is handsome in every detail. At 2 o'clock each day there's a "Back of the House" tour which gives you a look into its workings. At any time ask at the desk for the self-guiding art tour folder. In galleries are Hawaiian quilts and *tapas* hung as tapestries, and fine Oriental and Pacific art treasures. Manta rays perform at night in a flood-lighted cove off a lookout terrace. To the north you find a restored old Hawaiian wall and remnants of a *heiau,* shrine, and other walls.

The next hotel is going up on a cove at Hapuna, 1/2 mile south, adjacent to a state park blessed with wide powdery beach, mild surf, cabins and campground, pavilion with changing rooms, cooking grills—and no throng.

Rough paved road goes south a couple more miles through Puako where more Parker Ranch marginal land will be transformed by hotels, houses, and parks. Now you pass modest vacation homes, a few on stilts over shoals that yield shells and colorful fish. Hoku Loa Church, which missionary Lyons built in 1858-60, has been made like new. In the bush to the south, you'll find the coral stone walls of an abandoned house of the same era. Note the new Catholic church in the round, with soaring roof and fine use of lava. Near the end of the road, a trail (indicated by a warrior sign) leads to some of Hawaii's most sophisticated ancient figure carvings spread all over fields of *pahoehoe.* The first are just 600 feet inland, but follow arrows another 2,000 feet to the big group, and then 200 feet farther to a third collection at trail's end. Another petroglyph field, at Anaehoomalu, will become accessible when still another resort town starts rising on one more siphoned-off chunk of Parker Ranch.

Visit the two outstanding *heiaus* just south of Kawaihae (to be the nucleus of a historical park). Pu'ukohola, a National Historic Landmark, looks like a fortress guarding the road and is even more impressive when you walk up onto its 224 by 100-foot rock platform. Kamehameha built this last sacrificial temple for his war god Kukailimoku (the image is in Bishop Museum) because a prophet said it would assure his becoming ruler of all the islands. Keoua, his last rival for control of this island, was slain as he landed at Kawaihae for the dedication in 1792, and Kamehameha offered up his body on this spot. Older Mailekini, below the road, was later made a fort to protect Kawaihae. Close by is Spencer Park on Ohaiula Bay with bountiful sand, *kiawe* trees for shade, and a pavilion whose design was inspired by the form of Pu'ukohola.

Kawaihae is where the first cattle were landed and, in 1803, the first horses; where stranded British sailors Isaac Davis and John Young lived when they were advisors to Kamehameha and helped him build a superior army and navy; and where the first missionaries paused before sailing on to Kailua to ask the king's permission to land. Today this is the port where young cattle from West Hawaii ranches are transferred from trucks onto barges bound for Oahu feed pens; and where bulk sugar is stored in a huge shed—rather than conventional silos as at Hilo—and pushed onto a freighter by bulldozers (call Kawaihae Terminals, Inc., for a plant tour). The town has a small marina and a factory that turns out plywood products from the island's eucalyptus, *koa*, and *'ohi'a*. For respite from the heat and glare, visit the general stores, Chock Hoo, or Doi's (next to their orchid nursery) where townsfolk take refreshments out to the canopied terrace to watch harbor doings while children check on the pet monkeys.

The road from Kawaihae north 11.4 miles to Mahukona (route 27) lets you loop Kohala. It spans raw coast—black rock under a blanket of *kiawe*—with a string of coves splendid for snorkeling. If you're traveling it south, you face at once all the volcanoes but Kilauea and a 40-mile sweep of coast.

North Kohala

Here is the Hawaii of several decades ago, remarkably untouched, somnolent, but with a secure position in history as the birthplace and boyhood home of the first Kamehameha. When Kamehameha was growing up, there was taro all over the hills and valleys and the region was the island's most populous. Taro and native villages gave way to five sugar plantations, each with mill towns and gracious baronial estates, but high costs have long since reduced the field to one company.

The parched cattle country of the west turns to verdant cane fields and high pastures as you move east. At Mahukona, once Kohala's sugar shipping port and now nearly abandoned, you can swim and fish from the old landing or at a beach park. From Mahukona light, you can follow a jeep track ½ mile south to Koaie, a fishing settlement from the 13th century to 1915 and part of a 1 by 4-mile *ahupua'a* (land tenure unit), Lapakahi, the state is excavating and will partially reconstruct for a historical park. Remains of the economically-related farming community are upland a couple of miles and not yet accessible. The archaeological "dig" on this last undisturbed site of its type is the largest and most intensive ever undertaken in Hawaii; already relics from a half-dozen levels have provided many answers as to how average Hawaiians lived down through the centuries.

The mile-long road from route 27 to Kapaa Beach Park crosses an old cane railroad bed and gives access to excellent snorkeling grounds—go off the park's old Hawaiian canoe landing. Walk five minutes to the north, then around a fence to ruins of another village occupied until about 1915 (stone terraces, walls with steps, house platforms, burial cairns). Kohala Kim Chee Factory lies right on route 27. Each morning but Sunday almost a ton of cabbage is converted into the popular Korean hot pickle relish.

The turnoff to Upolu Airfield is also the way to Mookini Heiau (follow warrior signs), the state's first Registered National Historic Landmark and one of two sacrificial temples of the highest rank (the other was Wahaula, page 75) built in the 13th century by the Tahitian priest, Paao. Much remains of the 250 by 130-foot platform and surrounding walls; there's a boulder upon which—it is said—victims were strangled. Kokoiki,

Hapuna, *Big Island's finest beach, is partly state park. It attracts body surfers in winter, swimmers any time.*

Gilt and bronze statue *of Kamehameha in Kapaau is twin of one before Honolulu's Judiciary Building.*

the district just west, was the birthplace of Kamehameha I. Kohala residents hold occasional shark hunts at Upolu Point—when they have a ranch animal carcass to attract the monstrous killers into deep water off rocks where hunters stand to harpoon and shoot them.

Hawi, 7 miles from Mahukona, is the best known of a handful of settlements with picturesque old houses and store fronts, churches and temples, along the eastern 7 miles of route 27. They're separated only by patches of jungle or a green sea of swaying cane tops. Hawi is the Big Island's northernmost town and the location of Kohala Sugar Company's office (call there to arrange a visit to its mill 3 miles east). Displayed out front are *papamu*, Hawaiian "checkerboard" boulders. Close by is the stack of the first mill of one of the early plantations. Hawi has an interesting Jodo Temple, and its Sacred Heart Church is notable for an early stained glass window.

From Hawi, route 25 winds for 20 miles back to Waimea along steep flanks of the Kohala Mountains covered with sweet grasses, cactus, rocks, wild fennel and morning glory, and windbreaks of Norfolk pines, eucalyptus, and ironwoods. About midway, stop at Kahua Ranch picnic shelter for an expansive view of the Kawaihae coast. Mauna Horeba Chapel at ranch headquarters contains a Jean Charlot fresco. The road crests above Waimea, at 3,564 feet, where some say Kamehameha planned his island-conquering strategy; the plateau represented the sea, and all the visible peaks (the three big volcanoes, Puu Waawaa, even Maui's Haleakala), islands.

If you follow route 27 east of Hawi, you come upon a gilt-and-bronze figure of Kamehameha in front of the district court house in Kapaau. This is the original statue the Hawaiian government commissioned from an American sculptor working in Italy. It was finished in 1880, lost at sea, recovered, and put here—after a replica of the statue had been made and placed before Honolulu's Judiciary Building.

Kapaau has a couple of quaint temples (one off a road that goes uphill beside the court house); diminutive St. Augustine's Episcopal Church (in a yard with large gravestones and tall, aged palms), dedicated in 1884 by a largely British congregation; and the district's prize, Kalahikiola (¼ mile up a marked side road), the church designed by missionary Elias Bond who also started Kohala's first sugar plantation to make work for the Hawaiians. The meeting house is monumental considering its era and the way it had to be built. For six long years ending in 1855, parishioners hauled its stones from ravines, and to make mortar, brought sand from the shore, coral from the sea, and wood (for burning coral) from the mountains. Beyond the grounds, set off by a stone arch, are the empty frame buildings of the old Kohala Female Seminary which Bond started. The road to the church passes macadamia nut groves and the mission homestead, white buildings framing a generous lawn with fruit and shade trees, still occasionally used by Bond's descendants.

About 2 miles east of the church turnoff, a warrior marker points to Kamehameha Rock, a huge boulder the ruler is supposed to have carried from the sea to a nearby *heiau*. In gulches between Kapaau and Niulii (a scattering of houses in jungle), villagers still grow wet land taro and sweet potatoes (mostly the latter) the old Hawaiian way. Look down Waikane Gulch as you pass and you'll see how they have diverted the stream through rock-terraced plots—water from one dribbles into the next and so on down the hill. A thick pandanus forest now screens Niulii's quaint Japanese graveyard from the ocean it once overlooked. Take a side road down to the cove below, to Keokea Beach Park, a grassy flat with an old *heiau* crowned by a jaunty lookout pergola. Another pavilion shelters picnickers and campers from the region's heavy rains. The sea may be too wild for swimming, but you will find an inlet protected enough for boats and a stream bed to explore. An adjacent bluff is faced with caves; according to legend, one leads into the *heiau* that sits on top.

Kohala Ditch Country

For the motorist, this luxuriant world ends about 1½ miles beyond Niulii at the lookout over broad, green-carpeted Pololu Valley and off down a coast of splendid, uninhabited gorges. For the hiker, this is the start of a spectacular journey (a wet and slippery one) along a 40-mile network of trails into Pololu and other valleys named Honokane-Nui, Honokane-Iki, Honokea, and Honopue (see Hiking, page 69).

The Kohala Ditch Trails give access to an elaborate waterworks (ditches, tunnels, intakes, pipelines, pumps) built early in this century to carry the rainwater that favors these canyons to cane fields on lee slopes. Kohala Ditch Company men navigate the course on sure-footed mules. You're welcome to hike, but except for the 15-minute walk down to Pololu's beach, consult Kohala Sugar Company, Hawi, on your itinerary and sign a liability release.

The trail system snakes in and out of valleys and over plateaus between. It is well-graded but hangs on sheer *pali* as it crosses several gulches. You gawk at seascapes and waterfalls, ford streams, hear native birds, brush wild orchids, ferns, ginger, *ti*, gardenias, and native trees.

To hike the full distance, you'll want to stay at the company's cabin complexes, and usually there's space available. Honokane Camp is about halfway along, 'Awini near the farthest point. In one day, you can cross upper Pololu (and run under Kapoloa Falls but feel only mist) into Honokane-Nui, criss-cross its stream nine times on the way up to 850-foot man-made falls, and return by way of Pololu beach.

The network stops short of two large breaks in the east end of the Kohala Mountains, Waimanu and Waipio valleys, accessible only from Honokaa (this page). Clouds that press down upon the swamp between Honopue and Waimanu often conceal even prominent landmarks.

A 4-mile jeep road goes from Waimea up through pastures and an evergreen forest onto the crest of the Kohala Mountains, passing a lookout into Waipio at the head of a rear canyon. Arrange with the State Forestry office in Hilo to pick up a key for the locked gates, or take a tour (page 69). The summit is a bog, with native lobelias, violets, ferns, sedges, and stunted trees. You are most likely to escape fog in the morning.

Hamakua District

Hamakua for most people is the cane field fringe of Mauna Kea's long northeastern slope that route 19 spans for most of its 55 miles from Waimea to Hilo. There are no resorts. There are a lot of detours you can make to quaint plantation towns and gulches burrowed out of the coastal bluff by streams with waterfalls fed by Mauna Kea's winter snows and a year-round abundance of rain.

And there's a special place—Waipio Valley—that can hold you on the Hamakua Coast a day or more.

From Waimea to Honokaa, 16 miles and an overall drop of 1,500 feet, you see truck farms, new homesteads, pastures punctuated with eucalyptus, misty forest, and finally an expanse of bright green sugar cane. At Waimea's outer edge, a dirt road, the middle part of which calls for 4-wheel-drive, wanders off over the side of Mauna Kea for some 40 miles to Humuula in the Saddle. About 8 miles up, at Mana, is the prim little white house of John Parker and several generations of Parkers, now a family museum.

The highway bypasses Honokaa, but be sure to turn into this strongly Portuguese settlement perched on the hillside. Box buildings along its main street are in various pastel colors. Note the People's Theatre (since 1930); two pretty frame churches—the rambling Methodist sanctuary (formerly Congregational serving Filipinos, then Koreans), and the Catholic Our Lady of Lourdes, with yellow steeple; Hotel Honokaa Club and Andrade's, lively with cane planters and Aloha-shirted *paniolo* on Saturday nights; and Nakashima's Store, another of those institutions with unbelievable stock—especially hardware.

Drive downhill to the classic plantation camp at Haina, overlooking the Honokaa Sugar Company mill above the sea; houses and gardens are red and green. Halfway down is the Hawaiian Holiday macadamia nut factory; tours (work days, 8-4) also cover candy-making—and samples.

Waipio Valley

Honokaa is also the gateway to Waipio Valley, the awesome gap that checks the northward advance of Hamakua's cane. It is the most accessible visiting place along the primitive *pali* coast of the mile-high Kohala Mountains, but even so, the only road in calls for a 4-wheel-drive vehicle or hiking—or an all-day tour (see page 69).

In a passenger car, you can drive 10 miles (route 24) to the lookout park on Waipio's east rim where the descent begins. You approach through steep hills of cane, 1,000 feet above the sea, and through Kukuihaele, a wisp of a village, whose stores have a surprising assortment (fresh film, decorative household wares—as well as foodstuffs).

At the lookout, you gaze upon one of nature's masterpieces. Below, a stream lazes along a 6-mile-long valley checkered with taro patches and bounded by 2,000-foot-high walls. A white ribbon of surf unwinds up the coast and disappears behind a bold headland. The old horse trail that zigzags up the opposite bluff crosses deeply furrowed tableland to the next big valley, Waimanu (see Hiking, page 69), resplendent with waterfalls including one that is reportedly the highest in the state.

It's a steep mile down into Waipio Valley; the grade reaches 26 per cent. Then you follow dirt roads and wheel tracks, splash through mud and across streams, plow through thickets of ferns, ginger, guavas, *noni* apples.

When white men first visited Waipio, in 1823, they found a continuous garden of taro, bananas, and sugar cane, fishponds, several *heiaus*, and a place of refuge. They learned from the nearly 1,500 inhabitants about sojourns of early kings, one of whom had sacrificed 80 people before demands of his god were satiated. Here, in 1780, Kamehameha received his war god from reigning chiefs and was thus singled out as future ruler. Chinese immigrants came in the late 1800's and grew rice until the 1930's (you can see remains of a wooden temple). Waipio still has a couple of dozen taro farmers, and a few still live in the valley. There's a *poi* factory (visit mornings), but most growers stuff their crops in gunny sacks and haul them out by jeep or truck for processing.

Near the end of the downhill course, a road branches to the beach, passes Lalakea Fishpond, crosses gray sand dunes festooned with *naupaka*, and lands you near the main stream where you can dip (ocean swimming is usually hazardous—huge waves, rip tides). On the ocean face of the 900-foot bluff you descended is a "come-and-go" waterfall—the run-off from an irrigation ditch above, sometimes dry from July to October.

The road inland turns into a network, but most people find their way to the Peace Corps camp (visitors welcome) and to Nanaue Falls on the valley's far side. It's easy to spot the broad road (on the near side of the camp) to a private park going in on a level ridge 1/4 mile from Hiilawe Falls, a natural cascade that drops 1,000 feet from the top of a side canyon. When a *heiau*-like pavilion of steel and bronze glass is complete, you will be able to buy lunch as well as picnic at this view point. Hiilawe Stream flows past the Peace Corps village and furnishes its water. Periodically recruits bound for Southeast Asia live in the native houses, learn languages and how to grow rice and taro, tend a water buffalo, and fight mosquitoes. You'll see a Borneo longhouse, Nepalese stone house, and Thai, Philippine, and Malaysian huts.

Nanaue Falls drop into a series of swimming pools; you can safely climb rocks to two above ground level. You'll discover other waterfalls, large and small, some with swimming holes.

Honokaa to Hilo

If you stick to the wide, smooth highway from Honokaa to Hilo, you'll see cane fields above and below (ending in cliffs above the sea), span gulches on widened bridges of an old standard-gauge railway, and arrive before you

know it. But even if you're in a hurry, stop at one of the bridges to see the trestle underneath and the old road winding in and out of the canyon. If it is clear, you can see Mauna Kea. In the morning its high grazing lands and brown and black lavas and cones are distinct; in the afternoon, the lofty dome is but a silhouette, usually with a mantle of clouds.

You can follow by-paths (some of them sections of the old Belt Road) to visit jungled gorges, parks, rocky points, and country towns with picturesque mills.

Between Honokaa and Paauilo, a side road marked "Kalopa" takes you uphill along Kalopa Gulch into a 600-acre recreation center gradually being developed with trails, shelters, and cabins, and featuring a 100-acre aged forest with perhaps Hamakua's largest *'ohi'a*. Water is in, and you can cover about 3 miles in an ordinary car, another 1 1/2 miles in a 4-wheel-drive. Turn off the highway into Paauilo, a classic plantation town with buildings like a stage set. At Laupahoehoe go down to the grassy park out on the wave-pounded peninsula. The coastline views are splendid from this finger of a lava flow, which had a settlement before the 1946 seismic wave rolled in. You can see ruins of the school and a monument with the names of 24 teachers and pupils who lost their lives.

Waikaumalo Park lies uphill from the highway (between Ninole and Honohina villages) along a stream with swimming holes. Wind down into Kolekole Gulch on the old road to reach Kolekole Park, almost under the highway bridge. It also has splash pools in a stream you can follow out to sea. Drive across the stream on the old road bridge to wind back up the other side of the canyon past Hakalau mill where cane still arrives in an old-fashioned wooden flume on a trestle over the gulch.

Turn off again to tiny Honomu where you can count five churches and temples and see traditional Buddhist trappings in the Odaishisan. Take route 22 through sugar land for 2 more miles to Akaka Falls State Park. You can picnic in this 66-acre aboretum of giant gingers, ferns, *ti*, azaleas, orchids, and bamboo, and walk an easy loop trail through a stream-eroded gorge so deep and thickly-canopied that little sun gets through—but be prepared for rain. Akaka Falls (the state's largest easily-accessible waterfall) drop 442 feet over a mossy precipice in Kolekole Stream.

The Pepeekeo-Onomea-Papaikou section of the old road is a pretty stretch bordered with areca palms and African tulip trees. It passes sheltered Onomea Bay and an interesting notched point (the result of a sea arch that collapsed) and offers uphill views of trestled highway bridges. Drive several miles uphill on route 21 (turn off at Mauna Kea Sugar Company) to reach Kaiwiki Park, a play and picnic field surrounded by cane and with a sweeping view of Hilo and its bay.

A 442-foot drop in Kolekole Stream forms beautiful Akaka Falls; park is delightful for picnicking, strolling.

The Saddle and the Big Mountains

The scenery is entirely different on this alternate route (about 55 miles) between Hilo and Waimea. The Saddle Road (route 20) crosses the lonely pass between Mauna Loa and Mauna Kea. It's paved, but rough and narrow, gives access to hunting grounds and rugged roads up the state's two highest mountains.

Through the Saddle

From Hilo you go from 'ohi'a and fern forest into barren plateau—lavas that have crisscrossed into the Saddle over thousands of years. You traverse 9 miles of an 1855 flow from a Mauna Loa eruption that lasted 13 months, longer than any other in historic time. Farther on you cross lava from a 1935 outburst that threatened Hilo's water supply until the course of the flow was changed by aerial bombing. The swirly *pahoehoe* surrounds Puu Huluhulu, a Mauna Kea cinder cone that looks as if it had been set upon the Saddle floor; sandalwood grows on its south side. Watch for two side roads; the first goes south up to Mauna Loa Observatory (page 92), and the next, north into Parker Ranch's Humuula Station, starting point for roads up and around Mauna Kea (this page).

Pohakuloa Camp (part of Mauna Kea State Park) is set in game bird grasslands at 6,500 feet; the air is dry and crisp—and downright cold at night. You will find native trees, picnic grounds, lodgings for hunters, skiers, and family groups (see Camping, page 67), and a feature attraction—the *nene*. Normally Pohakuloa's pens have 30 pairs of this native Hawaiian goose which had become almost extinct when a breeding project was started here some 20 years ago. Since then the birds have also been bred and reared in captivity at other places (notably England and New England) and several hundred released into their preferred habitat (arid land at 6,000 to 7,000 feet) on Mauna Loa, Hualalai, and Haleakala. Usually you are allowed to visit the friendly *nene* (2½ feet high, grayish and white, with black head and semi-webbed feet) and other rare native fowl, Laysan and Hawaiian (Koloa) ducks.

For the last 15 miles, to where it meets route 19 just 4 miles south of Waimea, the Saddle Road gradually descends 3,000 feet through fine pheasant country with views of the lava-scarred mountains. Big Islanders tell of mysterious things which are said to happen in the windy, desolate Saddle before eruptions (cars rattle, or eerie lights appear).

Mauna Kea

For those who would take up the challenge, the state's highest peak stands waiting to be climbed. But it's a lot easier to 4-wheel-drive it to the 13,796-foot summit (see Driving Rough Country and Skiing, page 69) or even to maneuver a passenger car up to a viewpoint at the 9,600-foot level.

You drive hard cinder a precipitous 6½ miles from Humuula Junction to Hale Pohaku, a timberline camp at 9,200 feet in Mauna Kea State Park (see Camping, page 67). Look for pheasant and quail, skimming the emerald grasses that carpet cinder cones; grazing herds; and wild game, particularly the big Mouflon sheep. You can drive ½ mile above the camp to Kilohana Lookout, an inspiring place in the sky so far above the Saddle that the big swell on the opposite side, Mauna Loa, appears deceptively close. The few trees seem out of place at this extreme elevation.

Two routes go on to the summit: a 6-mile foot trail and a 4-wheel-drive road whose use is controlled by the State Parks office (it is open to hikers). The cinder road serves the highest (13,780 feet) major astronomical observatory in the world and two lesser ones.

From the giant University of Hawaii-National Aeronautics and Space Administration observatory (5 stories high with 60-foot dome and 88-inch telescope), scientists can study the moon and other planets far from population centers, lights, or electronic beams. A smaller observatory has a 20-foot dome and a 24-inch telescope and matches one in use by the Air Force.

Hikers should note that the road has a gentler grade and firmer surface than the trail. But since the trail is not bad going downhill (you sink in cinders, but just run), you can make a loop. Start at dawn in order to climb the lowest and steepest part before the sun is hottest and to get back before afternoon clouds roll in. The air is so thin you can take but a few steps before stopping to gulp for it. In winter, temperatures can drop from 50° to 15° and blizzards blow up.

At the foot of a cinder cone, at 13,200 feet, is Lake Waiau, about 400 feet across and 15 feet deep. Because of a mysterious impervious bottom, the water doesn't seep away through the porous lava.

The summit is a cluster of cones of various hues, and your reward for plodding up to it is the magnificent view —of the other volcanoes, clouds in wisps or fluffy layers, fields of cinders and hardened lavas, perhaps glistening snow. The foot trail spirals the north side of the summit, but you can plunge down the soft south slopes and join it below the lake. At about 12,000 feet, (along the trail or at the end of a ¼-mile footpath from the road) is Keanakakoi Cave, the world's most extensive ancient adze quarry and a National Historic Landmark. There are imperfect tools discarded in a pile of chipped rocks. You can hunt for other quarries, even glacial scratches on the lava.

From Humuula Junction, a gravel road winds northeast along Mauna Kea's slope, through grazing lands interrupted by clumps of trees. At 7,000 feet you are above the Hamakua rain forest and often enveloped in clouds. The route becomes a 4-wheel-drive trail and passes close to a mortared-stone monument in a grove of

On top of the world —*strange landscape of Mauna Loa is reached by crushed-cinder road through broken lava.*

Douglas firs—a memorial to the botanist and explorer for whom the tree was named. David Douglas was found dead in a cattle trap at this spot in 1834; how he was killed is still a mystery. About 20 miles farther along, near Mana, the trail turns again into a graveled, passenger-car road and comes out on route 19 at the edge of Waimea.

Mauna Loa

The road up Mauna Loa is unique in two respects: It is the highest in the Pacific open to passenger car travel, and it climbs terrain said to resemble the surface of the moon more than any other place on earth. On a 17-mile course of crushed cinders, you wind from the Saddle up to an isolated scientific community at 11,150 feet (weather and geophysical observatory, solar research unit, Atomic Energy Commission facility).

Go on a clear morning, and have your car tuned for high altitude; sign a State Fish and Game waiver at the unmanned checking station at the start.

Roadside features are hardened lavas—jet black, silvery, brown, reddish—of shapes so fantastic as to stimulate even the most sluggish imaginations. In the lower reaches are ridges and valleys and peaks of jagged *aa* which, when mist courses through them, look like a furious ocean. Farther up are expanses of *pahoehoe* that resemble beaten eggs—close up the brittle material looks like rope and petrified wood. Near the top is more *aa*.

About 3½ miles up, you cross a road that ends nowhere—a prisoner-built segment of an abandoned Hilo-Kona route. From 8,300 feet on, you follow Stainback Highway (it is not negotiable between Kulani Honor Farm and this point) and take in sweeping views of the Saddle and Mauna Kea—unless clouds hang low. Visit the weather station—and warm up; in winter snow banks are not uncommon.

If you're determined to go on to the summit, you can ask permission at the observatory or from Hawaii Volcanoes National Park officials to drive a rock and cinder track—for 4-wheel-drives and skillful drivers only, and generally limited to official use. Or you can walk the 3 miles to the rim of Mokuaweoweo, a firepit 600 feet deep and 3 miles long. Cracks in its overlapping layers of lava are still warm, and wisps of steam rise from many cinder cones. Readings from seismometers in the caldera are relayed over 4 miles of wires to recorders at the observatory.

It takes at least a half day to hike around the firepit to the national park cabin on the opposite rim. To hike across is quicker and more interesting—and tougher. But all walking in the rough *aa* so high up is exhausting—even hiking the Mauna Loa Trail downhill from the summit cabin to Kilauea takes all day.

Clouds hang low *over Iao Needle and green-clad walls of Iao Valley. Easy paths lead into cool ravine.*

MAUI...the Valley Island

Hospitable Maui has a slogan, *"Maui no ka oi,"* which means "Maui is the best." You can judge that for yourself along with the mounting number of other visitors sampling its jungled valleys, ribbons of sand, cool grasslands, vast crater, and notable remainders of Hawaiian history.

It is said (although debated) that Maui was named for a demigod, a legendary superman who fished the Hawaiian Islands from the sea and lassoed the sun to give them daylight.

With 728.8 square miles, Maui is Hawaii's second largest island, and really a double one, shaped like a bust statue whose head and trunk are two volcanic peaks of different age. First came the West Maui Mountains which have been eroded into a series of deep gorges such as Iao Valley which burrows right into the center of Puu Kukui, the 5,788-foot summit and Hawaii's second rainiest peak (more than 400 inches a year). The great mass of Haleakala which rises to 10,023 feet in the southeast is a newer, rounded dome. In between—like the neck of the statue—

is a low sandy isthmus, just 7 miles wide, a valley formed by erosion from the once separate islands and the reason for Maui's nickname, the Valley Isle.

Most of Maui's 40,000 people live in or about the "big" towns—Wailuku, Kahului, Lahaina—or in the growing number of houses on Haleakala's north and west slopes. The fertile isthmus and mountain foothills are planted to sugar cane and pineapple; Hawaiian Commercial & Sugar Co. is one of the largest cane sugar plantations in the nation and operates two mills. Ranching, including the raising of thoroughbred horses, is an important industry up on Haleakala; and from its Kula region come fine cut flowers and vegetables—like popular Maui onions. On top of the mountain is "Science City," with observatories and tracking stations. The island has a rum distillery, fruit juice plant, and crafts manufacturers; but it is tourism that has Maui astir. Its 2,500 hotel rooms will be more than doubled during the next few years, mostly in big spreads that take advantage of west coast beaches and fair weather.

Festivals

Lahaina Whaling Spree (May); a spirited replay of the town scene during whaling days, with costumes and beards, water sports, *lu'au* in the old prison yard, Missionary Memorial church service under the giant banyan tree. **Makawao Rodeo** (usually over Fourth of July). **Maui Historical Society garden party** (summer), held at a gracious estate or ranch home. **Maui County Fair** (October), Kahului; oldest county fair in Hawaii and most true to its billing.

How to Get There

Maui lies 70 miles southeast of Oahu, and Aloha and Hawaiian Airlines planes stop at Kahului Airport all through the day coming from both Honolulu and the Big Island. (On a full-fare Honolulu-Hawaii island flight, a Maui stopover costs only $5.) From Honolulu, Hawaiian has a daily round-trip flight to Hana Airport (via Kahului), and Royal Hawaiian Air Service calls several times. Royal Hawaiian Air Service, Air Hawaii, and Sky Tours Hawaii operate commuter flights to Kaanapali Airstrip, and the first two make Maui-Big Island connections. Lahaina is the Maui port of call on Matson cruises.

Where to Stay

Maui's luxurious resort community, Kaanapali, stretches back from several miles of swimming beach, has four big hotels, cottage colonies, two golf courses, airstrip, shops, dining spots, and more hotels and a Whaler's Village shopping complex on the way. Hotels on the water are the Sonesta Beach, Maui Hilton, Royal Lahaina, and Sheraton-Maui whose main structure is built on a famous promontory, Black Rock (legendary spirit leap of dead souls). Actually this resort region extends from Lahaina, just south, with its colorful Pioneer Inn (page 100), to Napili Bay several miles north and dominated by the sprawling, informal Napili Kai Beach Club with housekeeping units. In between there are apartments and cottages (many of them condominium apartments or cottage clusters run as hotels).

A less populous destination is Hana on the verdant east coast. Here you'll find the prestigious Hotel Hana Ranch, its 60 rooms spread over a 20-acre garden; the Hana Kai, with deluxe apartments; other housekeeping spots; and nice, furnished, low-cost cabins (for 6 people) in nearby Waianapanapa State Park (for reservations write State Parks office, Wailuku).

In the Central Maui hotel base—closest to the main airport, most convenient for moving different directions to sightsee—are the Maui Beach, Maui Hukilau, and Maui Palms hotels on Kahului Bay, with medium-priced and deluxe rooms, and a scattering of small, modest places uphill in Wailuku.

Another massive west side resort region is developing from Maalaea Bay to Makena. Now you find spacious Maui Lu at Kihei (Polynesian cottages, restaurant, pool, beach, gardens), other small apartment complexes, and bigger ones going up. Soon work will begin to turn 1,500 scrub acres fronting 2 miles of coast north and south of Wailea Beach into Wailea Pua Kuleana (City of Flowers), which one day will have 11,000 hotel units, houses, apartments, golf course, and a town center without automobiles. It will be 2½ times Waikiki's size but of low profile.

Maui also has inexpensive mountain inns such as Hotel Iao Needle just above Wailuku, and Kula Lodge and Silversword Inn in Kula; and near Lower Paia, beach cottages such as Club South Pacific (a Club Mediterranee approximation). The Maui Isle Hawaii Visitors Bureau, Wailuku, is up to the minute on all hotels and often knows of apartments or cottages to rent for a month or longer.

Getting Around on the Island

You can rent a car, jeep, or dune buggy from transportation agencies at Kahului Airport and Kaanapali Airstrip (better reserve ahead), and at Hana arrange for a U-Drive at your hotel. Lahaina agencies have motor scooters for rent. There is some scheduled shuttle service from the main airport to Lahaina-Kaanapali-Napili hotels. Package tours—to Kula, Iao Valley, Lahaina, or a combination of these—leave from Kahului Airport, where you can also arrange a tour to Hana or Haleakala. Major Hana and Lahaina region hotels arrange local sightseeing trips. Valley Isle Aviation (Kahului Airport) offers charter service between airfields, will give you a

Luxury resorts *overlook Royal Kaanapali Golf Course and 3-mile beach at its edge. This is Royal Lahaina Hotel.*

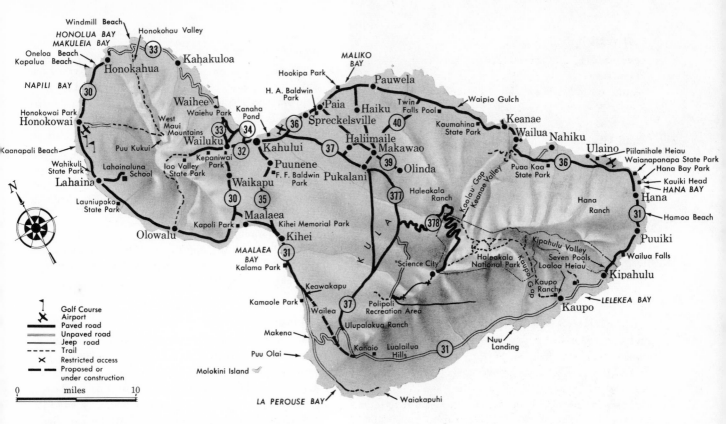

Map legend:

Golf Course
Airport
Paved road
Unpaved road
Jeep road
Trail
Restricted access
Proposed or under construction

0   miles   10

1-day air and ground tour (i.e., Kaanapali to Hana and back). Buses run all day and into the night between Lahaina and Napili, stop at all the hotels and apartments. After early 1970 you'll be able to ride over a 6-mile Lahaina-Kaanapali scenic route on the antique train of the Lahaina-Kaanapali & Pacific Railroad. The replica of the turn-of-the-century Kaanapali Coast cane haul line will have a 400-foot trestle. Terminals will be modeled after quaint depots of the period.

Maui's Hawaii Visitors Bureau office is at 2133 Main Street, Wailuku. Kahului Airport has a State Visitor Information counter.

It takes at least two days to drive Maui's main roads and visit the principal sights. Even with more time, you're in for one or more long days of sightseeing if you try to cover all of the island by car from any one hotel base.

From the Wailuku-Kahului hub it's about 40 miles to the top of Haleakala (route 378, reached from three directions), about 130 miles around the base of the mountain (routes 36, 31), and about 60 miles around the West Maui Mountains (routes 30, 33). But driving trips take longer than the distances indicate. The roads from Honokohau to Waihee and from Kaupo to Makena are difficult for ordinary cars. Tours avoid them and drive-yourself agencies require you to drive them at your own risk. If you would explore you'll go anyway, but check road conditions and rent a sturdy, high-slung car—or better, a jeep.

Recreation on Maui

Picnicking and Camping

Camping is permitted in most county and state parks which have rest rooms and drinking water, and usually pavilions, tables, showers, electricity, and grills. You'll need a permit from the Maui County Department of Parks and Recreation, Wailuku, to camp (with tent or camper vehicle) at Honokowai, Kihei Memorial, Kalama, Kamaole III, Waiehu, H. A. Baldwin, Hookipa, and Hana beach parks.

To use campgrounds at Kaumahina and Waianapanapa parks and Polipoli Recreation Area, or to reserve Waianapanapa cabins (page 107) or Polipoli Cabin (small charge), get in touch with the State Parks office, Wailuku. Haleakala National Park (Box 456, Kahului) has Hosmer Grove campground, and low-cost crater-trail cabins which you must reserve (see Haleakala, page 103). Church and organization camps—Y-Camp Keanae and camps Maluhia, Piiholo, Pecusa, and Olowalu—are often available to families (write Maui Isle Hawaii Visitors Bureau, Wailuku). You'll come upon spots to camp along unpopulated coasts, beside streams, or in a village church or school yard. You can rent equipment in Kahului from Hawaiian Rentals and Maui Rents (branch in Lahaina), campers from most firms listed on page 12.

For picnicking, note Iao Valley State Park, Keanae Lookout, Kapoli Park, and Ulupalakua Ball Park.

A refreshing dip in the stream at Keanae and a picnic on its shore can be a pleasant break in the drive to Hana.

Swimming, Surfing, Shelling

Maui's west coast is almost a fringe of sand, with one spot after another good for swimming except when the sea is very rough. Other shores are dotted with sandy swimming coves. These are the parks that have ocean swimming and rest rooms or complete bathhouses: Kamaole I, Kalama, Kihei Memorial, Kapoli, Launiupoko, Wahikuli, Honokowai, Kapalua (Fleming's), Waiehu, H. A. Baldwin, Hookipa, and Hana. Several hotel beaches are outstanding: Kaanapali (3 miles long), Napili, Hamoa (for guests of Hotel Hana Ranch). Good places for a plunge lie along uninhabited strips: Waihee; north of Kapalua (Honolua Bay is the most sheltered spot); in front of the Japanese cemetery at Kaanapali; Olowalu; parts of Keawakapu, Wailea, and Makena.

In many a gulch you'll find crisp fresh-water pools big enough at least for a dip. Note Twin Falls, Puaa Kaa State Park, Hinamoo pool in Nahiku's stream, Keanae's stream, the mouth of Ulaino stream, Waianapanapa Cave,

Kipahulu's Seven Pools. Kepaniwai Park's swimming and wading pools are fed by a mountain stream.

Surfing. There's some surfing off the Keawakapu shore, in Maalaea, Hana, and Hamoa bays, and at H. A. Baldwin and Hookipa beaches. In the Lahaina region, surf off Lahaina town and Launiupoko Park for average waves; go north to Honokahua (also called Ball Park or Stable Point), Makuleia (Slaughterhouse Beach), and Honolua for bigger thrills. Arrange for boards and instruction at the major resort hotels or rent boards from Pacific Buggies U-Drive or Kaanapali Activity Center at Kaanapali Airstrip.

Shells wash in at Waiehu and Waihee, around Hana, and at Olowalu. At Camp Pecusa (Olowalu), and at the pebbly end of a crescent of gray sand ½ mile north of Olowalu, look for "Hawaiian diamonds" (quartz).

Fishing

You can troll the channel waters between Maui, Kahoolawe, Lanai, and Molokai for marlin, *mahimahi, ono, kawakawa, 'ahi,* and *ulua.* Several charter boats are moored in Lahaina Harbor. Get information on them at Kaanapali Activity Center or nearby hotels, or write Pacific Game Fishing Unlimited, 1777 Ala Moana, Honolulu. Maalaea Boat and Fishing Club sponsors periodic open tournaments.

At deluxe west side hotels and Hotel Hana Ranch you can rent fins, face masks, and snorkels, arrange diving trips with an instructor-guide. Try spear fishing for eels, octopus, and small fish off Lahaina, Makena, Waiehu-Waihee, Spreckelsville, and around Hana.

There are good spots for surf casting (for *ulua, papio,* and *'o'io*) and pole fishing off rocks (for *'u'u* and *'aweoweo*) along every shore. Villagers at Keanae, Wailua, Hana, Kaupo, and Lelekea Bay have skiffs or motor-powered outriggers and might take you trolling or surround-net fishing for *akule.* There are piers to fish from in Kahului, Hana, and Maalaea bays; you can pick *'opihi* off rocks near the Bell Stone above Kahakuloa, at Makena, and Nahiku; at times *o'opu* can be taken with a hook and line in streams.

A reservoir at Wailuku is stocked with catfish, bass, and tilapia but you'll need a license and permit—both obtainable at the State Fish and Game office, Wailuku.

Boating

Sailing craft and glass bottom boats leave Lahaina Harbor on scheduled cruises and charter trips. To find out about various boating possibilities, inquire at the wharf, nearby hotels, or Kaanapali Activity Center. You can go out for an hour to view colorful reefs and deep sea formations that yield Lahaina's famous black coral, cruise for part of a day or by sunset up and down the Lahaina roadstead, or go for an entire day across to Lanai for a tour, picnic, and swim. Water skiing is available, too, and at the major resorts (including Hana Ranch), there are kayaks, outrigger canoes, small sailboats, or outboards to skipper yourself.

Hiking and Horseback Riding

Hikers and riders should focus on Haleakala and the Hana Ranch. See page 105 for the crater trails and the trail out through Kaupo Gap. Frank Freitas (Box 50, Makawao), who conducts crater horseback trips, also takes riding parties (minimum of 4) into the Olinda grasslands on the side of the mountain. Kula Lodge and Silversword Inn will arrange rides for their guests.

From near Haleakala's summit you can walk down a 5½-mile jeep road to Polipoli Spring, cabin, and campground, then on several trails through a forest of redwoods, pines, cedars, and eucalyptus. A 5-mile loop trail around the spring is being developed.

Hotel Hana Ranch guests (and sometimes others), by arranging a day ahead, can hire horses and a guide by the hour to ride the 7,000-acre ranch's network of bridle trails, perhaps to Hamoa Beach, a bamboo forest, Waianapanapa State Park, or Ulaino. The trails are also pleasant to walk. Trips of 2 to 4 days up Kaupo Gap into the crater are feasible only by horseback and require several days' notice. The short, steep Niniao Pali Trail at Kaupo is a fine day's hike through open pasture and guava forest to a lookout above a deep valley rimmed with waterfalls.

To hike just a day on the miles-long Maui Ditch Trail (all but valley sections overgrown), start from Kopiliula Falls west of Nahiku and cross Keanae Valley. The terrain is easy—but so is getting lost during downpours. Arrange with East Maui Irrigation Company, Paia.

In West Maui, Iao Valley State Park has short scenic trails (see page 99). To cross the West Maui Mountains —generally up through Iao Valley, out at Olowalu—is very rough going and requires State Department of Health typhoid clearance (the trail penetrates restricted watershed). You can join a monthly rain-gauge-reading party on a tough climb up Honokohau Valley to Puu Kukui (write John Stegmuller, Maui Land & Pineapple Company, Kahului). It's 4 hours up and 2 hours down; expect to sink to your knees in mud in a bog where native violets and a few West Maui silverswords grow.

Visitors can join Mauna Ala's monthly hikes, alternating between a Sunday family outing and a Saturday challenge for the experienced. Write the hiking club (Box 869, Wailuku) for a schedule and more about Maui's trails.

Paliku cabin, *in rain forest at the east end of Haleakala Crater, is a favorite destination for hikers and riders.*

Hunting

You can hunt pheasants, doves, and quail on weekends and holidays during season (usually November 1 to mid-January) in the Kula-Kahikinui Game Management Area, reached by Walker Road, then Polipoli Access Road (dirt) from Upper Kula Road (route 377).

Goats may be taken on Haleakala's north and south slopes. Access is from the park (firearms permit from park headquarters is required) or from below with permission from Kaupo, Ulupalakua, or Haleakala ranch managers who sometimes allow hunting on ranch lands. James Smythe, Lahaina, takes hunting parties into the West Maui Mountains after a sporty breed of wild boar and domestic pigs gone wild. Wild boar inhabit the forest reserve above Nahiku, rough country where you'll need a resident guide (and his dogs). Mammal seasons are all year; get permits and hunting licenses from the State Fish and Game office, Wailuku.

Golf

Maui has four courses: the celebrated Royal Kaanapali and a par-64 course at Kaanapali; Maui Country Club, Spreckelsville; Waiehu municipal links. Hotel Hana Ranch has an 18-hole par-3 pitch-and-putt course.

Bicycling

You'll find bicycles to rent at several hotels (west side and Hana) and Maui Rents (Kahului and Lahaina).

Central Maui

Wailuku and Kahului are Maui's "twin cities," and—together with the plantation settlements of Puunene, Waiehu, and Waihee—they form the island's hub. The two towns are great rivals and very different.

Wailuku, charmingly situated on West Maui Mountain slopes at the mouth of Iao Valley, is the county seat (Maui County includes Lanai and Molokai) and long-time business center. Narrow, hilly streets with wooden shops, tree-shaded residential lanes, and a gracious civic center give it an old-Hawaii look despite a handful of new buildings, evidence the town is not to be outdone by its enterprising neighbor.

Kahului, just 3 miles downhill on the bay, is the busy port and new commercial and residential center, but its population has yet to match Wailuku's 7,000.

Pick up a map of the area (and don't hesitate to ask directions) and meander over a few out-of-the-way roads: monkeypod-lined Puunene Avenue with mill and remaining plantation camps; Beach Road, then Lower Main Street (route 34), from Kahului to Wailuku—note the Chinese cemetery on the steep bank as you enter the hillside town; route 341 through Paukukalo Hawaiian Homesteads to Waiehu; Wailuku's Lower Market Street (route 33) for picturesque buildings (see Happy Valley, below).

Some Places to Visit

Treasure Craft of Hawaii, near airport, makes more than 100 Hawaiian-design ceramics pieces. Call ahead to tour.

Kanaha Pond, between airport and Kahului. Ancient royal fishpond, now Hawaii's most important native waterfowl and migratory bird refuge (particularly for Hawaiian Stilt). Wildlife expert Joseph Medeiros gives tours by appointment; call State Fish and Game office, Wailuku.

Hawaiian Commercial & Sugar Co. mill, Puunene. Call a day ahead to arrange a tour which includes a Joseph Seagram and Sons rum distillery next door.

Jodo Mission, Molokai Hema at Niihau Street, Kahului. Small masonry Buddhist temple with onion-shaped domes.

Ka Lima O Maui, 727 First Street, Kahului. Rehabilitation Center where Hawaiian craft products are turned out by handicapped workers and sold here and at a shop in Wailuku.

Kahului Harbor, Maui's only deep-water port, is location of state's first bulk sugar plant, fueling base for several hundred Japanese fishing boats each year.

Turn-of-the-Century Railroad Coach, now a lounge in front of The Landing restaurant in Kahului. It belonged originally to Oahu Railway, was used for Kahului-Haiku scenic rides just before freight-passenger Kahului Railroad (1881-1966) went out of business.

Kahului Shopping Center has some 35 shops with a variety of interesting foods and other goods along a monkeypod-shaded mall. Try Tasaka's Guri Guri sherbet.

Hawaiian Fruit Growers Exchange, on Beach Road, Kahului, packs concentrates of guava, papaya, and passion fruit, much of the latter grown on trellises just out of town. Call ahead for tours given from June to January.

Aloha Poi Shop, 800 Lower Main, Wailuku, is a place to see how *poi* is made; but telephone first.

Shishido Manju Factory, 758 Lower Main, is famous for *mochi* cakes.

Wailuku Churches. Kaahumanu Church, on High Street, is Maui's oldest, built in 1837 of plastered stone. It's of mission style with handsome spire viewed against a mountain backdrop. Wailuku Union, also on High Street, is opulent by contrast, a small stone Gothic built in 1911 to replace an 1867 predecessor. Church of the Good Shepherd, 2140 Main Street, a 1911 Episcopal sanctuary (founded 1866), is stone, has interior details of native woods, an unusual stained glass window behind the altar. St. Anthony's, on Mill Street, is an elaborate Spanish Mission-style compound started in 1919 and extended 20 years later. From its first (1855) wooden church, Father Damien was assigned to the Molokai leprosy colony.

Hale Hoikeike, off Iao Road, Wailuku. Museum with early native implements, 19th-century pieces, and interesting book and gift shop (Mon.-Sat. 10-3:30). Buildings are the home built in 1841 by Edward Bailey, head instructor of the Wailuku Female Seminary, with 20-inch-thick stone walls covered with plaster held together by mixing in human hair, and hand-hewn sandalwood beams; and the kitchen-dining room of the school, an 1838-39 addition to its original building (now gone).

Music Sales, 40 Market Street, Wailuku (branches in Kahului, Lahaina). One of Hawaii's largest producers of hula accessories has inexpensive feather gourds, bamboo sticks, etc.

Happy Valley, a part of old Wailuku on route 33, has balconied living quarters above open-front shops and taverns, including the valley namesake, which serves good Hawaiian food.

Halekii and Pihana heiaus (marked turnoff uphill from route 341). Halekii, 150 by 300-foot temple of worship used during reign of Kahekili (1765-1795), who held all islands but Kauai and Hawaii, has partially-restored gray stone walls, terraces, and post holes and is explained by a diagram. Pihana, at the end of a path 300 feet farther up, was a sacrificial temple consecrated in 1779.

Maui Jinsha, in Paukukalo off route 341, is an unusual—for the Islands—Shinto complex. Sacred objects lie behind the temple in a raised building that also has traditional roof symbols—protruding horns and barrel-shaped ridge piece.

Waihee churches. At Waihee Congregational Church, a simple stone and plaster structure from the 1860's, services are still conducted in Hawaiian as well as English. A pretty Catholic neighbor, St. Anne's, is of wood and has stood only a few decades.

Wailuku's Hale Hoikeike, *built as a home in 1841, now houses a fascinating collection of old Hawaii relics.*

Iao Valley

From Wailuku, you can drive for 3 miles (route 32) into Iao Valley, never far from the rushing stream. This spectacular gorge, often called Hawaii's Yosemite, is hemmed in by forested walls almost a mile high. It was here that forces of Kamehameha the Great and the king of Maui fought the battle in which so many Maui warriors were slaughtered it is said their corpses dammed Iao Stream. You pass Kepaniwai ("damming of the waters") Park which has man-made swimming and wading pools fed by the stream; picnic shelters; Chinese, Filipino, and Japanese gardens with pavilions from Asia; and a monument commemorating the arrival of the first Japanese immigrants in 1868. To come are Portuguese, Hawaiian, and Early American gardens with pavilions, and a large social pavilion.

The road ends in Iao Valley State Park where you'll see 2,250-foot Iao Needle, a green-clad pinnacle that juts up 1,200 feet from the valley floor. From the turn-around are easy walks down to the stream, up to a shelter viewpoint for a look farther into the hushed ravine, or into the interior tableland — wet, but strikingly scenic.

Around the West Maui Mountains

The loop from Wailuku around the West Maui Mountains (routes 30, 33) is less than 60 miles, but it includes one of those stretches — Honokohau to Waihee (see page 103) — where car renting agents don't want you to go. Anyway, instead of driving the loop all at once, you'll probably want to stay awhile on the Lahaina-Kaanapali-Napili Coast. From there you can venture on around the point when the road is right—or anytime in a jeep.

Wailuku to Lahaina

You travel a fast, smooth, 22-mile course on Honoapiilani Highway (30) from Wailuku to Lahaina. The road across the isthmus to Maalaea Bay hugs the lower slopes of the mountains and passes tiny Waikapu village. Drive down into Maalaea, a settlement around a small boat harbor facing Haleakala, with a popular boat and fishing club (restaurant above), pretty Kapoli Park, and a small *torii*-marked shrine at water's edge.

Next comes a particularly scenic drive along the tops of seashore cliffs, then a descent to the narrow Olowalu plain where cane fields slope up to mile-high mountains broken by Ukumehame Gulch, and other deep gashes.

Olowalu is remembered for an eighteenth century massacre: An American trader, seeking revenge for a stolen boat and murdered crewman, lured the natives out to his vessel, then slaughtered them with cannon fire. Within a

A cloud cap *casts soft shadows on ridges and valleys of the West Maui Mountains just behind Lahaina town.*

mile south of monkeypod-shaded Olowalu settlement, you pass two church camps. At Camp Olowalu you'll find Lanikila Congregational Church, an 1859 treasure (still used) that is soon to be rebuilt with funds collected as plate offerings at the annual Whaling Spree's "missionary church service." Windows are just cutouts in the stone walls; the earth floor has a stone path aisle; the roof is missing, but a monkeypod tree provides a canopy just open enough for a view of the mountain tops. At Camp Pecusa you can swim and look for "Hawaiian diamonds" (high-grade quartz).

At Olowalu settlement note Ichiki country store—it has electric eye doors; and Chez Paul, Maui's only French restaurant—and it's fine indeed (make reservations). Just north, then .6 mile up a marked cane field road are the Olowalu Petroglyphs, carved several hundred years ago on outcroppings along a pass through the mountains. A stairway goes up to a viewing platform. A half mile north of Olowalu is another "Hawaiian diamond" hunting ground with surfing waves offshore. You'll find more surf off mile-long Launiupoko Beach Park.

Lahaina

Lahaina is where modern Hawaiian history began. Kamehameha the Great had a residence here after he conquered Maui in a bloody battle in Iao Valley. Some of the first missionaries from Boston came ashore here in 1823.

At Baldwin Home Museum *you see missionary doctor's house, study-dispensary the way they looked in 1840's.*

Kamehameha III lived at Lahaina when he granted religious freedom and drew up Hawaii's first laws and first constitution. In the middle years of the century, whalers came by the thousands to winter in this little port, anchoring their ships offshore in the roadstead. (A fictional account of Lahaina's kings, missionaries, and whalers is part of James Michener's gaudy 1959 bestseller, *Hawaii*.)

Lahaina is still partly the town it has been for the last century: sleepy, friendly, a bit beaten up like the celebrated South Seas ports. Streets are narrow, sidewalks few, trees old and spreading, family gardens a tropical hodge-podge, and friendly dogs run loose everywhere. Most houses are simple cottages, most trading takes place in false-front wooden buildings, and the biggest sign is the "Jesus Coming Soon" neon on the Gospel Mission.

But Lahaina no longer exists just to sell gas, groceries, and booze to West Maui's cane and pineapple workers. There are new shopping complexes, restaurants, bars, condominiums—but for tourists. Most are in keeping with the town's Restoration Plan, to refurbish the best of the weathered buildings, particularly on Front Street, encourage harmonious new building, and restore or rebuild a few structures from each period of its 19th-century history—from early monarchy days through the beginnings of plantations and influx of workers from the Orient. The plan is the joint effort of state and local government and a private foundation. Lahaina is a National Historic Landmark, its center section under Historic District protection.

The town is just the right size for walking, or bi-cycling. It's nearly flat, stretched out for about 2 miles along the water, but only 4 blocks deep. Most of the historic places lie between Shaw and Papalaua streets—just over a third of a mile—along and within a couple of blocks of Front Street. Get a copy of the *Lahaina Historical Guide*, with map, or the Lahaina walking tour brochure (both available at hotels and stores), look at the model of the town plan in the Lahaina Restoration Foundation office behind Baldwin Home—then explore.

Reminders of Monarchy, Missionary, Whaling Days

Pioneer Inn, built in 1901, is two stories with wrap-around verandas; a new wing, in matching style, contains some smart shops. Porches are popular Wharf Street and harbor lookouts; side porch is part of barroom which has cargo and tonnage lists from whaling ships that called in 1843. House rules of 1901 are posted in rooms.

Small Boat Harbor, bounded by wharf, breakwater, and yacht and sampan moorage along shore, is departure point for sailing cruises and fishing charters and best channel vantage point. Eventually piers will be located north of wharf and a beach will take their place. Now local boys scramble out to the breakwater to swim and surf, and others to view Lahaina from its salt-water front yard. Offshore view is of Kahoolawe, Lanai, Molokai.

The Carthaginian, moored opposite Pioneer Inn (daily, 9-5; adm. fee). Three-masted Danish schooner turned whaling square-rigger for film *Hawaii* is now a whaling museum. The vessel is 130 feet long, carries 17 sails.

Hauola Stone, off point north of ship, is ancient chairshaped healing rock: Hawaiians sat in it, dangled their feet, let waves wash over them. Steps may be built to it so that today's visitors can try the cure-all.

Old Court House, built in 1859, is now Lahaina Art Gallery (open daily). Cannons out front are from a ship, probably Russian or British, that sank around 1800. National Landmark plaque is south of building. At two corners of grounds are reconstructions of ruins of the old fort (1832-1854), actually a compound used chiefly to confine unruly seamen.

Carthaginian, *square-rigger that once cruised the Baltic Sea, is now a whaling museum. View is from Pioneer Inn.*

The pace is easy *in Lahaina. Morning coffee drinkers enjoy corner of Pioneer Inn porch.*

This is Wharf Street, *with Old Court House in foreground. Pioneer Inn (with verandas) is favorite place to watch the passing scene.*

Banyan Tree, planted in 1873 to commemorate 50th anniversary of the arrival of Lahaina's first missionaries, is largest in the Islands, covers entire square (about ⅔ acre) behind Court House. A labyrinth of secondary trunks and posts now supports its canopy. Lahaina Art Society holds Saturday shows under it.

Baldwin Home Museum (guided tours daily, 9-5; adm. fee). Baldwin Home, restored New England-style residence of medical missionary Dwight Baldwin and his family from 1836-1868, was built in 1834-35 of plastered coral and hand-hewn 'ohi'a beams, has original furnishings, other period pieces. Adjoining Dispensary-Study contains Dr. Baldwin's medical kit, medical and theological books, and other early physicians' trappings. Master's Reading Room next door, Maui's oldest building (1834) with coral stone walls 2 feet thick, was put up by ships' officers and the mission, has storeroom downstairs, reading-meeting room above.

Spring House, now part of a restaurant, was a turn-of-the-century liquor storage vault; whalers' watercasks were rolled from the beach to a hand pump that stood nearby.

Hale Paahao, the refurbished 19th-century lockup, has walls of coral block taken from old fort and put up in 1854 by prisoners themselves (mostly rowdy seamen); a guardhouse, and a cell-block inside the compound, with 10 cubicles.

Seamen's Cemetery has only one inscribed marble slab and the fragment of another left. Buried here was a cousin and shipmate of author Herman Melville, who himself, as a young seaman-deserter, spent three fugitive weeks in Lahaina in 1843.

Marine Hospital, on Front Street north of Papalaua, functioned as such from 1840-1865, then became in turn a girls' school, vicarage, and residence.

In the future some long-gone buildings will be reestablished in replica on their sites. Seaward of the library: a two-story brick house put up before 1800, used by Kamehameha the Great (excavated remains are on exhibit); a thatch "long house" in which Hawaii's first constitutional legislature met in 1840; a small stone building—the original Hawaiian customs house and first United States post office in the Sandwich Islands. Near Baldwin Home: Rev. William Richards' home, Hawaii's first coral stone house; a missionary-built seamen's chapel and reading room; a cook house, adobe house, and visitors' cottage. Near Holy Innocents Church: the palace and residence of Kamehameha III. Canal Street will again resemble the waterway and marketplace where whalers came in lifeboats to barter for provisions.

Churches, Temples, Cultural Institutions

Waiola Church (originally called Wainee) was built in 1952, but its history dates back much farther. Maui's first Christian service was conducted here outdoors in 1823 by two missionaries brought to Lahaina by Keopuolani, queen of Kamehameha the Great and mother of Kamehameha II and Kamehameha III. Since 1832, when the first permanent building went up, the mission has been re-established again and again after fires and windstorms damaged its churches. In the cemetery, planted with fragrant plumerias and ancient palms, are gravestone inscriptions going back to 1823, including one for Keopuolani herself.

Hale Aloha was built in 1858 by Wainee Mission for an English school, parish house, occasional services. It's now crumbling but will be restored.

Maria Lanikila Church was built in 1928 to replace an 1858 frame structure whose establishment followed the celebration of Maui's first Catholic Mass on Lahaina beach in 1841.

Church of the Holy Innocents is a 1927 Episcopal church with paintings of a Hawaiian madonna and child and Hawaiian staffs of life—taro, fish, and breadfruit. It will be rebuilt in restoration style. Episcopal services at Lahaina go back to 1862 —the first in Hale Aloha.

Jodo Mission near old Mala Wharf (which inter-island ships used from 1922-41) has a Japanese Cultural Park commemorating first immigrants, with giant bronze statue of Buddha imported from Japan.

Hongwanji Temple has the largest Buddhist congregation and dates back to 1904. The present building was built in 1927. A tiny **Shingon Buddhist Temple** is on Chapel Street. The **Chee Kung Tong** (or Wo Hing) Chinese mutual aid society building, dating from 1912, has Oriental grilles on Victorian verandas and shrines still in use.

Restaurants and Shops

Lahaina itself has three kinds of eating places—bona fide restaurants, bars with food, and lunch counters—and in many, impromptu entertainment is usual at night. But west side visitors can choose a variety of cuisines in restaurants spread out over a dozen miles—from Olowalu to Napili. Several provide courtesy transportation from hotels. The larger places and hotel dining rooms have scheduled shows most nights.

Shops have the usual Hawaiian costumes and jewelry, woven and wood pieces, imports from the Orient and South Seas, and of course, black and pink coral—fun to shop for where the craft originated and divers go after it. In town note the restoration complexes—Pioneer Inn, Whaling Port Arcade, Arbor Shops (a remodeled bowling alley), which has Lahaina Restoration Foundation's Lahaina Book Shoppe (good Hawaiiana including records); old establishments like the bakery, dry goods store, mango and papaya stand, Lahaina Poi Factory—*poi, kulolo* and *haupia* (coconut puddings) to take out—and markets, some with Lahaina-made *pupus* (hors d'oeuvres); Lahaina Yacht Club; Martin Gallery (paintings).

To Lahainaluna

Lahainaluna Road shortened to L'Luna on signs) takes you from Lahaina past Pioneer Mill (the sugar company dates from 1860) on a 1½-mile climb (with a panoramic view coming down) to Lahainaluna School, started by missionaries in 1831, chiefly to train teachers. The oldest American school west of the Rockies, L'Luna has

Hawaii's first newspaper *was printed in this coral stone building on the campus of Lahainaluna School.*

been a public school since 1923. It is also a boarding school, agricultural school, and vocational school—and there's no other in the country quite like it. On the tree-shaded campus is Hale Pa'i, built in 1836 of plastered coral to house the press used to print textbooks and Hawaii's first newspaper. Now a printing museum, it has a working model of the original press and a collection of the early printing—newspapers, money, tracts, hymnals, a Bible, and a Hawaiian-English dictionary.

Lahaina to Honokohau

At Lahaina's north edge, you'll find remains of a Royal Coconut Grove (young palms are growing to take the place of ones planted in 1847 and succumbing to wind, old age), and Wahikuli Beach Park—Sand Box Beach (a favorite of local residents), improved with more sand, shade trees, places to picnic and change clothes.

Not all of Kaanapali is hotels and golf courses. Uphill from the highway, there are still cane fields, and even a plantation camp, Puukolii, with numbered houses, old trees, and two churches (one abandoned).

Continuing north, you'll pass small beaches (including Honokowai Beach Park), tourist compounds, scattered bungalows and tiny wooden churches, and finally Napili Bay with informal inns that share one another's resources (grocery stores, restaurant). A road up the mountainside, between two rows of Norfolk pines, leads to Pineapple Hill, plantation home turned dining spot.

Beyond Napili are a series of beaches favored — and nicknamed—by the local people. Kapalua Bay (Fleming's Beach) is the exquisite, palm-fringed crescent of sand you've seen pictured in travel folders. It's still a little park, with picnic tables and rest rooms, but soon a 350-acre resort and residential development will go up here and over the pineapple-covered hills to the north. Oneloa (Beach Camp) Beach is ½ mile farther, beyond the lighthouse. Honokahua (Ball Park or Stable Point) Beach (where only experts swim and surf) is at the foot of a gulch in Honokahua village. It is opposite a tiny green church and grassy playing field set in a eucalyptus grove.

A half mile farther at Makuleia Bay (Slaughterhouse Beach) teen-agers haul their boards down a path from the road above for winter surf. About two miles beyond, a short spur (walk if it is muddy) levels down to Honolua Bay which surfers rate tops and yachtsmen praise as an anchorage; campers use a grassy clearing where there are firepits and water. Swimmers can avoid the pebbly beach by walking down a boat ramp.

Honokohau to Wailuku

Windmill Beach, 1½ miles farther, is usually windy and its water rough; but on glassy days it is splendid for diving. At Honokohau Valley, the route number changes to

33 for a narrow, twisting, up-and-down gravel road (some 15 miles, but being improved) that bears the euphemism, Kahekili Highway—it follows the course of an old royal horse trail. Honokohau is a jungle of fruit trees. Drive into the valley a little way to see taro cultivated beside the stream and orchids on the slope.

Between Honokohau and a lighthouse at the island's north point, you cross weathered sandstone bluffs of various hues. There's a blow hole on the jagged coast not far south of the lighthouse, and just before you dip down into Kahakuloa village you can try whacking a roadside boulder known as the Bell Stone with a rock or something hard. No special resonance results but the stone is well worn from eons of trial bangs.

Kahakuloa, in the midst of cattle country and guarded to the south by a bold headland, is a cluster of wooden shacks with iron roofs fringed by a patchwork of taro at the mouth of a green valley. Villagers still pound *poi*, raise pigs, fish, beat the washing on rocks in the stream—but watch television. For 9 more miles, you wind along cliffs above fern gulches that stretch to the sea. Just after you reach paved road, a spur goes into Waihee Valley where more taro is grown. Waihee, 4 miles from Wailuku, has its churches (page 98), musty remains of a sugar mill, a beachcombers' shore and snorkelers' reef.

Haleakala

In the overlook atop Haleakala, Maui's 10,023-foot volcano, a National Park Service marker points out that the paved road you just traveled is the only one in the world that in just 40 miles takes you from sea level up so high. It doesn't need to tell you that the climb and summit views are spectacular. Off to the southeast are the tops of Hawaii's Mauna Loa and Mauna Kea floating in a sea of clouds. As you turn clockwise, other islands and the rest of Maui come into view—unless clouds below blanket them. The air is bracing, probably 30 degrees cooler than that you left behind. In winter you may encounter snow and temperatures below freezing.

Haleakala National Park takes in the summit and astonishing crater of this dormant volcano which last erupted about 1790, low down on its southwest flank. It was from the crater rim that the demigod Maui allegedly snared the sun; thus the name Haleakala—"house of the sun." The crater is a vast depression carved out of Haleakala's dome by centuries of erosion and partially filled by later volcanic activity with colorful cones and windswept banks of cinders. It is 7½ miles long, 2½ miles wide, 21 miles around, 3,000 feet deep, and covers 19 square miles.

The park has recently been enlarged to 23,000 acres

Sun-warmed sand *and a feathery fringe of palms — this is Kapalua (Fleming's) Beach, a photographer's delight.*

by the inclusion of part of Kipahulu Valley and the Seven Pools at its mouth—some 4,300 acres. The lower region will gradually be developed for recreation, but virgin forest above 3,100 feet is a preserve for scientific purposes. Besides rare native plants, it has native birds (among them several honeycreepers including the Maui Nukupuu) long considered extinct.

The Drive to the Top

Call park headquarters for a weather prediction before you start the 1½-hour drive from Kahului to the summit (routes 37, 377, 378). Coloring in the crater shows up best in the afternoon, but after 10 A.M., clouds often roll in. You climb through cane fields, then pineapple, into the Kula upland—note eucalyptus groves, commercial flower gardens. From the turnoff onto route 378, you follow a serpentine up through pastures (with pheasant and quail as well as cattle), and perhaps a layer of clouds, into a wasteland of rock and weird plants.

Park headquarters (open daily, 7:30-4) is at 7,030 feet, a mile past the entrance. Here you obtain the permit required for going into the crater even a short way and can get help in planning crater trips. You can also pick up a free park map-guide and leaflet on silverswords, a low-cost *Hiker's Guide,* and booklets on the plants, wildlife, geology, and history. You can picnic and camp in Hosmer Grove, ½ mile below park headquarters, amid North American pine, cedar, juniper, and spruce trees,

Slopes of smooth cinder *lie below rocky rim of Haleakala Crater. Clouds billow in through Koolau Gap.*

deodar from India, cryptomeria from Japan, and eucalyptus from Australia; trees are labeled along a short trail.

There are several places to stretch your legs in the 9½ miles between park headquarters and the top. At 8,000 feet, walk a mile on Halemauu Trail to the crater rim to look across Koolau Gap, down Keanae Valley, and upon the trail ahead zigzagging down the crater wall. The view is similar from Leleiwi Overlook, which has interpretive exhibits and is only a 350-foot walk from the road. Here, at 8,800 feet, is the best place to see the Spectre of the Brocken which may occur in late afternoon (you see your shadow against clouds and encircled by a rainbow).

There's a road to Kalahaku Overlook, just above, which once had a rest house where travelers on foot or horseback stayed before the Haleakala road was built. Today you'll find exhibits on the crater's cones and lava flows and an enclosure of Haleakala's famous silverswords. These rare relatives of the sunflower are a species which evolved in and is unique to this isolated habitat (except for a few plants on the Big Island). The plants grow 7 to 30 years as mounds of silvery spiney leaves before blooming. Then blossom stalks shoot up as high as 9 feet from May to November and produce 100 or more tiny purplish flowers. After they bloom, the plants die—but not until they have dropped seeds to start others.

At the top are two observatories with displays: Haleakala Visitor Center (daily, 8:30-3:30; ranger on hand)

on the rim at 9,745 feet; and Puu Ulaula Visitor Center (always open, unmanned), ½ mile up on Red Hill, the summit.

The exhibits at Haleakala Center explain the crater's features and formation. You look down on slopes of cinder blown by the easterly trade winds against the rocks of the original rim, cut by Koolau Gap on the north and Kaupo on the south. Beyond Koolau, the peak, Hanakauhi ("Maker of Mists"), often protrudes from a blanket of clouds. On the opposite rim, Haleakala Peak stands out like a fortress above Kaupo Gap. Symmetrical cones of varied hues may look like small mounds of sand, but each is several hundred feet high; the largest, Puu O Maui, rises 1,000 feet from the crater floor. In remarkable contrast to the naked summit slopes are the meadow and stand of trees at the crater's east end, 7 miles away, where the annual rainfall is 250 inches.

From Haleakala Center a trail goes up 380 yards to White Hill, past ruins of stone wind barriers Hawaiians built for sleeping enclosures. The hill is andesite, lighter in color and with more silicon and sodium than most Hawaiian lava. Here is where Sliding Sands Trail starts. A walk down a little way gives you the feel of the crater, but it's a tiring climb back at this altitude.

From Puu Ulaula Center you have a 360-degree panorama—of the crater and, on a clear day, West Maui and all the Neighbor Islands but Kauai and Niihau. It's rare to be "all socked in," unable even to see a piece of the chasm. You can continue for a mile beyond the park, along dead-end Skyline Drive through "Science City," with its domes and antennae for communications and space study. You'll have a precipitous view down to the Lualailua Hills and the south coast desert.

Crater Hiking or Horseback Trips

To qualify as a true crater-goer, you should go down inside. The park service maintains 30 miles of well-marked trails and three rustic cabins (with everything but food) for 12 persons. It charges each cabin-user a small daily fee and takes reservations only 6 months in advance. In summer (through September), the best time for crater-visiting, cabins are hard to get on short notice. If you want to hike or ride horseback for the usual two or three days, write Haleakala National Park (Box 456, Kahului) and give exact dates, the number in your party, and which cabins (Kapalaoa, Paliku, Holua) you wish to use. Or ask the park service to work out your itinerary and hold the cabins necessary.

Frank Freitas (Box 50, Makawao) is the park service-sanctioned guide for horseback trips (horses are not rented for unguided trips). He takes parties of up to 7 persons, gets permits, arranges for cabins, and provides horses, food — and the cooking. He also offers a pack service to hikers who want supplies taken into the crater. No guide service is available or necessary for hikers, or riders who have their own horses.

Two main routes into and through the crater are each about 10 miles long and meet near Paliku Cabin at the east end. Sliding Sands Trail takes you from the top down and along the south face to Kapalaoa Cabin (about 6 miles); then you go northeast for 3½ miles to Paliku.

On Halemauu Trail you descend the west wall to Holua Cabin (4 miles), then go 6 more miles, mostly eastward, along the center of the sloping floor. Cross trails and side trails on the bottom connect the two routes and lead to various points of interest.

If you're going full circuit, go in on Sliding Sands and out on Halemauu (avoid Sliding Sands as a way out); drive two cars to the park so you can leave one at the start of each trail—or someone will have to hike extra miles up the road. For a long (12 miles) day's hike or horseback ride, go down Sliding Sands, cross the floor on Ka Moa O Pele Trail, and climb out on Halemauu. A good overnight trip (and there's no car problem) is to take Halemauu all the way to Kapalaoa Cabin one day (about 8 miles) and return the next. In a half day you can make a round trip on Halemauu as far as Holua Cabin. The 8-mile Kaupo Gap Trail between Paliku and Kaupo village on the south shore is practical going downhill—an alternate way out (arrange to be met).

Here are some of the things to see down in this weird environment: native shrubs with unusual flowers or berries; sandalwood trees; lichen, or Hawaiian Snow, the first plant to appear after a lava flow in higher altitudes; mountain *pili,* distinct from the lowland variety once used for grass houses; stone altars, shelters, and platforms, evidences of early Hawaiian encampments; volcanic dikes, remnants of the divide that once separated the heads of Keanae Valley (Koolau Gap) and Kaupo Valley.

Rare silversword plant *blooms only once, then dies. Easiest place to see plants is at Kalahaku Overlook.*

North of Kapalaoa is Bubble Cave, formed when molten lava was forced up by gases and stayed in that position until it cooled; later part of the top fell in and created a natural opening. At rainy Paliku, large native trees (*'ohi'a, kolea, 'olapa*), tall grass, and ferns create a green haven in the barren waste. Here you occasionally see the *nene,* or Hawaiian goose (the state bird). From Paliku, hike Lauula Trail (2.3 miles) to the top of Kalapawili Ridge for a look into the Kipahulu forest and down Kaupo Gap.

On Halemauu Trail you pass Bottomless Pit, an old spatter vent which looks like a well about 10 feet across. It has a bottom, 65 feet down, so keep away from the crumbly edges. Nearby are Pele's Paint Pot, a colorful pass between cinder cones; and on a cross trail, Pele's Pig Pen, a half-buried spatter vent. Near Holua Cabin you'll find the Silversword Loop Trail, lava tubes (don't enter them), and old Hawaiian adze quarries.

Going Around Haleakala

The 130-mile route around mighty Haleakala is a possible—but not recommended—one-day drive. Fortunately it divides naturally at Hana on the east coast where there are places to stay and to camp. Unfortunately, both the north coast road (route 36) from Kahului to Hana (some 50 miles), and the southern route (31), about 75 miles long, much of it over a rough, unpaved road (see page

Hawaii's state bird, *the nene, is sometimes seen here. Once almost extinct, it was reintroduced in park in 1962.*

Japanese bell *at Buddhist temple in Lower Paia is sounded by swinging wooden shaft against it.*

109), are easier driving toward Hana. On route 36 you're then on the inside lane when the road edges cliffs high above the sea. On route 31 heading northeast—toward the wind—dust blows past the car and not into it.

Traveling the entire loop is worth putting up with a little discomfort. With time for only a part, take the easier, more scenic northern road. And don't miss the splendid country that stretches 20 miles north and south of Hana town. There are several ways to see the area: You can stay in Hana and explore; make a day-long round trip from Central Maui on route 36—and go south as far as Kipahulu (drive yourself or arrange a tour); drive one way and fly the other; or take a one-day air tour that includes motoring in the Hana region (see page 94).

The Northern Road to Hana

Plan 2½ hours to drive the Hana Highway (route 36) from Kahului as you'll negotiate hundreds of curves, most of them on the last 30 miles of narrow road. You start on a straight course through cane fields, bypassing Spreckels-ville's gracious homes, and Maui Country Club (to see them, drive route 32 past the airport, then east on a dead-end road that parallels the beach).

Just before Lower Paia, you'll find H. A. Baldwin Park on the beach and beside it, Rin Zai Zen Buddhist Mission notable for its graveyard with Okinawan-style family mausoleums—like miniature houses. Right in the little plantation town are an art gallery in a remodeled theater and a handsome Soto Buddhist Temple with a massive gong alongside that is struck 18 times at dawn and dusk. The graveyard above a sandy cove has markers carved with Japanese characters.

Take a side road inland marked to Maui High School to see the ruins of Hamakuapoko Mill which functioned from 1890 to 1906. This was where the first American flag was raised after annexation. Turn left just before the school, and you'll see the vine-covered stone walls in a cane field. For more on the roads up through this plantation country, see Kula Route, page 110.

The highway passes Hookipa Beach Park and Maliko Bay, and—about 20 miles from Kahului—an easy-to-reach swimming hole, Twin Falls, fed by the divided watercourse of a mountain stream. There's a sign at the start of a short trail 1¾ miles beyond Kakipi Gulch.

By now you're on a road that hangs on ferny, pandanus-laden cliffs that drop off to the pounding surf. It twists in and out of green gulches adorned with sparkling pools and waterfalls, in a jungle of breadfruit, *koa, kukui, 'ohi'a,* and paperbark trees, groves of bamboo, tangled *hau* and guava, giant *a'pe* leaves, wild ginger, even rubber trees. In this country people still live off land and sea and are respectful of the legends breathed by every cliff and hollow. Villages are but a sprinkling of houses and a general store, and you'll spot one-room schools and century-old churches. One, Kaulanapueo Church in the Huelo region, is beautifully kept and used once a month. Turn downhill at the church sign just before Kailua town.

Shady Kaumahina State Park sits atop a cliff overlooking Honomanu Gulch and Keanae Peninsula to the south. Far below you'll glimpse Honomanu Bay's black sand beach where natives fish and swim. Then from several high points you look down upon Keanae and Wailua, their cluster of houses, church steeples, banana groves, and taro patches like South Seas scenes.

Take the side road down onto Keanae Peninsula, past the pebbly cove where villagers launch their skiffs, wooden houses where you may find someone pounding taro in the back yard, and the coral stone church, more than 100 years old that its few member families have refurbished—with aid from other churches. Watch the surf pummel the lava shore—the jagged rocks glisten from their constant washing. On a clear day, Haleakala looms up to the south. Ask if you can walk through the fenced taro fields at the end of the road to the stream. From the rocky beach at the mouth of the stream, there's a good view south along the jagged coast. You can swim upstream, between cliffs hung with ferns and ginger, into an oval pool with a waterfall so forceful you can only thrash your way up to the foam.

There's another part of Keanae above the peninsula—more houses, a store. Just before you reach them the road goes inland and bridges a gulch; you can walk to swimming holes above and below the bridge.

The spur road to Wailua village passes the churches, some houses fronted with rows of *ti* and crotons, and ends above a narrow cove at the mouth of the stream. Here villagers put out in fishing boats and children body surf with homemade boards in the late afternoon while their elders relax on their porches and read, or just sit. Quaint St. Gabriel's with its painted trim of red hearts is known as the Miracle Church. It is said that in 1865 when its builders set out to dive for coral and sand, they found them heaped on shore by waves. Some graveyard markers have photographs; most are decorated—usually with artificial flowers in bottles of water.

Take the road inland past Wailua's other row of houses for a close look at the taro and bananas grown for Central Maui and Honolulu markets. The geometrically terraced plots are in a gently-rising valley guarded by mountain walls and as neat as a memorial park. Irrigation water trickles downhill from one patch to another in the old Hawaiian manner and the strips between for walking are carefully power-mowed.

From Keanae Lookout you have a two-way view: down over Wailua to the sea which breaks against Keanae Peninsula in the distance, and up through Keanae Valley to Koolau Gap in Haleakala's rim. The narrow road bridges a rushing stream and waterfalls in almost every gulch and for a time follows a portion of open ditch, part of the system which carries water from Haleakala's north slopes to the Central Maui agricultural belt. A sign points out the Maui Ditch Trail (see Hiking, page 97). Stop for a dip at Puaa Kaa State Park where you can choose between two crisp, fern-banked pools, each with a waterfall.

Three miles of rocky road take you down through Nahiku village, now mostly forest-covered, past its few scattered houses, school, and two churches, to ruins of the landing used at the turn of the century to unload equipment for building irrigation tunnels through the mountain. You'll see trees left from Nahiku's rubber plantation of more than 50 years ago and can try out two good swimming holes: one reached by a path from the turnaround at the landing, and the other, Hinamoo, about 400 feet from the bridge a few turns above.

The road on to Hana crosses much grazing land. A branching 3-mile jeep road leads to Ulaino where a rushing stream drops into a natural fresh-water swimming pool at the ocean's edge. About half way you pass close to a National Historic Landmark, Hawaii's largest discovered *heiau*, Piilanihale, near Kalahu Point. Its 340 by 425-foot platform has terraces on two sides that rise to 50 feet; a 10-foot wall about 10 feet thick encircles the other sides. Piilanihale is believed to have been built by a Maui chief in the sixteenth century, and other ruins nearby indicate this was the site of an entire village.

A side road to Hana Airport cuts through a pandanus forest. Another (2 miles from Hana) goes to Waianapanapa State Park, with cabins (see page 94). There's a footpath to Waianapanapa and Waiomao caves, two lava tubes near the sea, filled with water and said to be connected. In Waianapanapa cave, a legendary princess was killed by her jealous husband—he swung her by the feet and bashed out her brains on the cave's roof. Hawaiians tell you the mineral deposits you see are her brains mixed with blood and that cave water still runs red in April, the month the slaying occurred. Certainly Waianapanapa is a properly spooky place to swim. Daring souls take a flashlight and swim underwater—past a point where the roof arches down—into another chamber with a rock ledge said to be the throne where the princess hid. Waiomao's pool is too shallow and stagnant for swimming.

Out on a point you'll see a natural rock arch and blow hole, and on the grassy ledge over the sea (you can hear water gurgling underneath), are three old burial grounds that are still in use. Below, fringing Pailoa Bay, is Honokalani black sand beach; scout for beach glass and swim when the bay is calm. You can walk an old Hawaiian shoreline trail all the way to Hana; sections are paved with smooth stones, now eroded. About 1/4 mile north, toward the airport, the trail passes early surface graves, on top of the clinkery *aa* rock, and a small *heiau*.

Like a patchwork quilt, *taro plots on Keanae Peninsula stretch out below as you look down from the road.*

Hana

Hana town (population 600) is inhabited mostly by part-Hawaiians who work on the Hana Ranch or its resort. Evidences of the area's once-large Polynesian settlement are taro patches, banana clumps, and bits of stone terraces in nearby gulches. Subsequent sugar plantations were marginal and finally sold, and since 1944, the fields have been converted to grazing land for 5,000 white-faced Hereford beef cattle. Drive a mile to the top of Mount Lyons, a cinder cone above town, to a stone cross on a torchlighted platform, a memorial to Paul Fagan that overlooks the ranch and hotel he founded.

One of few modern notes for miles around is Hana's compact shopping center, with even a wide-screen theater. But "Main Street" still has the Hasegawa General Store, subject of a popular song, and a fascinating Buddhist temple, part missionary, part Oriental in style; and Sunday services are still conducted in Hawaiian and English at century-old Wananalua Church, built of lava rock by hand over a 20-year period.

From the Hana school, site of an early war *heiau*, walk to the summit of Kauiki Head, the fortress-like cliff guarding Hana Bay. Here armies of Kamehameha and the king of Maui tangled with slingshots. From Hana pier you can walk along the base of the cliff to a plaque on the ocean side that marks the birthplace of Kamehameha's wife, Kaahumanu, in a cave above; then, for a good off-shore view of the bay, cross a little wooden bridge to a rocky islet with an automatic lighthouse. The bay is always calm for swimming in front of the community pavilion (rest rooms, showers). Don't let the gray coloring of the sand disturb you—that's just decomposed lava mixed in. On the north side, off Hana Kai Resort, is Keanini Surf—for boards. Drive through Waikaloa settlement on the north shore, through a dense *kamani* grove and past old-time Hana houses—box-like, dark green, their gardens overflowing with red *ti*. Walk from the school down the south side of Kauiki Head to an old Japanese cemetery, then on to a small red cinder beach and tiny ocean swimming pool guarded by a lava dike.

Hana to Kaupo

South of Hana you travel route 31, an increasingly bad road with an impressive name—Piilani Highway. At the edge of town a dirt road goes off to Lehoula Beach, one of two beaches reserved for Hotel Hana Ranch guests. The other is Hamoa, a few miles on and along a side road loop that passes remains of Hale O Lono Heiau (on the inland side) and turns north along rocky Haneoo Beach, where you can walk through a lava arch. Offshore you'll see the outline of once-sacred Kuula's fishpond (Hawaiians will not disturb the stones). You can walk to Koki Beach (swimming is unsafe) below the hill north of the stretch of the loop road nearest Hana. The fire goddess, Pele, is said to have left her bones on this hill when she finished her Maui work and assumed a new body before leaving for the Big Island.

At Puuiki, drive up the hill to St. Peter's, descended from East Maui's first Catholic church. Perhaps someone in the village will guide you to the pictographs of Waiohonu Stream, located on cliffs about 200 yards inland of the bridge but hard to find. The unexplained figures, quite like a child's "match men," were painted with a red dye which has withstood years of weathering.

On Muolea Point, with its grove of coconuts, are stone ruins of royal summer houses; you can walk down to them over the meadow. Where the road turns into Wailua Gulch, you'll see two mighty falls toppling hundreds of feet of water off Haleakala's slopes. The concrete cross on a high mound between road and sea is a memorial to Helio, a Hawaiian who became a Catholic in 1840 and converted several thousand Mauians to his new faith even before the Catholic priests arrived on the island. Near a plaque, a trail down the Hana side of the divided gulch leads to ruins of Helio's village, Wailua. South of Wailua Falls are gnarled *kukui* trees on the mountainside, remains of a sacred grove. A few more turns bring you to the "Virgin by the Roadside," a shrine with a marble statue from Italy. Every day it is draped with leis, and once a year a pilgrimage is made to it from all Hana Catholic churches.

Demonstration *of poi pounding, lei making, exhibits of Island fruits, flowers on grounds of Hotel Hana Ranch.*

From the bridge over Kipahulu Valley's Oheo Gulch, you look uphill or down on the justly-famous Seven Pools, now part of Haleakala National Park. One pool drops into another all the way to the sea. It's easy to swim in those below the bridge—a path goes down the south bank; and you can hike up the stream bed to several above. You can also hike up through pasture south of the stream to Waimoku Falls at 1,200 feet (called Kipahulu Falls on roadside marker). Paved road ends at Kipahulu Ranch headquarters, near an old mill stack and restored mission church (white, green trim) with chandeliers to hold candles. You look up the valley to Haleakala's rim from its banyan-shaded front yard, or down to the sea from its cliff-top graveyard.

The *pali* (cliff) drive on to Kaupo is exciting when the one-lane gravel road hugs the edge of rocky cliffs above the water and dips straight down into gulches. If you meet a car (quite unlikely), one of you may have to back up to find a safe shoulder. The country is drier here, with open pastures divided by lichen-covered stone walls, and abundant *hau* and *koa haole* trees. The road edges so close to Lelekea Bay that a heavy sea will send spray right into your car. You'll see a few outrigger canoes on the rocky beach. A switchback trail visible on the hillside just south is the remains of the old king's highway.

Kaupo's quaint Hui Aloha Church and tidy graveyard sit out on a grassy peninsula, an inviting place to picnic or camp. You can explore nearby ruins of a mission school, and a *heiau* on the hill above the road. A larger temple, Loaloa, is at the start of Kaupo Gap Trail, behind the school off the spur road to Kaupo Ranch headquarters. A National Historic Landmark, it has a platform of several hundred square feet, was probably built about 1730 by a Maui king, Kekaulike.

Kaupo to Ulupalakua

You have come about 20 miles from Hana, have more than 20 to go over a road even worse before you reach civilization again at Ulupalakua Ranch. Stop at Kaupo Store (open odd hours) whether you need something or not. It has a hitching rail for horses, doubles as post office (all mail goes in one box which people hunt through).

In this lonely, desolate country are rewards for the explorer: ruins of old settlements few have seen, some perhaps not even discovered. You'll have more exciting views of the coastline and distant Hawaii island as you dip down to the sea at old Nuu Landing where there are village ruins and a salt pond. Here the road widens and you climb gradually toward Kanaio through a bizarre landscape that includes a Hawaiian dryland forest, more pastures, fields of yellow poppies, old lava flows, cinder

Kipahulu's Seven Pools *cascade into one another out to the sea—a dramatic spot for a picnic or refreshing swim.*

cones. About a mile beyond Nuu you cross a dry river bed, gutted by centuries of flash floods; you can walk up to a pool at the head of the gulch where there are caves and petroglyphs. Halfway or more is the old Kahikinui ranch house and nearby, below the road, the crumbling stone foundation of Santa Ynez Church, worshipping place of some Hawaiian Catholics whose arrest in the 1830's contributed to the subsequent granting of religious freedom.

You go along at an elevation of 1,500 feet but always there's the blue sea below with tiny, crescent-like Molokini island, still a revered home of ancestor spirits to some Hawaiians, and Kahoolawe, the uninhabited target island, hardly more forsaken than where you are. Down below are a few grueling jeep trails, including one which continues as a foot path to La Perouse Bay, past burial caves at Waiakapuhi. Between Kanaio and Ulupalakua you look down upon the surprisingly fresh-looking lava from Haleakala's last eruption some 200 years ago. Part of it flowed from Puu Mahoe, a cone just above the road. You can see Puu Olai cinder cone, a Makena landmark, jutting into the sea.

It's like finding an oasis to reach park-like Ulupalakua Ranch, Maui's largest, with its green lawns and knolls and stately trees (jacaranda, eucalyptus, camphor, pine, cypress). On the shoulder above the road just past the sign, "Hawaii 37 Ends," you'll find a Hawaiian sacred boulder to which offerings are still sometimes made. It is supposed to be a man molded in lava by Pele, the volcano goddess, whom he had angered. Ulupalakua's verdure is said to result from the beneficence of a double-faced rain god which stands (out of sight) near the rambling frame ranch house built in 1857 by sea captain James Makee, who grew sugar here for 20 years. Cattle-raising was started after his time. You can see the Makee mausoleum on Keekeehia Hill, ruins of the Makee mill, and the signal gun Makee fired to welcome visiting ships to the bay nearly 2,000 feet below. Hawaii's last king, Kalakaua, had a hideaway cottage on the grounds, and the ranch office is in the Makee-built jail.

You can continue on route 31, down 4 miles of dirt road to Makena, then north along the coast through Kihei; or stay on high ground and take paved route 37.

The Kula Route

The high road and its offshoots travel Kula, where stands of eucalyptus break grasslands, farmers and gardeners grow plums, persimmons, delphiniums, and carnations, and you may have to stop to let a herd of cattle pass. St. John's Episcopal Church, a 1906 frame building with Chinese characters over the doorway and contemporary faceted-glass windows by Erica Karawina, was founded by a Chinese Lutheran minister who taught Chinese language and culture to immigrants' children. On the hill above are the walls and bell (but not the floor) of the 1852-53 Haleakala (or Keokea) Church of David Malo, early Christian convert who became an educator, minister, and historian. Kula's treasure is the 1897 Catholic Church of the Holy Ghost (on Old Kula Road above the highway). Its octagonal shape and several Portuguese inscriptions show the heritage of the original parishioners —mostly Portuguese immigrants. Note the exquisite steeple, gilded wooden bas reliefs, and large Austrian-made altar shipped in sections around Cape Horn.

From route 377 a dirt road climbs 10½ miles to Polipoli Spring, in a recreation area at the edge of a redwood and mixed hardwood forest (see Camping, Hiking, Hunting, pages 95 and 97). A car with high clearance is usually equal to the trip, perhaps even for another 1,000 feet to the top of Polipoli cinder cone, a Haleakala ridge vantage point from which you see West Maui, Kahoolawe, and Hawaii. A jeep trail continues to the summit. You can hike it up or down but to drive (advisedly

down), get permission from the State Forestry office, Wailuku. The spring is actually a man-made tunnel; the forest (with trails) contains some 35,000 redwoods planted in 1927, some now 4 feet in diameter and 80 feet tall.

Highway 37 is the direct way to Kahului, but if you have time take route 40 from Pukalani Junction past Dick's Hawaiian Crafts (original wood pieces) to Makawao, then any of several roads to shore. Tree-lined Baldwin Avenue passes side roads to Haliimaile (an attractive plantation town) and Mauna Olu College (in some historic buildings), and goes by Rainbow Park (summer-blooming shower trees). If you go down to Haiku, ask the way to the Japanese folk garden.

South Seas and Old West meet at Makawao, but its Club Rodeo serves gourmet food and fine wines. Its dominant church, Makawao Union, is English Country Gothic. Route 39 climbs 5 miles up rainy slopes to Olinda. Watch for coral stone Pookela Church, missionary-built in 1850; small farms; large residences, one the nucleus of the state's only girls' boarding school, Seabury Hall; and Olinda Honor Camp which sells woodwork.

The Makena-Kihei Route

Where route 31 meets shore, go south a mile to Makena's 1838 Keawalai Church, still well-kept. It was a busy place when Ulupalakua was planted to sugar and Makena was Maui's second-ranking port. Adjacent graves, some marked with photographs, are built above ground—Hawaiians found the lava too hard for digging.

If the rocky, rutty road is dry, continue south 3 more miles to La Perouse Bay, named for a French explorer who anchored in 1786, was greeted by the natives, then sailed away and mysteriously disappeared at sea. You'll pass ruins, go through an enchanting kiawe forest with openings to smooth beaches and views of Puu Olai promontory and Molokini and Kahoolawe islands, bump your way over Haleakala's last lava flow, see fishermen's shacks, campers' tents, and cactus that sprouted from a few plants introduced by Latin American cowboys.

From Makena Junction north to Kihei, you travel 8½ dirt and paved miles along a sandy shore with lava points, coral reefs, more kiawe, beach parks, beach homes, and growing hotel cottage and apartment colonies—the beginnings of massive resort development (see Where To Stay, page 94). Kihei's St. Theresa Church has a Hawaiian madonna carved in wood. Ask at Kilolani Church how to get to the ruins of David Malo's Kalepolepo sanctuary. Crumbling stone walls, 2½ feet thick and probably 130 years old, lie ¼ mile into kiawe forest south of town, edged by forlorn Lihue Cemetery. From Kihei, take route 35 to Kahului, or route 31 past Maalaea Bay, then route 30—left to Lahaina, right to Wailuku.

Towering cliffs, *broken by green-carpeted valleys untouched by roads, mark the windward coast of Molokai.*

MOLOKAI...the Friendly Isle

Molokai is today's closest approximation of old-time Hawaii—with the exception of Niihau, which is privately owned and cannot be visited by the public. This island lies closest to Honolulu and abounds in typical Hawaiian scenery, yet has only an infant tourist industry. The inhabitants have been almost indifferent to the hordes of vacationers passing by on flights to Maui and Hawaii, but all strangers are welcomed with good-natured amiability. This unaggressive attitude toward visitors is a refreshing — though sometimes exasperating — travel experience.

Hawaii's fifth largest island is one of plantations and pastures, little farms and big ranches, arid plains and lushly grown mountains. On a map it is shoe-shaped, long (37 miles), and narrow (10 miles). It was formed by two major volcanic domes. The western end of the island, first to be built up, is now a tableland called Mauna Loa that rises to only 1,381 feet. The jagged mountains of the northeast, topped by 4,970-foot Kamakou, were formed later by the East Molokai volcano. Kalaupapa, the little tongue of land that juts out from the north coast, is like an afterthought; Kauhako, the volcano which created it, is much younger.

Molokai is called the Friendly Isle now, but it was the Lonely Isle for half a century after sufferers of leprosy were first segregated on naturally-isolated Kalaupapa Peninsula 100 years ago.

Until recently the scarcity of water in the right places has been the island's biggest problem. A 5-mile tunnel to carry water through the mountains from wet, uninhabited Waikolu Valley to the thirsty western plains has already upped pineapple production and encouraged the growth of seed grain and other crops. Another big development push will come when the world's largest rubber-lined earth reservoir, at Kualapuu, is finished in 1970. With an assured water supply, plans are in the works for a tourist mecca. Near the turn of the century, Molokai's population was only 1,000, but the increased agricultural activity has already pushed the figure close to 6,000.

The western third of the island is Molokai Ranch, Ltd., much of it leased to pineapple growers. Before long, some 6 or 8 miles of the western shore will become a mammoth residence-resort area to be called Kaluakoi. On the other side of the island, a big development is coming at Keawanui—in fact over all the southeast coast to

Kalaupapa's light, *now automatic, is one of Pacific's strongest, sits atop one of country's tallest lighthouses.*

Halawa Valley. The center of the island has homesteaders, most of whom grow pineapple for the large companies. A cinder-sand shipping industry that serves Oahu has Molokai prepared for its own building boom.

You can see the Island's produce at the Molokai District Fair at Kaunakakai in August.

How to Get There

Molokai lies 26 miles southeast of Oahu and is just 9 miles from Maui. Aloha Airlines, Hawaiian Airlines, and Air Hawaii have daily flights between Honolulu and Molokai Airport at Hoolehua, about a half hour trip. Most return flights start on Maui and some stop on Lanai. Sky Tours Hawaii and Royal Hawaiian Air Service stop on call at Molokai Airport.

Between Honolulu and Kalaupapa Airport, Air Hawaii, Royal Hawaiian Air Service, and Sky Tours Hawaii have daily flights; some trips include stops at Molokai

Airport (Hoolehua) and Lanai. Air Molokai has tours and charter flights to all Molokai airstrips and to all Neighbor Islands except Kauai. A Kalaupapa visit is a separate trip that must be made within a day (there are no places to sleep or eat). But there's time to tour the peninsula between morning and afternoon flights, and on the return trip you can get off at Hoolehua and stay over to see the rest of the island. You have an hour-long Kalaupapa visit on the all-islands-in-a-day trip of Sky Tours Hawaii.

One day is practical for Molokai proper, too, if you're content to drive just to the most celebrated places — Halawa Valley and the lookouts over Kalaupapa. But the best reasons for going to Molokai — to explore and to "get away from it all" — take more time.

Where to Stay

Molokai's first all-around tourist resort, the Hotel Molokai, is a few miles east of Kaunakakai on the island's south shore. Molokai Seaside Inn, a cluster of frame cottages and a restaurant at the edge of town, is unpretentious and inexpensive. The Kaunakakai Hotel in town caters to local businessmen.

Puu O Hoku Ranch Lodge is a resort for hunters. Situated at 700 feet on 22 square miles of rolling green hills at the island's eastern tip, it has a sweeping channel view, beaches, trails, swimming pool, and airstrip.

Hale Kai, at Kawaikapu, has cottages where everything is furnished except groceries (write Harold S. Wright, Box 939, Honolulu).

Getting Around on the Island

Molokai has rental cars—including a few jeeps—and guided tours. Make reservations through your hotel, airline, or a travel agent so that you will be met at the airport. Air Molokai (see How to Get There) will give you a bird's eye view of the island.

The island has just a few roads. Main routes are numbered and paved except for a few terminal stretches where you must contend with dirt and dust (generally red), rocks, ruts, and sometimes mud. A passenger car will get you most places during normal weather.

Kamehameha V Highway (45) follows the shore for 29 miles from Kaunakakai (8 miles from the airport) to Halawa, the island's easternmost point. Route 46 goes west from the airport through Molokai Ranch land to the Libby McNeill & Libby plantation headquarters at Mauna Loa (the village and post office are called Maunaloa). From here a private road climbs to Mauna Loa's summit, Puu Nana. Other roads, with locked gates, branch out to beaches; to Hale O Lono Harbor (where Papohaku sand is shipped, and outrigger canoes are launched in the annual

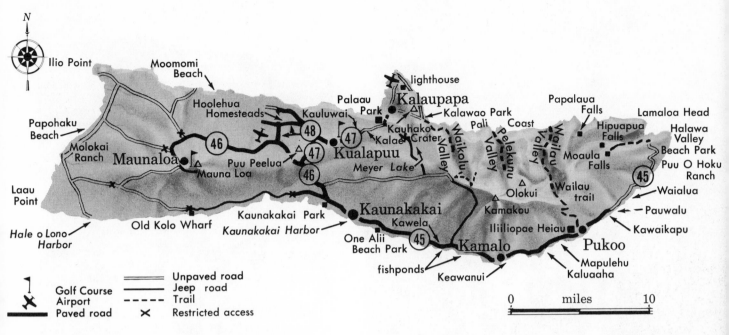

Aloha Week Molokai-to-Oahu race); and to the western points, Laau, and Ilio. You can sometimes get permission to use these roads at plantation headquarters or at the Molokai Ranch office in Kaunakakai. Route 47 goes to Palaau State Park and lookouts over Kalaupapa, route 48 to the Hoolehua Homesteads and more pineapple fields.

Sightseeing on Molokai is not without obstacles and frustrations. The compelling destinations are at the ends of unpaved roads, whereas the good roads take you through the less interesting country. Give-away maps do not show some place names, and some marked points of interest are difficult to find, disappointing, or on private property.

On the following pages you'll find directions for getting permission to visit the worthwhile places. Most landowners are trusting and informal and generally agreeable to trespassing by tourists who ask first.

Recreation on Molokai

Picnicking and Camping

Palaau Park, high in a handsome forest, covers some 233 acres and has a campground, picnic tables, shelter, rest rooms, and drinking water. Another fine spot for mountain camping is a meadow with a stream a few hundred yards east of Waikolu Valley Lookout. (Get permission to camp from the Division of Forestry in Kaunakakai or Honolulu.)

On weekends you'll see tents pitched here and there along the southeastern shore and people cooking out. One Alii Beach Park just east of Kaunakakai is a county-approved campsite with pavilion, rest rooms, drinking water, and wading pool (get permit from county agent, Kaunakakai). Adjacent Del Monte Park has several pavilions. Get permission to use this employee recreation area from the Del Monte Corporation in Kualapuu.

You can camp on the shores of Halawa and Wailau valleys and use water from the streams. The beach on the south side of Halawa is a county park with pavilions, rest rooms, showers, picnic and barbecue facilities. A grove of trees just above is a good place to camp. Wailau is accessible only by boat or long, arduous trail.

A Hawaiian Homes Commission Recreation Center at Moomomi Beach on the north shore has a pavilion and water. You can camp, fish, swim in a sheltered cove, and gather beach glass. To use the area, you'll have to pay a fee and get a key to the gate from the commission office in Hoolehua.

For just a picnic, there's hardly a finer spot than Kalawao Park.

Another pretty place is Kaunakakai Beach Park, in Kamehameha V's coconut grove.

Swimming

Shoals that fringe the shore from Kolo eastward are protected and safe, but mostly too shallow or silty for swimming. Farther north, around Waialua, are some deeper coves with sandy beach. The west end of the island has a handful of beautiful beaches but the roads to them are private and the water is frequently rough. When the sea is calm it's safe to swim at the entrances to Halawa, Wailau, and Pelekunu valleys, and their streams are fine

At Kalawao Park *you can picnic on grassy bluff above sea and watch surf crash into cliffs of Pali Coast.*

Hikers at Halawa. *From base of Lamaloa Head you look across bay to Halawa Cape, the island's eastern tip.*

for a dip. For an exhilarating plunge try the startling-cold fresh water in the pool beneath Moaula Falls (see Halawa Valley, page 118).

Hiking

The Wailau Trail across the island is for experienced hikers only. From Mapulehu you can walk over the mountains and out to the mouth of Wailau Valley in one day, camp there overnight, and walk back out the next day. The leeward ascent is on an easy-to-follow jeep trail (call Mrs. Pearl Friel at home or at the Bank of Hawaii in Kaunakakai for permission to cross private land). The descending trail is too overgrown to be discernible. You have to follow the stream out — for three or four hours.

Ask your hotel to find you a guide to take you up along the Waialua River to Pakaikai, homesite of an ancient chief, or if you are a good hiker, you can make your own way. Start east of the river, climb the ridge, circle around and come out at the top of the falls.

To hike in Halawa Valley you need permission from Puu O Hoku Ranch. It's an easy walk up to Moaula Falls (see Halawa Valley, page 118). To go on to the smaller pool at the base of Hipuapua Falls is tough — you have to scramble over rocks. You can also hike a jeep trail up the north wall of the valley, past Papa Heiau to the top of Lamaloa Head, and from there continue through forest and grasslands to where 1,000-foot falls drop into Papalaua Canyon.

From Wailau Valley you can walk about 2 miles west along the shore. A switchback trail connects Kalaupapa with Upper Molokai, and from Kalawao Park you can walk to Waikolu Valley (see Kalaupapa, page 119). Off the Waikolu Valley Lookout road are nine jeep or foot trails, most of them just a mile or two to the edge of the forest, but a few longer, out to spectacular view points (see Upper Molokai, page 115).

Fishing

Penguin Bank, a submarine shelf that juts 27 miles into the sea from Molokai's southwest corner, is one of Hawaii's most fertile fishing grounds. Fishing boats out of Honolulu frequently go here, and you can also charter a boat in Kaunakakai; tour operators will make arrangements. With a boat you can skin dive between Kolo and Kaunakakai. Spear fishing is good off Wailau and from Halawa south to Kamalo; shore casting and spin fishing, particularly for 'o'io and *ulua*, from Halawa all the way to Kaunakakai, and along west coast beaches.

Hunting

Molokai's public game management areas total 40,000 acres, all on the leeward side. Goats and boar may be hunted all year and birds on weekends and holidays during season (usually November 1 to mid-January). You obtain daily permits at the State Fish and Game Division office in Kaunakakai. Axis deer season is short (generally several weekends starting in late spring); hunting dates and areas are assigned at public drawings held at Fish and Game offices in Kaunakakai and Honolulu, where you can also get more information and buy annual hunting licenses. (When the India axis deer were given to Kamehameha V, they were released first on Molokai.)

Mammal hunting on private lands is unrestricted. Guests at the hunting lodges and Hotel Molokai go after deer, goats, and birds (in season) under a package that includes guide, equipment, license, and an assurance of game. Tour operators can direct you to guides for hunting in public areas and to a few who have hunting rights on private lands.

Golf

The island has two 9-hole courses. At Ironwood Hills Golf Course above Kualapuu, non-members pay a small greens fee and should make a reservation. The Mauna Loa course is for Libby McNeill & Libby employees, but visitors can call and usually arrange to play as guests.

Kaunakakai

Small Kaunakakai is a lively place. Virtually all Molokai trading takes place in wooden buildings (being restored to their former "plantation town" character) along its wide main street. Barges loading pineapple, and fishing boats add color to the big, busy wharf. People drive to town at least once a week to buy groceries and gossip. Saturday is the most popular day, and that night dances or parties go on at the inns—Kane's, Seaside, Mid-Nite, and Hele On which has dancing and shows every night but Monday.

The foundation of the home of Kamehameha V lies next to the wharf, and a park on the shore just west of town—take route 46—is in the extensive coconut grove he had planted 100 years ago. In several plots on the outskirts of the village, seed grains (mostly corn) are grown to supply Mainland farms in the Midwest.

Upper Molokai

You climb 11 miles from Kaunakakai to the crest of the island high above Kalaupapa, the last mile over an unpaved road (routes 46, 47). Route 48 branches toward the airport and Hoolehua Homesteads and offers a view over the gigantic new reservoir. From Kualapuu you can see a Hoolehua landmark, Puu Peelua, or Hill of the Caterpillar God, which got its name from a legend in which a Molokai girl's lover turned out to be a giant caterpillar. When the people tried to burn it, it released

Fortress-like cliffs *isolate Kalaupapa Peninsula from rest of Molokai. View is from lookout at Palaau Park.*

millions of small caterpillars, or army worms, now the island pest. Kamehameha the Great camped for a year at Kauluwai to get his troops conditioned and provisioned before attacking Oahu—which is visible from this high ground on clear days.

About 3 miles beyond Kualapuu is the FAA long-range Communication Center and Receiver Station for the Pacific Missile Range and the Apollo program. Visitors are welcome, and you will be fascinated by the types of antennae.

At Kalae — marked but inaccessible or not worth trying to find — are remains of a sugar mill, Molokai's first *kiawe* tree, and Waialala Spring, which, according to tradition, only one person could approach at a time.

Palaau Park

The road ends on a 1,600-foot cliff where the steep trail zigzags down to Kalaupapa, the only access by land to the settlement. The topside view of the cliffs stretching to the east is as awesome as the sight of the little peninsula laid upon the sea like a carpet; but a better vantage point is the lookout in Palaau Park. The park road, near the end of route 47, is a drive through a beautiful wilderness of *koa*, paperbark, ironwood, and cypress trees. It ends about a half mile beyond the main picnic area near a campground with pavilion and picnic table. Beyond is a small arboretum which has 40 species of trees labeled. A little farther along is the site of a new, larger pavilion and picnic area to be completed in 1970.

From here there are two short trails to walk. A footpath arched with ironwoods that has a cathedral quality leads to the Kalaupapa overlook (and another picnic table). You can make out the wharf, churches, lighthouse, landing field, crater, and other features of the peninsula whose story is told on a plaque at the viewing point. The other walk is along a truck trail carpeted with ironwood needles to a remarkable phallic rock. Walk about 200 yards, then turn right onto a narrow footpath that climbs about 50 yards to a starkly realistic image fashioned out of a 6-foot-high stone. Early Hawaiian women made offerings to the rock to achieve fertility (the rock was also supposed to have had power to make crops grow).

Waikolu Valley Lookout

You travel 10 long miles on a gravel and dirt road (much of it one lane wide) to reach the Waikolu Valley overlook. A passenger car will do in dry weather, but in a jeep you're not only safer but can explore some spur trails. The turn-off from route 46, opposite Molokai Aggregate Company, is marked "to Molokai Forestry Camp," which you reach just after leaving pasture land for forest reserve; it's a good place to check road conditions beyond. The forest, planted since 1900 as watershed, is splendid with pines, cedar, eucalyptus, 'ohi'a, ferns, and clumps of ginger.

When you've covered 9½ miles, watch for a sign that says Lua Moku Iliahi. It marks the Sandalwood Boat, a large depression in the ground the size and shape of a

Keawanui view *includes taro patch, walled fishponds built in semicircles out from shore.*

ship's hold, dug more than a century ago and used to measure the amount of sandalwood a ship could carry. Hawaiian chiefs bartered the wood for trinkets and whiskey and finery from white traders who in turn sold it at great profit, especially in China where it was prized.

At Waikolu Valley Lookout you step to the edge of a deep, narrow gorge laced with high waterfalls. This is the valley from which Kalaupapa takes its water supply and which sends irrigation water to the leeward plains — you can spot the tunnel. Waikolu is usually clear in the morning and you can see the little islet offshore. But in the cloud-filled valley of an afternoon you may see the rare Spectre of the Brocken — your shadow on the clouds framed by a rainbow.

A few hundred yards farther brings you to some abandoned buildings at the edge of a soft meadow sprinkled with plum trees. From here a foot trail (soon to become a road) goes to the head of Pelekunu Valley, and the main road becomes a jeep road going south for 12 miles to route 45 at Kawela. It has fine views of the fishponds below and of the islands of Lanai and Maui. Soon this stretch will be improved to take passenger cars.

If you have trouble turning a large car around at Waikolu lookout or at the meadow, back up to one of the jeep trails that take off from the lookout road. There are six up to the lookout and two beyond, most just a mile or two to the edge of the forest. The most interesting is Puu Kauwa, a 3-mile spur that connects with route 47 above Kalae. It overlooks Waihanau Stream and Kalawao and passes tiny Meyer Lake at 2,000 feet; but to drive or walk it, you need permission from Meyer Estate. Puu Kauwa is the prettier approach to Waikolu Valley Lookout and going out, or downhill toward Kalae, you can often make it in a passenger car. Check with State Division of Forestry offices in Kaunakakai or Honolulu for more information on this network of roads and trails.

The Southeastern Coast

Kaunakakai to Halawa (route 45) is less than 30 miles, but you should count on three to four times as many minutes to drive and sightsee. Beyond Mapulehu the road is rough, narrow, and winding, but with views to compensate for its shortcomings. You look across the narrow channels to Lanai and Maui. Inland are steep green mountain slopes topped by 4,970-foot Kamakou.

This coast has the only remaining concentration of fishponds in Hawaii (there are still a few scattered ponds on Oahu). These and several *heiaus* comprise the Hoku-kano-Ualapue National Historic Landmark complex. The ponds, a few still being used commercially, were built by Hawaiian kings and chiefs as long ago as the fifteenth century to fatten and store the good eating fish they wanted always available. They were enclosed by coral or basalt walls an average of 5 feet wide and 2 to 5½ feet high, and in many cases more than 2,000 feet long. Each had one or more breaks with grills just open enough to let in young fish, which became too fat to get out again once they had eaten.

There were once 58 ponds from Kolo to Waialua. Some have been deliberately filled in, others entirely or partially destroyed by silt from run-off or tidal action.

However, a few are being repaired and put to work again by the Oceanic Institute (the scientific relative of Sea Life Park at Makapuu, Oahu), which in 1965 began a five-year Rockefeller Foundation-supported project to experiment with fishponds as a possibility for increasing the tropical world's protein sources. You'll find Oceanic's field station beside its Alii Pond (26 acres, 2,700 feet of wall) on the Halawa side of One Alii Beach Park. Hotel Molokai is on the other.

Besides Alii, look for these ponds in either commercial or scientific use: Keawanui, a little beyond the Smith-Bronte flight marker (54½ acres, 2,000-foot wall, pre-16th century); Ualapue at Kaluaaha, offshore from Mystic Spring (with a wall 8 to 19 feet wide); and Kupeke, just east of Pukoo (alongside the road).

At Kawela, a couple of miles beyond Alii Pond, are signs pointing to a city of refuge (which you can't see) and a battlefield.

Kamalo has a pier for small boats. Your next stop should be St. Joseph Church, a tiny classic frame chapel with a tall steeple, the second (1876) Father Damien built on this side of the island before his noted St. Philomena Church at Kalawao. A mile farther on is a monument marking the spot where, in 1927, Ernest Smith and Emory Bronte crash-landed their plane in a clump of *kiawe* trees to end the first civilian transpacific flight, 25 hours and 2 minutes long.

Soon, another marker points to two *heiaus*—important ones, but barely discernible up on the ridge. Farther on, Loipunawai Mystic Spring emits fresh water just a few feet from the salty ocean. It's within a circular stone wall beneath some banana trees. Next comes Ah Ping's store which has the kind of fascinating hodge podge you expect in a general store.

Kaluaaha Church (a half mile farther) is Molokai's earliest—built by one of the first missionaries. Its 3-foot-thick walls of plastered stone went up in the 1840's. The buttresses, iron roof, and faded red steeple came later. The steeple has fallen, but will be restored, complete with its 1844 bell. Inside you'll find hymnals and an 1860 Bible printed in Hawaiian and perhaps some announcements written in Hawaiian on the blackboard. Father

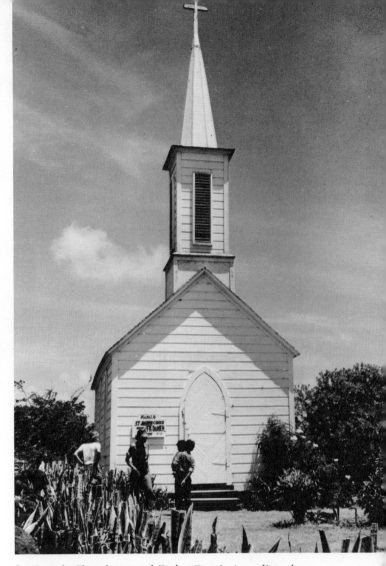

St. Joseph Church, *one of Father Damien's earliest, has clapboard walls but fine old glass windows, bronze bell.*

Damien's Our Lady of Sorrows Church, built two years before St. Joseph Church and recently rebuilt, is just down the road in a palm grove with a mountain backdrop.

Be content just to read about most marked places of historic interest from here on (they're hard or impossible to see) and observe instead how the people live today. At scattered houses, be they beach shacks or neat cottages, you'll see nets drying and laundry flapping in the breeze (especially on Saturdays). And it's fun to chat with families out swimming, fishing, cooking, and camping on weekends.

Iliiliopae Heiau is said to have been built by thousands of *Menehune* who formed a line from the Wailau shore over the mountains to Mapulehu — the Wailau Trail — and passed stones from hand to hand. To visit this massive old sacrificial temple — and you should — ask permission and directions from Mrs. Pearl Friel (call her at home or at the Bank of Hawaii in Kaunakakai). It's a 10-minute walk inland from the Wailau Trail sign on an

Derelict church *in Halawa Valley was built a century ago as branch of Kaluaaha mission, has an elaborate pulpit.*

overgrown road with several gates, then through fenced pasture. The platform seems as big as a football field and its actual size is awesome — 286 feet west to east, and 87 feet north to south. Moreover, stones are piled solidly to a height of 12 feet except for terraces on two sides.

From Pukoo to Waialua you pass the site of a royal taro patch, the stack of an 1870-1900 sugar mill, a legendary Shark God hill, and a roadside rock said to have been an ear that could hear enemy approaches. After you leave fishponds, at about Pauwalu, you'll spot occasional swimming places, sandy strips and coves along a shore increasingly broken with high and rocky points.

Soon you're climbing through Puu O Hoku Ranch and looking over rolling hills to turtle-shaped Mokuhooniki, an islet off the eastern tip used for bombing practice in World War II. From here is your best view of West Maui, too, with Haleakala looming shadow-like behind. Beyond the ranch buildings, between the road and the sea, you'll spot a dense stand of trees that is a sacred *kukui* grove, burial place of Lanikaula, a famous Molokai prophet for whom it is named. The *kukui,* Hawaii's state tree, is also the flower of this island.

Halawa Valley

Finally the rough road zigzags down the ridge into Halawa Valley, guarded to the north by mighty Lamaloa Head.

Here, in reach of an ordinary car (and about the only such vestige of old Hawaii that is) you'll find the South Seas of stories and paintings. The valley is broad (a half mile), deep (3 or 4 miles), and green-carpeted, and backed by cliffs with two high falls to fill the stream that meanders out to sea. Hundreds of people once lived in Halawa and even a few decades ago taro farmers and fishermen were active. There are still a few houses, but jungle has gradually encroached on the geometric taro layout. Except for the county roads and the beach park at the south, the valley belongs to Puu O Hoku Ranch. Ask permission before you stray very far, but plan a few hours to explore, in the morning when it's usually clear.

At the foot of the ridge the road forks. One leg goes down to the shore, where you can swim in the bay if it's calm or at the mouth of the stream (it's about 100 feet wide, at least 4 feet deep). The other road goes into the valley a little way, past two churches and some houses (without telephone and electricity) almost hidden in the lush foliage. The dollhouse-like church is still used; its more grand neighbor is a century old and now deserted.

Halawa's *pièce de résistance* is Moaula Falls, a pleasant hour's hike (take along mosquito lotion); but be wary of going if it has rained recently. The lower part of the main trail up the far side of the valley is overgrown now and to get to it you have to ford the wide part of the stream (there's a locked gate on the ranch jeep trail that crosses a bridge). An easier route is to walk up the road (you can't turn a car around) to the last house, then follow a trail of sorts alongside a water pipe. You'll cross a couple of irrigation ditches and a narrow part of the stream (there are rocks to step on), but don't lose sight of the pipe. When you come to a water tank, you pick up the main trail (and the pipeline continues alongside). You'll spot many abandoned taro patches, and in the tangle of *hau*, *kukui*, mangoes, surinam cherries, *liliko'i*, and ginger, may stumble onto chunks of old stonework.

The falls drop out of a towering cliff with such force that the surface of the 150-foot pool below is a mass of bubbles. According to legend, you should swim only if the *mo'o* (lizard) is happy; you toss in a *ti* leaf and if it floats, all is well. Even if it sinks, the mountain-cold water is too good to miss; it's like swimming in champagne. Dive under the falls where the slap of the water is like a good sound spanking.

Pali Coast

The coastline from Halawa to Kalaupapa is one of Hawaii's most spectacular, with towering green cliffs and waterfalls that plunge hundreds of feet into the ocean or disappear halfway down as winds blow them into a mist. The cliffs are honeycombed with caves; one at sea level is navigable to some 200 feet inside the island; another navigable tunnel makes a right turn back to the sea.

Only from a boat or plane can you see it all. Airplane sightseeing tours take you by, as do regular inter-island flights whenever they travel the north route between Oahu and Maui. For a closer and longer look, you can hire a boat or small plane.

Wailau Valley

Wailau, largest of the few valleys that break the 2,000-foot *pali,* is accessible only by boat or hiking across the island. Remote, untrodden, it's truly a place to go and live off the land. There is no protecting reef off this windward shore; so boat trips are usually possible only from the first of May to mid-September when the sea is calm enough to land a craft on the stony beach.

Wailau is about a mile wide and stretches inward almost 5 miles to Mount Olokui, some 4,600 feet above the valley floor. During or after rainfalls — and it rains almost every day or night — the sheer walls all around literally drip with waterfalls which nourish the stream that runs out to sea. You can wade into this stream and gather *hihiwai*, a tasty fresh-water shellfish. Bananas, pineapple, sugar cane, taro, hydrangeas, and ginger are just some of the fruits and flowers that grow wild.

Until 1919 Hawaiian families living in the valley had

When sea is calm, *you can land a boat near Papalaua Falls and walk along the shore, over sea-washed boulders.*

a contract to supply *pa'i 'ai* — *ti* leaf bundles of pounded taro — to the settlement at Kalaupapa. Then they were underbid by Oahu taro growers who could ship at lower cost out of Honolulu. Soon everyone left Wailau, and no one lives there permanently now. A few Hawaiians camp during the summer to hunt and fish. They are very hospitable; if they've had any luck hunting, they may fry some goat meat for you.

The trail to the head of the valley (and thence over the mountains to Mapulehu) is overgrown; you have to make your own way along the stream. The terrain is fairly level, but the hike takes three hours or more.

Barring rough seas, you can walk the shore for almost 2 miles west, until you reach the mighty cliff which bars entrance into Pelekunu Valley. You can land a boat at Pelekunu in summer, and there's an indistinct trail into the valley from Wailau (over the ridge). Pelekunu's ridges are generally alive with goats.

Kalaupapa

It's easy now to visit Kalaupapa, the tiny (4¼ square miles) peninsula that juts out from the north coast's fortress-like cliffs. For almost a century, this isolated low tableland (250 feet) was a place of banishment for sufferers of leprosy; to most others it was a place of mystery and a source of pitiful and horrible tales.

During the last 25 years there has been a great fall-off in new cases and sulfone drugs have been effective in checking the disease. Patients are no longer exiled here and most of today's 165 are arrested cases. These can leave, but with family ties severed, many consider Kalaupapa their home and are happy with the simple, self-contained life of this scenic hideaway.

The settlement welcomes visitors, and there's no hazard to health if you follow the rules. You must have a permit to enter (small children are not allowed and minors over 12 only under special restrictions), and should apply two days ahead of time at the State Department of Health in Honolulu, or ask your airline to get it.

The only way in or out is by air—unless you take the 3⅛-mile zigzag trail along the abrupt mountain wall.

There's time between the regular morning and afternoon flights (see How to Get There, page 112) for the inexpensive 3-hour auto tour offered by ex-patients. You can substitute your own itinerary, but an escort is required. Take a picnic lunch; Kalaupapa has no restaurant or public store.

Molokai Lighthouse is near the paved runway for small planes, but you'll see it long before you land. Its beam is more than twice as bright (2,500,000 candlepower) as any marine light on the Mainland's West Coast.

Often when you drive from the airport to town your eyes are drawn to unusually high sea spray, the result of nature's contest between the relentless rollers and the

Quaint figures, *temple shapes, even a replica of a grass shack are among gravestones in Kalaupapa cemetery.*

gusty winds which hit them head on. The old graveyard that stretches along the shore is divided into sections for the various religions.

Kalaupapa has four churches, a community hall (patients give seasonal choral concerts), a general store, two bars (beer and wine only), and a wharf where barges come three times in the calm summer with rice, canned food, feed, lumber, and fuel (mail and fresh and frozen food are flown in). Three-fourths of the patients — the married ones — live in trim cottages, have gardens, TV, and do their own cooking. Patients need not work, but about half take jobs. An unusual note is the absence of children. They are particularly susceptible to leprosy, and new babies are placed elsewhere.

It is 2½ miles across to Kalawao, the peninsula's easternmost district, on a road that dares you to reach its 35-mph speed limit. The colony was started at Kalawao. For years conditions were primitive and unsanitary; water was carried from a tiny stream a mile away. After building of a pipeline from Waikolu Valley, the settlement gradually moved to the Kalaupapa side, which is drier and less windy. A spur road up to windswept Kauhako, the 450-foot summit, gives you a look into the crater's opaque green pond (connected with the sea) and at the stone piles — remains of 100-year-old house enclosures — that dot the landscape.

Kalawao has two historic churches. Protestant Siloama, built in 1871 before a backdrop of mist-shrouded peaks, is still used and was recently rebuilt. Note its doorway inscription, in Hawaiian. St. Philomena, better known as Father Damien's church, is in two sections — a frame chapel in the rear built in 1872 and the larger masonry part he added. The colony's first white resident, Damien devoted himself to relieving victims' suffering from 1873 until he died in 1889 after contracting the disease. His body was sent to Belgium in 1936, but a large bust of this martyr who has been proposed for sainthood is in the church graveyard. Sculptress Marisol's Damien is one of two statues representing Hawaii in the U.S. Capitol; its replica is in the State Capitol rotunda.

The road ends at Kalawao Park where you can picnic on a grassy bluff above the sea and watch the surf crash into the cliffs beyond. You can walk on down to Waialeia Valley cove, which attracts driftwood, and along the shore a mile to Waikolu Valley.

Ask your driver to take you into the lava tube, a mile's drive from Kalawao over pastureland (for cattle), then a 75-yard walk. You enter through a roof cave-in and walk out to a ledge above the sea. Nearby is an old platform, remains of an unsuccessful landing place.

If there's time before your plane leaves, you might want to go through town to the fine sand beach at the base of the cliff and gather shells.

Fresh from the field—*pineapple never tasted so good! Machine harvests up to 25,000 pineapples in an hour.*

LANAI...the Pineapple Island

Lanai is synonymous with pineapple-growing in the minds of most people and is generally overlooked as a vacation spot even by Islanders. To be sure, Lanai has lots of pineapple — more than 15,000 acres. Its claim to being the "world's largest pineapple plantation" is made on a sign at the airport.

But if you want a bit of Hawaii to yourself, if you prefer roughing it to the trappings of tourist resorts, you'll delight in exploring the little-traveled shores, verdant mountains, and wide open desert of this small island just a half hour by air from Honolulu. Lanai has a fine swimming beach, a miles-long "shipwreck" coast made to order for beachcombers, good hunting and fishing. You can drive or hike to lookouts above deeply-eroded gulches, and search for — and find — many remains of old Hawaii. You'll encounter plantation life in its purest form; most of Lanai's 3,000 people work for the pineapple company and live in Lanai City, a model plantation town.

Sixth in the island group in size—just 17 miles long and 13 miles wide—Lanai is an extinct volcano with a single crater, Palawai. Some say "Lanai" means a swelling or hump; if you look at the island from Maui, you will see that the name fits the contour of the land which rises in a smooth, curved ridge from the southern base to an altitude of more than 3,000 feet and then slopes down again to the northern tip. Deep gulches cut into the ridge on the east side down to the mile-wide coastal plain. On the west side the ridge drops down to a plateau of 1,500 to 2,000-foot elevation, ending in cliffs above the sea. Vegetation on the plateau is scrubby, but gulches and hillsides on the windward side have luxuriant growth. Rainfall in high areas averages 42 inches a year; in lower areas, 12 inches.

One of the legends of Lanai is that the island was inhabited only by ghosts or evil spirits for 1,000 years after the Polynesians had settled the other islands. Then Kaululaau, nephew of the Maui king, was punished for one of his mischievous acts by being banished to Lanai. He was not expected to survive, but Kaululaau went all over the island fighting the ghosts and made the island a safe place for humans to live.

Spreading kiawe trees *at Manele Beach provide shade for camp. The weather here is almost always dry.*

Protected pool *for youngsters is carved out of lava at Manele Beach. Swimming beach is Lanai's finest.*

Protestant missionaries arrived on Lanai in 1835, and 20 years later a Mormon colony was started in Palawai Basin. The colony later dissolved because the leader, Walter Murray Gibson, was cut off by the church for refusing to turn over his land acquisitions. His land eventually passed on to sugar interests, then cattle ranchers, and by 1910 most of the island had been bought up by one ranching company. Thus, when Dole Company purchased this firm in 1922, it virtually bought the island. It still owns all but a few parcels which include house lots sold to employees. Dole has turned a semi-wasteland into an exotic fruit basket out of which comes nearly an eighth of the world's pineapples.

How to Get There

Hawaiian Airlines stops at Lanai every afternoon and three mornings a week on flights each way between Honolulu and Maui airports, with stops on Molokai. Air Hawaii, Royal Hawaiian Air Service, and Sky Tours Hawaii serve Lanai daily on trips between Honolulu and Maui's Kaanapali Airstrip. There's time between a morning arrival and afternoon takeoff to see the easy-to-reach sights.

A 65-foot glass bottom boat operated by See Under Sea sails to Lanai from Lahaina, Maui, daily on an 8-hour tour that includes 5½ hours of beach time and touring.

Where to Stay

The island's one hotel is Lanai Inn, a comfortable white frame former plantation home with veranda on a pine-covered hillside in Lanai City. It has 3 triple, 5 double, and 2 single rooms, all with bath. Rates include meals—home-cooked.

Getting Around on the Island

Lanai City has a taxi, and its two car rental agencies have jeeps, which you need to really explore the island. The only major paved roads radiate from Lanai City to Kaumalapau (route 44), to the northeast coast (route 44), and to Manele (route 441).

Dirt roads which criss-cross the pineapple sections are generally good. Others are often in too bad condition for passenger cars and during rainy weather may be impassable even in a jeep. Before starting out for off-beat areas, ask the manager of Lanai Inn for directions and road condition information. He can also help you plan hiking, hunting, and pack trips.

You can take a 4-hour Gray Line tour, which takes in many of the island's scenic spots. Passengers on the glass bottom boat from Lahaina (see How to Get There) arrive at Lanai in time to join this tour.

Recreation on Lanai

Picnicking and Camping

Picnicking and camping are permitted almost everywhere except in the pineapple fields. Manele Beach is the only improved camp site; it has showers, rest rooms, picnic tables, and barbecues.

Swimming

Hulopoe Bay ranks high on the list of Hawaii's best swimming spots; it is safe except when the sea is extremely rough. Along the shore are Manele Beach, which

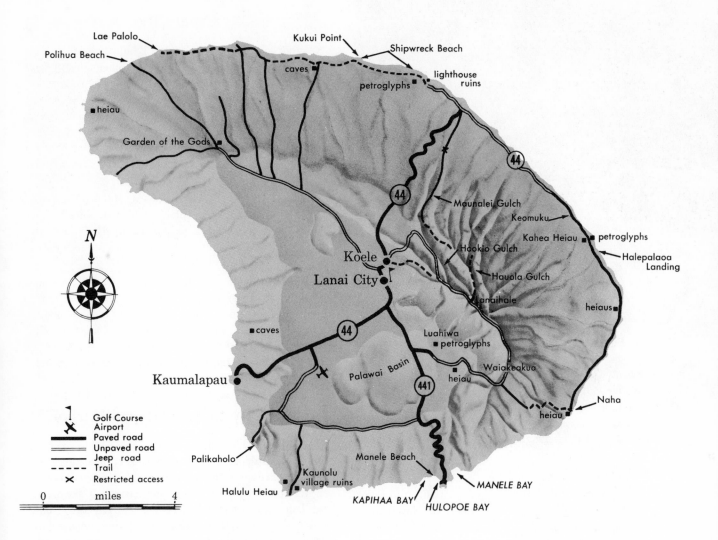

has *kiawe* trees for shade, and a pool for youngsters carved out of the black lava. Children can also swim in shallow, sandy coves along the windward coast.

Hiking

Lanai's most pleasant hikes are in the cool, forested mountains. You can walk up to Lanaihale on two different routes: On one (about 4½ miles), you hike a foot trail that starts near Koele and leads to Munro Trail (Lanaihale Road), then walk along the road through the rain forest to the summit; on the other (2½ miles and easier going), you climb the southeastern section of the road. Short trails go from it onto side ridges, one to the lookout over Hauola Gulch. For a triangle hike of 3 or 4 miles, walk from Koele to Munro Trail, turn north on the road and follow it along the ridge above Hookio and Maunalei gulches and on back to Koele.

At Shipwreck Beach you can walk the shoreline for several miles. You can take a hot, dry, cliff-top walk for 2 miles from Kaunolu to Palikaholo, and follow an old Hawaiian paved trail for a mile or more uphill from Naha; both routes connect with jeep trails at each end.

Fishing

Trolling for *mahimahi, ahi, aku, ono, kawakawa,* and *'ulua* is good off the coast from Kaumalapau to Manele Bay. There are no charter boats, but Lanai's boat owners moor their craft at Kaumalapau or Manele harbors where you can try your luck at arranging a trip. The reef-protected shoals along the windward coast are ideal for spear fishing and netting. Except for good casting for *'ulua* off Polihua Beach, the coastline generally is unsuitable for surf casting and pole fishing. At rocky beaches you can gather *'opihi* (small shellfish) by day and *pipipi* (sea snails) at night—you just pick them off rocks.

Hunting

During seasons set each year, the entire island is open to hunting on Sundays and holidays, except for pineapple fields, areas near main roads, and Maunalei Game Reserve.

Luahiwa petroglyphs are not easy to find, but they're among the best such carvings found in the Islands.

Bird season—for pheasants, chukar and Francolin partridge, barred and lace-neck doves, California valley and Gambel's quail—generally runs from November 1 to mid-January (Sundays only). There are special annual seasons for deer and mouflon sheep and a year-round goat season with a bag limit of two goats per day. Would-be sheep and deer hunters are too numerous for the abundance of game and therefore must file an application to participate in drawings to hunt. Drawings are held at State Fish and Game Division offices in Honolulu and Lanai City about a month before the start of the seasons. These offices also sell annual hunting licenses and will tell you where to get required daily permits (free).

You can arrange for guides, dogs, and jeeps at Lanai Inn. During both bird and mammal seasons, inter-island airlines run hunter's flights from Honolulu to Lanai.

Robin Hood hunters can stalk deer and goats on weekends and weekdays after working hours in a large bow hunting reserve on the lee side of Lanaihale from Koele to Manele Road. Bag limits are three deer a year and two goats a day; permits are required.

Golf

A 9-hole course near Lanai City is maintained by Dole Company for public use. There are no greens fees.

Lanai City

No other settlement in the Islands is quite like Lanai City. Situated at 1,600 feet, just below the mountains, it has a climate like a California mountain town in summer—comfortably cool days, crisp nights. It has evergreens, too—hundreds of stately Norfolk Island pine trees, planted by the pineapple company, which tower over the neat rows of square, pastel-colored, iron-roofed houses. The village is very still at night—until the siren sounds at 4:30 A.M. to awaken field workers!

Home gardens, although tropical, also have azaleas, camellias, lilies, and other colorful temperate zone flowers which thrive at this elevation. For a truly flamboyant display, visit Ito's, a community garden that rises in terraces from the high road of the town.

Lanai City has plantation offices, a school, hospital, bowling alley, one theater (Oriental films several times a week), a few stores, a cafe, no bar, and more than half a dozen churches. Visit the ruins of the Church of Kihamaniania, a Protestant meeting house started in 1842 and completed in 1851. Some lava rock walls still stand.

Lanai City to Kaumalapau Harbor

The 6-mile paved road (44) from Lanai City to the harbor at Kaumalapau cuts through acres of pineapple, the fields broken only by red dirt roads which criss-cross them. You may see irrigating and harvesting machines; the latter load fruit onto trucks at the rate of 25,000 pineapples per hour. Planting and picking are done by hand, and during the harvesting peak in summer you see many women pickers, their heads all but covered with scarves, big hats, and goggles.

The road descends in curves to the harbor, backed by steep bluffs with the houses and gardens of a little village clustered on top. The company built the harbor to accommodate the barges which carry pineapple to the cannery in Honolulu, and at all times it has a smattering of fishing boats. At a 400-foot dock, cranes transfer as many as 1,300,000 pineapples a day from trucks to barges.

North of Kaumalapau the plateau ends in a bluff above the sea. To the south, jagged cliffs rise as high as 1,000 feet out of the water.

Lanai City to Manele

The 8-mile paved route (441) to Manele Bay is also lined with pineapple fields. On the way you can detour to the Luahiwa petroglyphs near the base of the steep slopes around Palawai Basin, but you'll need a guide or good directions to find them. You take a dirt road off the highway, then scramble up grassy banks to boulders which have one of Hawaii's most concentrated and best preserved collections of the ancient rock carvings.

Manele Bay has a new small boat harbor with a breakwater and piers used mostly for sport fishing boats. Low lava stone walls and platforms on the hill above are remains of early native houses. To the west is Hulopoe Bay with beautiful tree-fringed Manele swimming beach and an adjacent rock-rimmed pool for children. Bluffs along this coast were once submerged and marine fossils have been found as high as 1,200 feet.

Kaunolu Village

Probably the most extensive and best preserved ruins in the Islands are those of Kaunolu Village at the end of a rutty, rocky 3-mile jeep trail through grasslands south of the pineapple fields. Remains of 86 houses, 35 stone shelters, and various grave markings and garden sites are scattered across a point above the sea.

Now a National Historic Landmark, Kaunolu was once an active fishing community and a favorite recreation spot of Kamehameha the Great after he conquered all the islands. His house, on the edge of the eastern bluff above a usually-dry stream bed, overlooked the bay, the village, and Halulu Heiau out on a point on the west bank with cliffs on three sides.

Today you can see remains of this *heiau,* and, spread along the east bank, parts of rock platforms where grass houses once stood and sections of stone walls that enclosed them. Many boulders have petroglyphs, a few with bird-like figures peculiar to Lanai. A cave that was lived in has been partially excavated by Bishop Museum archeologists.

Kahekili's Jump, *a break in cliff through which fleeing warriors escaped—if they jumped clear of ledge below.*

From Kahekili's Jump, a break in a cliff above the sea, fleeing warriors are said to have leaped into the 12 feet of water 62 feet below. Their chances of survival depended mostly on whether they could clear the ledge of rock protruding 15 feet into the sea at the base of the drop.

From Kaunolu you can walk about 2 miles along cliff tops to Palikaholo, at 1,083 feet, the highest point in Lanai's coastline. You can also go from Kaunolu to Manele along the shore, but it is a difficult, rocky walk.

Garden of the Gods

You reach the Garden of the Gods about 7 miles along a dirt road out of Lanai City, but to find it a guide is almost necessary. The road goes first through pineapple fields, then through an area grown to lantana, *poha,* Norfolk pine, and eucalyptus. The Garden is a varicolored canyon of windswept sand with fantastic black lava formations standing all around, weird survivors of the decomposition and coloring wrought upon the less durable substances by wind, rain, and sun.

Dirt roads and jeep trails traverse the arid, uncultivated plateau that is northwestern Lanai. One road goes all the way to the white sands of Polihua Beach. Here surf casting is rewarding, but the strong current makes swimming dangerous.

Road to Kaumalapau *is one of Lanai's two major paved roads. The unpaved ones are best explored by jeep.*

The Windward Coast

Three miles along the narrow paved road (44) from Lanai City northeast to the windward coast lies a particularly pretty picnic spot—rolling green hills and grassy knolls, shaded by a few *lama* and *olopua* trees (once part of an extensive forest)—with a fine view over the 7-mile channel to Molokai. Then the road cuts a corkscrew course down to the shore.

Shipwreck Beach

At pavement's end you can drive west on a dirt road to an old lighthouse foundation, and along part of Shipwreck Beach, a stretch of 4 miles or more where a few hulks of old ships lie rotting and rusting on the reef and the shore—part sand, part black lava, part tidal flats—is littered with timbers and other remnants of once-proud vessels. Beachcomber shacks near the lighthouse ruin are built mostly of lumber from old, useless steamers purposely abandoned to this shallow reef graveyard.

From road's end walk about 100 yards west along a marked trail to Kukui Point where a score of petroglyph-covered boulders was discovered just a few years ago. Among the figures are strange "birdmen" like those at Kaunolu.

Glass fishing floats may come in anywhere along this windward coast from Lae Palolo to Naha, and occasionally you can find rare paper nautilus shells. There are intermittent shoals where youngsters can paddle.

The Road to Naha

From the end of route 44, a jeep road of gravel, then hard-packed sand, follows the northeast coastline a couple of hundred yards inland for about 15 miles to Naha, an old village site. A parallel road of sand and silt which hugs the shore has spots which become flooded during high tide. But to go beachcombing you can cross over to it on one of many connecting spurs. Clumps of *kiawe* trees here are so wind-bent they look like banks of tall wild grass. *Kiawes* along the somewhat protected inland route have old, gnarled trunks and branches that reach over the road in places to provide a lacy green canopy.

Keomuku, a ghost town on the coast road, consists of a few old houses, a church, and a school nestled in an oasis of palm trees. Just beyond the abandoned village you come to an old red water tower and windmill. Walk inland from the windmill to see the remains of Kahea Heiau on the bluff above. (The inland road passes right by it.) At the foot of the bank is a boulder covered with weathered petroglyphs. Stones from the *heiau* were used for the Maunalei Sugar Company's plantation railroad bed; you'll see ruins of the system here and there. Hawaiians claim the sugar company failed, in 1901, because it disturbed the temple.

Maunalei sugar was shipped to Maui for grinding from Halepalaoa Landing. The decking is now gone from the wharf, but you'll have a fine view from here of West Maui with Haleakala looming up behind.

Off Naha's narrow sand beach are good grounds for spear fishing, casting, and squidding. You can hike uphill from Naha for a mile or so along an old Hawaiian paved trail to a jeep trail through grasslands which meets Munro Trail (Lanaihale Road).

The Munro Trail

Lanai has beautiful forests, deep in gulches and high on mountain ridges. Munro Trail, a dirt road generally suitable for passenger cars, takes you to Lanaihale at the top of the island. On a clear day, from this 3,370-foot elevation you can see all of the major islands except Kauai.

The 7-mile route, formally called the George Munro Trail, extends from the southeast hills near Waiakeakua to Koele's rolling grasslands. Near the top of the ridge it cuts through a heavy rain forest of tree ferns and other exotic tropicals, most of them planted years ago by Hawaii's late naturalist, George C. Munro. Stands of Norfolk pines, in particular, were planted to increase the island's ground water, tapped for irrigation. Weather studies show that they collect moisture from the hill-hugging clouds.

A trail leads off to a lookout over 2,000-foot Hauola Gulch, Lanai's deepest ravine. From the road you can view the fortifications on Hookio Ridge at the head of Maunalei Gulch. Warriors used the man-made notches in the ridge both for protection and as bases for attack during a battle above this gulch in 1778 when the king of Hawaii massacred many Lanai natives.

Above Koele, the road overlooks the pumping station down in Maunalei Gulch, the island's watershed, which has tumbling waterfalls, a *kukui* grove, and lush valley plants. A jeep road from the windward coast part way into this gulch is usable only with permission from Dole Company.

INDEX